Internet Publishing and Beyond

Internet Publishing and Beyond

The Economics of Digital Information and
Intellectual Property

edited by Brian Kahin and Hal R. Varian

A Publication of the Harvard Information Infrastructure Project
in Collaboration with the School of Information Management
and Systems at the University of California at Berkeley

The MIT Press, Cambridge, Massachusetts, and London, England

Dedicated to the memory of
Paul Evan Peters (1947–1996)

Library of Congress Cataloging-in-Publication Data

Internet publishing and beyond : the economics of digital information and intellectual property / edited by Brian Kahin and Hal R. Varian.
     p.   cm.—(A publication of the Harvard Information Infrastructure Project)
  Includes bibliographical references and index.
  ISBN 0-262-61159-7 (alk. paper)
  1. Internet publishing—Economic aspects. 2. Intellectual property—Economic aspects. 3. Technological innovations—Economic aspects. I. Kahin, Brian. II. Varian, Hal R. III. Series.

Z286.I57 I58 2000
070.5'797—dc21   00-035154

Contents

Introduction

Brian Kahin and Hal R. Varian

The Internet has transformed the way information is accessed and used in business, education, and the home. Reproduction and distribution costs have virtually disappeared, at least for text. Management of behavior and transactions has become a core strategic focus. Large markets have become unexpectedly competitive. Advertising, which once seemed ill fitted to the one-on-one experience of the Web, has become a dominant force, buoyed by standardized software, economies of scale, and efficient consumer targeting. With the notable exception of the *Wall Street Journal* and *Consumer Reports,* few publishers have been able to impose subscription charges, except for online access to established print publications. Despite its unique content, the *Encyclopedia Britannica* has had to radically transform its business model from door-to-door sales of expensive printed volumes to an advertiser-supported Web site.

The present volume was conceived four years ago, when the peculiar economics of electronic commerce on the World Wide Web were beginning to take shape. Since then it has become clear that valued information is not just a vehicle for advertising on the Internet but a tool for a wide range of commercial strategies—a versatile, inexpensive tool for steering attention and shaping decisions, that can be programmed to respond to the cues of cookies and clicks. Atomized content—sentences, animations, linked words, pop-up windows—has become a means of engagement. Hyperlinks transport readers and viewers halfway around the world. But the links are not merely superfootnotes; they are networks that lead into communities and relationships, as well as transactions and other content. Context, not content, is king, and the context is the digital economy.

This dramatic rise in the use of the Internet raises several challenges to existing economic relationships and business models, which we examine in this book. Brad DeLong and Michael Froomkin lead off by contrasting conventional economics and the New Economy. In traditional economics, most goods are both rival and excludable, which means that one person's consumption of a good precludes another person's consumption of the same good and reduces the amount available to others. But information goods don't have these properties: My accessing a Web page has a negligible impact on your ability to view it. This means that conventional atomistic markets won't work well for information goods, and new forms of pricing and resource allocation are necessary. DeLong and Froomkin examine a variety of novel pricing and business practices and evaluate them with respect to their economic characteristics. They suggest that the nontraditional characteristics of information goods may well have profound effects on the structure of the New Economy.

Several of the issues surveyed by DeLong and Froomkin in their opening chapter are discussed in depth in subsequent chapters of the book. Hoffman and Novak lead off by describing experiences with a particular model of support that has been reasonably successful: selling advertising. They note several problems due to the immaturity the industry: the lack of standardization, the lack of information on effectiveness, the variety of pricing models for ads, and so on. Despite these issues, advertising expenditure on the Web grew from $550 million in 1997 to $2 billion in 1998, with forecasts of $13 billion by 2002. However, this is still only a small fraction of total advertising expenditures, which were about $285 billion in 1998.

Mings and White examine business models used in a particular industry: online newspapers. They look at subscription, advertising, transactions, and bundled (or partnership) models. There is currently much interest in viewing online newspapers as complements to print versions rather than as substitutes, since online news can provide a variety of additional features. The same is true of other media: Online resources can enhance a viewing experience on commercial or public TV, amplify magazine articles, and so on. It has often been observed that new media don't simply displace old media, but rather change the nature of specialization. Just as radio moved from dramatizations to music after the advent of TV, we may see newspapers change the nature of their offerings in response to online news.

The subsequent chapters in the book are concerned with economic analysis of intellectual property and information pricing.

Shy presents an interesting analysis of copy protection in a competitive environment. He first examines the case of a monopolist selling a product that exhibits network externalities, so that the value of the product depends on the number of users. He shows that in this case the monopolist may well want to be tolerant of illegal copies, even to the point of removing copy protection, since the presence of illegitimate copies may well enhance the value of the legitimate copies. He then analyzes the duopoly case, examining equilibrium in the choice of whether or not to implement copy protection. He shows that it is not an equilibrium for both firms to use copy protection: Competition will always force at least one of the firms to eliminate copy protection. Shy's analysis seems to be a good description of what happened to spreadsheets in the mid-1980s and poses a serious challenge to those currently contemplating various technological rights-management systems.

Bakos and Brynjolfsson analyze a particular pricing strategy known as bundling. In their model, consumers have independent valuations for a number of different information goods—think of articles in a newspaper on various topics. Some people value sports stories; other people value business stories; others value entertainment. A newspaper which bundles all the different stories together will have a less dispersed valuation by consumers than if it sold each story individually. It follows that the seller will be able to charge a higher price for the bundle than the sum of the prices it could charge for the separate components, and will therefor be able to make higher profits. Bakos and Brynjolfsson point out that bundling is especially attractive for information goods since there is generally a near zero marginal cost of production for such goods.

Chuang and Sirbu also examine bundling using a somewhat different model of consumer demand. In particular, they consider more detailed models of the decision to view or not to view a particular information good, as well as a more detailed model of production costs. They are able to delineate conditions under which bundling is more or less profitable than unbundled pricing and describe some empirical results about the scope of bundling in the pricing of academic journals.

Fishburn, Odlyzko and Siders examine a particular kind of bundling, subscription pricing. They are particularly interested in the competitive dynamics of a duopoly in which one firm charges a fixed fee per unit, while the other charges on a per-use basis. Their numerical models exhibit several forms of interesting behavior: sometimes there are stable competitive equilibria, but at other times there are price wars that are disastrous to both participants. They also discuss evidence that consumers have strong preferences for flat rate pricing, preferences that are not easy to incorporate into standard economic models.

Varian examines another form of pricing information which he refers to as "versioning." This means providing different versions of an information goods, such as an immediate and a delayed version, which appeal to different groups of consumers. This is essentially a form of quality discrimination, but with a few twists that make the analysis interesting. For example, for industrial goods, higher quality goods generally cost more to produce. But for information goods, the low-quality goods (e.g., the delayed version) often is a degraded version of the high-quality good, and this involves extra production steps, making such the low-quality good more costly to produce. Varian examines the profit-maximizing choice and the welfare effects of such pricing policies.

The theoretical analysis is helpful for understanding what kinds of effects might occur, but clearly some empirical analysis is called for. MacKie-Mason and Riveros describe an ambitious experiment in pricing access to electronic journals. They indicate a variety of services that such electronic publication can provide. They also describe another variation on bundling they refer to as a "generalized subscription," which allows the user to construct a bundle themselves, and they sketch an experimental design of an ongoing project involving Elsevier Science which may help resolve some of the issues of what type of pricing users prefer, at least in this particular industry.

Most of the papers in this volume were presented at a conference organized by the Harvard Information Infrastructure Project at Harvard Law School in January 1997. We greatly appreciate the willingness of the authors to revise and update their work presented at this conference. In certain cases, substantial changes were necessary because of so many years of "Internet time" have passed. We also want to express our appreciation to the other presenters at the conference and to Esther Dyson, Jeff MacKie-Mason, and Paul Evan Peters, who served as members of the steering committee along with the co-editors of this volume.

This project was co-sponsored by the Science, Technology and Public Program and the Center for Business and Government at John F. Kennedy School of Government; the Berkman Center for Internet and Society at Harvard Law School; the Council on Library and Information Resources, and the Coalition for Networked Information. Principal project funding was provided by grant from the W. K. Kellogg Foundation to the Harvard Information Infrastructure Project. Additional support for this publication was provided by the Class of 1944 Professorship at the University of California at Berkeley.

We dedicate this book to the memory of Paul Evan Peters, Executive Director of the Coalition for Networked Information from its inception in 1991 until his untimely death in November 1996. Paul was uniquely able to bridge different perspectives with stunning insight and humor. He created a remarkable sense of community not just around the Coalition as an organization, but around every debate on the form, implications, and future of digital information. Paul was one of the early visionaries of the Internet and a natural partner for this project. It is hard to believe that we have been without him for so long.

Speculative Microeconomics for Tomorrow's Economy

J. Bradford DeLong and A. Michael Froomkin

1. The Utility of the Market

Two and one-quarter centuries ago, the Scottish moral philosopher Adam Smith used a particular metaphor to describe the competitive market system, a metaphor that still resonates today. He saw the competitive market as a system in which

> every individual . . . endeavours as much as he can . . . to direct . . . industry so that its produce may be of the greatest value . . . neither intend[ing] to promote the public interest, nor know[ing] how much he is promoting it. . . . He intends only his own gain, and he is in this, as in many other cases, led by an *invisible hand* to promote an end that was no part of his intention. . . . By pursuing his own interest he frequently promotes that of society more effectually than when he really intends to promote it.[1]

Adam Smith's claim, made in 1776, that the market system promoted the general good was new. Today it is one of the most frequently heard commonplaces. For Adam Smith's praise of the market as a social mechanism for regulating the economy was the opening shot of a grand campaign to reform the way politicians and governments looked at the economy.

The campaign waged by Adam Smith and his successors was completely successful. The past two centuries have seen his doctrines woven into the fabric of the way our society works. It is hard to even begin to think about our society without basing one's thought to some degree on Adam Smith's. And today the governments that have followed the path Adam Smith laid down preside over economies that are more materially prosperous and technologically powerful than any we have seen.[2]

Belief in free trade, an aversion to price controls, freedom of occupation, freedom of domicile,[3] freedom of enterprise, and the other corollaries of belief in Smith's *invisible hand* have today become *the* background assumptions for thought about the relationship between the government and the economy. A free-market system, economists claim and most participants in capitalism believe, generates a level of total economic product that is as high as possible—and is certainly higher than under any alternative system that any branch of humanity has conceived and attempted to implement. It is even possible to prove the "efficiency" of a competitive market, albeit under restrictive technical assumptions.[4]

The lesson usually drawn from this economic success story is *laissez-faire, laissez-passer*: In the overwhelming majority of cases, the best thing the government can do for the economy is simply to leave it alone. Define property rights, set up honest courts, perhaps rearrange the distribution of income, impose minor taxes and subsidies to compensate for well-defined and narrowly specified "market failures"—but otherwise the economic role of the government is to disappear.

The main argument for a free competitive market system is the dual role played by prices. On the one hand, prices serve to ration demand: Anyone unwilling to pay the market price because he or she would rather do other things with his or her (not unlimited) money does not get the good (or service). On the other hand, price serves to elicit production: Any organization that can make a good (or provide a service) for less than its market price has a powerful financial incentive to do so. Thus, what is produced goes to those who value it the most. What is produced is made by the organizations that can make it most cheaply. And what is produced is whatever the ultimate users value the most.

You can criticize the market system because it undermines the values of community and solidarity. You can criticize the market system because it is unfair—for it gives good things to those who have control over whatever resources turn out to be most scarce as society solves its production allocation problem, not to those who have any moral right to good things. But—at least under the conditions economists have for two and one-quarter centuries first implicitly, and more recently explicitly, assumed—you cannot criticize the market system for being unproductive.

Adam Smith's case for the *invisible hand,* so briefly summarized above, will be familiar to almost all readers: It is one of the foundation stones of our civilization's social thought. Our purpose in this chapter is to shake these foundations—or at least to make readers aware that the changes in technology now going on as a result of the revolutions in data processing and data communications may shake these foundations. Unexpressed but implicit in Adam Smith's argument for the efficiency of the market system are assumptions about the nature of goods and services and the process of exchange, assumptions that fit reality less well today than they did in Adam Smith's day.

Moreover, these implicit underlying assumptions are likely to fit the "new economy" of the future even less well than they fit the economy of today.

1.1 The Structure of This Chapter

The next section of this chapter deconstructs Adam Smith's case for the market system. It points out three assumptions about production and distribution technologies that are necessary if the *invisible hand* is to work as Adam Smith claimed it did. We point out that these assumptions are being undermined more and more by the revolutions currently ongoing in data processing and data communications.

In the third section, we take a look at things happening on the frontiers of electronic commerce and in the developing markets for information. Our hope is that what is now going on at the frontiers of electronic commerce may contain some clues to processes that will be more general in the future.

Our final section does not answer all the questions we raise. We are not prophets, after all. Thus, our final section raises still more questions, for the most we can begin to do today is to organize our concerns. By looking at the behavior of people in high-tech commerce—people for whom the abstract doctrines and theories that we present have the concrete reality of determining whether they get paid—we can make some guesses about what the next economics and the next set of sensible policies might look like, if indeed there is going to be a genuinely new economy and, thus, a genuinely new economics. Moreover, we can warn against some pitfalls in the hope that our warnings will make things better rather than worse.

2. "Technological" Prerequisites of the Market Economy

The ongoing revolution in data processing and data communications technology may well be starting to undermine those basic features of property and exchange that make the *invisible hand* a powerful social mechanism for organizing production and distribution. The case for the market system has always rested on three implicit pillars, three features of the way that property rights and exchange worked:

• Call the first feature *excludability:* the ability of sellers to force consumers to become buyers, and thus to pay for whatever goods and services they use.

• Call the second feature *rivalry:* a structure of costs in which two cannot partake as cheaply as one, in which producing enough for two million people to use will cost at least twice as many of society's resources as producing enough for one million people to use.

• Call the third feature *transparency:* the ability of individuals to see clearly what they need and what is for sale, so that they truly know just what they wish to buy.

All three of these pillars fit the economy of Adam Smith's day relatively well. The prevalence of craft, as opposed to mass production, guaranteed that two goods could be made only at twice the cost of one. The fact that most goods and services were valued principally for their (scarce) physical form meant that two could not use one good: If I am using the plow to plow my field today, you cannot use it to plow yours. Thus, rivalry was built into the structure of material life that underpinned the economy of production and exchange.

Excludability was less a matter of nature and more a matter of culture, but certainly by Smith's day large-scale theft and pillage were more the exception than the rule:[5] The courts and the law were there to give property owners the power to restrict the set of those who could use their property to those who had paid for the privilege.

Last, the slow pace and low level of technology meant that the purpose and quality of most goods and services were transparent: What you saw was pretty much what you got.

All three of these pillars fit much of today's economy pretty well too, although the fit for the telecommunications and information-processing industries is less satisfactory. But they will fit tomorrow's economy less well than today's. There is every indication that they will fit the 21st-century economy relatively poorly.[6]

As we look at developments along the leading technological edge of the economy, we can see considerations that used to be second-order "externalities," that served as corrections, growing in strength to possibly become first-order phenomena. And we can see the *invisible hand* of the competitive market beginning to work less well in an increasing number of areas.

2.1 Excludability

In the information-based sectors of the next economy, the owners of goods and services—call them "commodities" for short—will find that they are no longer able to easily and cheaply exclude others from using or enjoying the commodities. The carrot-and-stick principle that once enabled owners of property to extract value from those who wanted to use it was always that if you paid you got to make use of it, and if you did not pay you did not get to make use of it.

But digital data is cheap and easy to copy. Methods do exist to make copying difficult, time-consuming, and dangerous to the freedom and wealth of the copier, but these methods add expense and complexity. "Key disk" methods of copy protection for programs vanished in the late 1980s as it became clear that the burdens they imposed on legitimate purchasers and owners were annoying enough to cause buyers to "vote with their feet" for competing products. Identification-and-password restrictions on access to online information are only as powerful as users' concern for information providers' intellectual property rights, which is surely not as powerful as the information providers' concern.[7]

In a world of clever hackers, these methods are also unreliable. The methods used to protect digital content against casual copying seem to have a high rate of failure.

Without excludability, the relationship between producer and consumer becomes much more akin to a gift-exchange relationship than a purchase-and-sale one.[8] The appropriate paradigm then shifts in the direction of a fundraising drive for a National Public Radio station. When commodities are not excludable, people simply help themselves. If the user feels like it, he or she may make a "pledge" to support the producer. The user sends money to the producer not because it is the only way to gain the power to use the product, but out of gratitude and for the sake of reciprocity.

This reciprocity-driven revenue stream may well be large enough that producers cover their costs and earn a healthy profit. Reciprocity is a basic mode of human behavior. Most people do feel a moral obligation to tip cabdrivers and waiters. People do contribute to National Public Radio. But without excludability, the belief that the market economy produces the optimal quantity of any commodity is hard to justify. Other forms of provision—public support funded by taxes that are not voluntary, for example—that had fatal disadvantages vis-a-vis the competitive market when excludability reigned may well deserve re-examination.

That excludability is a very important foundation for the market is suggested by the fact that governments felt compelled to invent it. Excludability does not exist in a Hobbesian state of nature: The laws of physics do not prohibit people from sneaking in and taking your things; the police and the judges do. Indeed, most of what we call "the rule of law" consists of a legal system that enforces excludability: Enforcement of excludability ("protection of my property rights," even when the commodity is simply sitting there unused and idle) is one of the few tasks that the theory of *laissez-faire* allows the government. The importance of this "artificial" creation of excludability is rarely remarked on: Fish are supposed to rarely remark on the water in which they swim.[9]

We can get a glimpse of the way the absence of excludability can warp a market and an industry by taking a brief look at the history of network television. During its three-channel apogee in the 1960s and 1970s, North American network television was available to anyone with an antenna and a receiver: Broadcasters lacked the means of preventing the public from getting the signals free of charge.[10] Free access was, however, accompanied by scarce bandwidth, and by government allocation of the scarce bandwidth to producers.

The absence of excludability for broadcast television did not destroy the television broadcasting industry. Broadcasters couldn't charge for what they were truly producing, but broadcasters worked out that they could charge for something else: the attention of the program-watching consumers during commercials. Rather than paying money directly, the customers of the broadcast industry merely had to endure the commercials (or get up and leave the room, or channel-surf) if they wanted to see the show.

This "attention economy" solution prevented the market for broadcast programs from collapsing: It allowed broadcasters to charge someone for something, to charge advertisers for eyeballs rather than viewers for programs. But it left its imprint on the industry. Charging for advertising does not lead to the same *invisible hand* guarantee of productive optimum as does charging for product. In the case of network television, audience attention to advertisements was more or less unconnected with audience involvement in the program.

This created a bias toward lowest-common-denominator programming. Consider two programs, one of which will fascinate 500,000 people, and the other of which 30 million people will watch as slightly preferable to watching their ceilings. The first might well be better for social welfare: The 500,000 with a high willingness to pay might well, if there were a way to charge them, collectively outbid the 30 million apathetic couch potatoes for the use of scarce bandwidth to broadcast their preferred program. Thus, a network able to collect revenues from interested viewers would broadcast the first program, seeking the applause (and the money) of the dedicated and forgoing the eye-glazed semiattention of the larger audience.

But this competitive process breaks down when the network obtains revenue by selling commercials to advertisers. The network can offer advertisers either 1 million or 60 million eyeballs. How much the commercials will influence the viewers depends relatively little on how much they like the program. As a result, charging for advertising gives every incentive to broadcast what a mass audience will tolerate. It gives no incentive to broadcast what a niche audience would love.

As bandwidth becomes cheaper, these problems become less important: One particular niche program may well be worth broadcasting when the mass audience has become sufficiently fragmented by the viewability of multiple clones of bland programming. Until now, however, expensive bandwidth combined with the absence of excludability meant that broadcasting revenues depended on the viewer numbers rather than the intensity of demand. Nonexcludability helped ensure that broadcast programming would be "a vast wasteland."[11]

In the absence of excludability, industries today and tomorrow are likely to fall prey to analogous distortions. Producers' revenue streams, wherever they come from, will be only tangentially related to the intensity of user demand. Thus, the flow of money through the market will not serve its primary purpose of registering the utility of the commodity being produced. There is no reason to think *ex ante* that the commodities that generate the most attractive revenue streams paid by advertisers or by ancillary others will be the commodities that ultimate consumers would wish to see produced.

2.2 Rivalry

In the information-based sectors of the next economy, the use or enjoyment of the information-based commodity will no longer necessarily involve rivalry. With most tangible goods, if Alice is using a particular good, Bob cannot be. Charging the ultimate consumer the good's cost of production or the free-market price provides the producer with an ample reward for its effort. It also leads to the appropriate level of production: Social surplus (measured in money) is not maximized by providing the good to anyone whose final demand for a commodity is too weak for that person to wish to pay the cost for it that a competitive market would require.

But if goods are nonrival—if two can consume as cheaply as one—then charging a per-unit price to users artificially restricts distribution: To truly maximize social welfare, we need a system that supplies everyone whose willingness to pay for the good is greater than the marginal cost of producing another copy. And if the marginal cost of reproduction of a digital good is near-zero, that means almost everyone should have it for almost no charge. However, charging price equal to marginal cost almost surely leaves the producer bankrupt, with little incentive to maintain the product except the hope of maintenance fees, and no incentive whatsoever to make another one except that warm, fuzzy feeling one gets from impoverishing oneself for the general good.

Thus we have a dilemma: If the price of a digital good is above the marginal cost of making an extra copy, some people who truly ought (in the best of all possible worlds) to be using it do not get to have it, and the system of exchange that we have developed is getting in the way of a certain degree of economic prosperity. But if price is not above the marginal cost of making an extra copy of a nonrival good, the producer will not be paid enough to cover costs. Without nonfinancial incentives, all but the most masochistic producer will get out the business of production.

More important, perhaps, is that the existence of large numbers of important and valuable goods that are nonrival casts doubt upon the value of competition itself. Competition has been the standard way of keeping individual producers from exercising power over consumers: If you don't like the terms the producer is offering, you can just go down the street. But this use of private economic power to check private power may come at a high cost if competitors spend their time duplicating one another's efforts and attempting to slow down technological development in the interest of obtaining a compatibility advantage, or creating a compatibility or usability disadvantage for the other competitor.

One traditional answer to this problem (now in total disfavor) was to set up a government regulatory commission to control the "natural monopoly." The commission would set prices and would do the best it could to simulate a socially optimum level of production. On the eve of World War I, when American Telephone and

Telegraph (AT&T), under the leadership of its visionary CEO, Theodore N. Vail, began its drive for universal coverage, a political consensus formed rapidly both in Washington and within AT&T that the right structural form for the telephone industry was a privately owned, publicly regulated national monopoly.

While it may have seemed like the perfect answer in the Progressive era, in this more cynical age commentators have come to believe that regulatory commissions of this sort almost inevitably become "captured" by the industries they are meant to regulate.[12] Often this is because the natural career path for analysts and commissioners involves some day going to work in the regulated industry in order to leverage expertise in the regulatory process; sometimes it is because no one outside the regulated industry has anywhere near the same financial interest in manipulating the rules, or lobbying to have them adjusted. The only effective way a regulatory agency has to gauge what is possible is to examine how other firms in other regions are doing. But such "yardstick" competition proposals—judging how this natural monopoly is doing by comparing it to other analogous organizations—are notoriously hard to implement.[13]

A good economic market is characterized by competition to limit the exercise of private economic power, by price equal to marginal cost, by returns to investors and workers corresponding to the social value added of the industry, and by appropriate incentives for innovation and new product development. These seem impossible to achieve all at once in markets for nonrival goods—and digital goods are certainly nonrival.

2.3 Transparency

In many information-based sectors of the next economy, the purchase of a good will no longer be *transparent*. The *invisible hand* theory assumes that purchasers know what they want and what they are buying so that they can effectively take advantage of competition and comparison-shop. If purchasers need first to figure out what they want and what they are buying, there is no good reason to assume that their willingness to pay corresponds to its true value to them.

Why is transparency at risk? Because much of the value added in the data-processing and data-communications industries today comes from complicated and evolving systems of information provision. Adam Smith's pinmakers sold a good that was small, fungible, low-maintenance, and easily understood. Alice could buy her pins from Gerald today and from Henry tomorrow. But today's purchaser of, say, a cable modem connection to the Internet from AT&T-Excite-@Home is purchasing a bundle of present goods and future services, and is making a down payment on the establishment of a long-term relationship with AT&T-Excite-@Home. Once the relationship is established, both buyer and seller find themselves in different positions. Adam Smith's images are less persuasive in the context of services—especially bespoke services that require deep knowledge of the customer's wants and situation (and of the maker's capabilities)—that are not, by their nature, fungible or easily comparable.

When Alice shops for a software suite, not only does she want to know about its current functionality—something notoriously difficult to figure out until one has had days or weeks of hands-on experience—but she also needs to have some idea of the likely support that the manufacturer will provide. Is it a toll call? Is the line busy at all hours? Do the operators have a clue? Will next year's corporate downsizing lead to longer holds on support calls?

Worse, what Alice really needs to know cannot be measured at all before she is committed: Learning how to use a software package is an investment she would prefer not to repeat. Since operating systems are upgraded frequently, and interoperability needs change even more often, Alice needs to have a prediction about the likely upgrade path for her suite. This, however, turns on unknowable and barely guessable factors: the health of the corporation, the creativity of the software team, the corporate relationships between the suite seller and other companies.

Some of the things Alice wants to know, such as whether the suite works and works quickly enough on her computer, are potentially measurable, at least, although one rarely finds a consumer capable of measuring them before purchase, or a marketing system designed to accommodate such a need. You buy the shrink-wrapped box at a store, take it home, unwrap the box—and find that the program is incompatible with your hardware, your operating system, or one of the six programs you bought to cure defects in the hardware or the operating system . . .

Worse still, the producer of a software product has every incentive to attempt to "lock in" as many customers as possible. Operating system revisions that break old software versions require upgrades. And a producer has an attractive and inelastic revenue source to the extent that "lock-in" makes switching to an alternative painful. While consumers prefer the ability to comparison-shop and to switch easily to another product, producers fear this ability—and have incentives to subtly tweak their programs to make it difficult to do so.[14]

2.4. The Economics of Market Failure

That the absence of excludability, rivalry, or transparency is bad for the functioning *invisible hand* is not news.[15] The analysis of failure of transparency has made up an entire subfield of economics for decades: "imperfect information." Nonrivalry has been the basis of the theory of government programs and public goods, as well as of natural monopolies: The solution has been to try to find a regulatory regime that will mimic the decisions that the competitive market ought to make, or to accept that the "second best" public provision of the good by the government is the best that can be done.

Analysis of the impact of the lack of excludability is the core of the economic analysis of research and development. It has led to the conclusion that the best course is to try to work around nonexcludability by mimicking what a well-functioning market system would have done: Use the law to expand "property," or use tax-and-subsidy schemes to promote actions with broad benefits.

But the focus of analysis has traditionally been on overcoming "frictions": How can we transform this situation in which the requirements of *laissez-faire* fail to hold into a situation in which the *invisible hand* works tolerably well? As long as it works well throughout most of the economy, this is a very sensible analytical and policy strategy. A limited number of government programs and legal doctrines will be needed to closely mimic what the *invisible hand* would do if it could function properly in a few distinct areas of the economy (such as the regional natural monopolies implicit in the turn-of-the-twentieth-century railroad, or government subsidies granted to basic research).

3. Out on the Cybernetic Frontier

But what happens when the friction becomes the machine?

What will happen in the future if problems of nonexcludability, of nonrivalry, of nontransparency come to apply to a large range of the economy? What happens if they come to occupy as central a place in business decision making as inventory control or production operations management does today? In the natural sciences, perturbation-theory approaches break down when the deviations of initial conditions from those necessary for the simple solution become large. Does something similar happen in political economy? Is examining the way the market system handles a few small episodes of "market failure" a good guide for understanding the way it will handle many large ones?

We do not know. But we do want to take a first step toward discerning what new theories of the new markets might look like if new visions turn out to be necessary (or if old visions need to be adjusted). It is natural to examine the way enterprises and entrepreneurs are reacting today to the coming of nonexcludability, nonrivalry, and nontransparency on the electronic frontier. The hope is that experience along the frontiers of electronic commerce will serve as a good guide to what pieces of the theory are likely to be most important, and will suggest areas in which further development might have a high rate of return.

3.1 The Market for Software (Shareware, Public Betas, and More)

We have noted that the market for modern, complex products is anything but transparent. While one can think of services, such as medicine, that are particularly opaque to the buyer, today it is difficult to imagine a more opaque product than software. Indeed, when one considers the increasing opacity of products in the context of the growing importance of services to the economy, it suggests that transparency will become a particularly important issue in the next economy.

Consumers' failure to acquire full information about the software they buy certainly demonstrates that acquiring the information must be expensive. In response to this cost, social institutions have begun to spring up to get around the shrink-wrap dilemma. The first was known as shareware: You download the program; if you like the program you send its author some money, and perhaps in return you get a manual, access to support, and/or an upgraded version.

The benefit of try-before-you-buy is precisely that it makes the process more transparent. The cost is that try-before-you-buy often turns out to be try-use-and-don't-pay.

The next stage beyond shareware has been the evolution of the institution of the *public beta*. This is a time-limited (or bug-ridden, or otherwise restricted) version of the product: Users can investigate the properties of the public beta version to figure out whether the product is worthwhile. But to get the permanent (or the less bug-ridden) version, they have to pay.

Yet a third stage is the "dual track" version: Eudora shareware versus Eudora Pro, for example. Perhaps the hope is that users of the free low-power version will some day become richer, or less patient, or find they have greater needs. At that point, they will find it least disruptive to switch to a product that looks and feels familiar, that is compatible with their habits and with their existing files. In effect (and if the sellers are lucky), the free version captures users as future customers before they are even aware they are future buyers.

The developing free-public-beta industry is a way of dealing with the problem of lack of transparency. It is a relatively benign development, in the sense that it involves competition through distribution of lesser versions of the ultimate product. An alternative would be (say) the strategy of constructing barriers to compatibility. The famous examples in the computer industry come from the 1970s, when Digital Equipment Corporation (DEC) made nonstandard cable connectors; from the mid-1980s, when IBM attempted to appropriate the entire PC industry through its PS/2 line; and from the late 1980s, when Apple Computers used a partly ROM-based operating system to exclude clones.

Fortunately for consumers, these alternative strategies proved (in the latter two cases, at least) to be catastrophic failures for the companies pursuing them. Perhaps the main reason that the free-public-beta strategy is now dominant is this catastrophic failure of strategies of incompatibility—even though they did come close to success.

A fourth, increasingly important, solution to the transparency problem is open-source software.[16] Open source solves the software opacity problem with total transparency: The source code itself is available to all for examination and re-use. Open source programs can be sold, but whenever the right to use a program is conferred, it brings with it additional rights: to inspect and alter the software, and to convey the altered program to others.

In the case of the "Copyleft license," for example, anyone may modify and re-use the code, provided that they comply with the conditions in the original license and impose similar conditions of openness and re-usability on all subsequent users of the code.[17] License terms do vary. This variation itself is a source of potential opacity.[18] However, it is easy to envision a world in which open-source software plays an increasingly large role.

Open source's vulnerability (and perhaps also its strength) is that it is, by design, only minimally excludable. Without excludability, it is harder to get paid for your work. Traditional economic thinking suggests that all other things being equal, people will tend to concentrate their efforts on things that get them paid. And when, as in software markets, the chance to produce a product that dominates a single category holds out the prospect of enormous payment (think Windows), one might expect that effort to be greater still.

Essentially volunteer software development would seem particularly vulnerable to the tragedy of the commons. Open source has, however, evolved a number of strategies that at least ameliorate, and may even overcome, this problem. Open-source authors gain status by writing code. Not only do they receive kudos, but the work can be used as a way to gain marketable reputation. Writing open-source code that becomes widely used and accepted serves as a virtual business card, and helps overcome the lack of transparency in the market for high-level software engineers.

The absence of the prospect of an enormous payout may retard the development of new features in large, collaborative open-source projects. It may also reduce the richness of the feature set. However, since most people apparently use a fairly small subset of the features provided by major packages, this may not be a major problem. Furthermore, open source may make proprietary designer add-ons both technically feasible and economically rational.

In open source, the revenues cannot come from traditional intellectual property rights alone. One must provide some sort of other value—be it a help desk, easy installation, or extra features—in order to be paid. Moreover, there remains the danger that one may not be paid at all.

Nevertheless, open source has already proven itself to be viable in important markets: the World Wide Web as we know it exists because Tim Berners-Lee open-sourced HTML and HTTP.

3.2 Of Shop-bots, Online Auctions, and Meta-Sites

Predictions abound as to how software will use case- and rule-based thinking to do your shopping for you, advise you on how to spend your leisure time, and in general organize your life for you. But that day is still far in the future.[19] So far, we have only the early generations of the knowledge-scavenging virtual robot and the automated comparison shopper. Already, however, we can discern some trends, and identify places where legal rules are likely to shape microeconomic outcomes. The interaction between the law and the market has, as one would expect, distributional consequences. More surprisingly, perhaps, it also has potential implications for economic efficiency.

Shop-bots

BargainFinder was one of the first Internet-based shopping agents.[20] In its first incarnation, in 1997, it did just one thing. Even then it did it too well for some. Now that BargainFinder and other intelligent shopping agents have spread into a wide range of markets, a virtual war over access to and control of price information is raging in the online marketplace. Thus, one has to ask: Does the price come at a price?

In the initial version of BargainFinder, and to this day, the user enters the details of a music compact disk she might like to purchase. BargainFinder interrogates several online music stores that might offer to sell it. It then reports back the prices in a tidy table that makes comparison shopping easy. Initially, the system was not completely transparent: It was not always possible to discern the vendor's shipping charges without visiting the vendor's Web site. But as BargainFinder's inventors said, it was "only an experiment."

Today, it's no longer an experiment. "Shipping and handling" is included as a separate and visible charge. The output is a handsome table that can be sorted by price, by speed of delivery, or by merchant. It can be further customized to take account of shipping costs by zip code, and results can be sorted by price or by speed of delivery. While the user sees the names of the firms whose prices are listed, it's a short list, and there is no way to know what other firms may have been queried.

Other, newer, shopping agents take a more aggressive approach. R-U-Sure, available at http://rusure.com, installs an application on the desktop that monitors the user's Web browsing. Whenever the user interacts with an e-commerce site that R-U-Sure recognizes, it swings into action, and a little box pops up with a whooshing noise. It display the queries it is sending to competing merchants' Web stores to see if they have a better price, and reports on the winner.

Competitor clickthebutton (http://www.clickthebutton.com) installs an icon in the taskbar, but pops up only when it is clicked. The company provides a full and impressively lengthy list of the sites it is capable of querying on the shopper's behalf.[21]

Bidding Services

Price competition is also fostered by bidding services and auctions. Bidding services such as http://www.priceline.com (hotels, air tickets) and http://www.nextag.com (consumer goods and electronics) invite customers to send a price they would be willing to pay for a commodity service or good. However, the price competition is constrained. There is no obvious way for consumers to learn what deals others have been able to secure, and the bidding services appear designed to discourage experimentation aimed at finding out the market-clearing price.

Priceline requires the consumer to commit to pay if his offer is accepted; Nextag does not, but tracks the user's behavior with a "reputation" number that goes up when a merchant's acceptance of a bid results in a purchase and goes down when an accepted bid does not lead to a purchase. Unlike Priceline, however, Nextag contemplates multi-round negotiations: "Sellers," it warns, "will be more likely to respond to your requests if you have a high rating."

At first glance, a highly variegated good such as a college education would seem to resist any effort at a bidding process. Nevertheless, ecollegebid.org (http://www.ecollegebid.org/) has a Web site that invites prospective college students to state what they are willing to pay and then offers to match it with a "college's willingness to offer tuition discounts." Although the list of participating colleges is not published, or even shared with competing colleges, executive director Tedd Kelly states that six colleges are set to participate and negotiations are under way with more than fifteen others. In its first five weeks, 508 students placed ecollegebids.[22] Once a college meets a price, the student is asked, but not required, to reply within 30 days, and to submit an application that the college retains the option of rejecting.

Auction Sites

Auction sites provide a different type of price competition, and a different interface with shopping bots. Users can either place each of their bids manually, or they can set up a bidding bot to place their bids for them. E-bay, for example, encourages bidders not only to place an initial bid but also to set up "proxy bidding" in which any competing bid immediately will be met with a response, up to the user's maximum price. Since E-bay gets a commission based in part on the final sale price, it gains whenever proxy bidding pushes up the price.

Perhaps the fastest-growing segment of the online auction market is aimed at business-to-business transactions. An example is Freemarkets (http://www.freemarkets.com), which boasts, "We created online auctions covering approximately $1 billion in 1998, and estimate we saved clients 2-25%. Since 1995, we have created online auctions for more than 30 buyers in over 50 product categories. More than 1,800 suppliers from more than 30 countries have participated in our auctions."

Meta Auction Sites

There are a significant number of competing consumer auction sites in operation. The profusion of auctions has created a demand for meta-sites that provide information about the goods offered on multiple online auctions. Examples of meta-sites include http://www.auctionwatch.com/ and http://www.auctionwatchers.com/.

Auctionwatch, like BargainFinder before it, has become too successful for some. E-bay initially requested that meta-sites not list its auctions. When Auctionwatch failed to comply, E-bay threatened auctionwatch.com with legal action, claiming that Auctionwatch's "Universal Search" function, which directs users to auctions on E-bay and competing services (Yahoo, Amazon.com, MSN, Bidstream, and Ruby Lane) is an "unauthorized intrusion" that places an unnecessary load on E-bay's servers, violates E-bay's intellectual property rights, and misleads users by not returning the full results of some searches.[23]

The claim that E-bay's auction prices or the details of the sellers' offers to sell are protected in the U.S. by copyright, trade secret, or other intellectual property law is bogus. (However, there are proposals in Congress to change the law in a way that may make the claim more plausible in the future.) Other hitherto untested legal theories may, however, prove more plausible. A claim that meta-sites were somehow damaging E-bay by overloading its servers, or a claim based on some kind of trespass, might find more support.

Whether meta auction sites do burden searchees' servers is itself a difficult factual issue. To the extent that many people who are not interested in bidding see the data on the meta-site, the load on E-bay is reduced. The current law is probably in the meta-sites' favor.

But there is uncertainty, and this uncertainty is compounded by the possibility of legislation.

Efficiency?

It is particularly appropriate to ask what the economically efficient solution might be at a time when the law is somewhat in flux. Most economists, be they Adam Smithian classicists, neoclassical Austrians, or more modern economics-of-information mavens, would at first thought instinctively agree with the proposition that a vendor in a competitive market selling a standardized product—for one Tiger Lily CD is as good as another—would want customers to know as much as possible about what the vendor offers for sale, and the prices at which the goods are available.

The reason for this near-consensus is that in a competitive market every sale at the offer price should be welcome: All are made at a markup over marginal cost. Thus, all online CD retailers ought to have wanted to be listed by BargainFinder, if only because every sale that went elsewhere when they had the lowest price was lost profit.

But not so.

A significant fraction of the merchants regularly visited by BargainFinder were less than ecstatic. They retaliated by blocking the agent's access to their otherwise publicly available data. As of March 1997, one third of the merchants targeted by BargainFinder locked out its queries. One, CDNow, did so for frankly competitive reasons. The other two said that the costs of large numbers of "hobbyist" queries were too great for them. A similar dynamic is currently unfolding in the online auction world: E-bay, the best-known online auction site, has started to block Auctionwatch's access to E-bay's data.

One possible explanation for the divergence between the economic theorist's prediction that every seller should want to be listed by BargainFinder or Auctionwatch and the apparent outcome is the price-gouging story. In this story, stores blocking comparison sites tend to charge higher-than-normal prices because they are able to take advantage of consumer ignorance of cheaper alternatives. The stores are gouging buyers by taking advantage of relatively high search costs.

Our utterly unscientific Web browsing supports the hypothesis that consumers have yet to figure out how to bring their search costs down—R-U-Sure may need a lot more publicity. Prices are in flux and do not appear to be behaving the way Adam Smith would predict. Random browsing among various delivery channels reveals wide price fluctuations, peaking at 40% on one occasion for consumer electronics items under $200. In this case, BargainFinder and its successors would indeed be valuable developments. They will make markets more efficient and will lower prices.

Another possibility is the "kindly service" story. Perhaps stores blocking BargainFinder, R-U-Sure, or meta-sites tend to charge higher-than-normal prices because they provide additional service or convenience. If commerce becomes increasingly electronic and impersonal (or if "personal" comes to mean "filtered through fiendishly clever software agents"), this sort of humanized attention will become increasingly expensive. To the extent that this additional service or convenience can be provided automatically, things are less clear.

In a sometimes-forgotten classic, *The Joyless Economy,* Tibor Scitovsky noted that the advent of mass production of furniture seemed to cause the price of hand-carved chairs to increase, even as the demand for them shrank.[24] As consumers switched to less costly (and less carefully made, one-size-fits-all) mass-produced furniture, carvers became scarce and business for the remaining carvers became scarcer. Soon only the rich could engage their services.

If the "kindly service" story is right, the rise of the commodity market creates a risk of a possible decline in service-intensive or higher-quality goods. Mass tastes will be satisfied more cheaply, yet specialty tastes will become more of an expensive luxury. On the other hand, the rise of shop-bots such as BargainFinder or R-U-Sure offers an opportunity for consumers to aggregate their preferences on a worldwide scale. Indeed, Mercata (http://www.mercata.com/) provides a service by which consumers can group together to put in a group buy for a product. The larger the number of units, the lower the price, although it is not clear that even the resulting price is always lower than what might be found by determined Web browsing. Thus, the transaction costs associated with aggregation of identical but disparate preferences, and

with the communication and satisfaction of individualized preferences, should be going down. As it becomes increasingly easy for
consumers to communicate their individualized preferences to
manufacturers and suppliers, and increasingly easy to tailor goods
to individual tastes—be it a CD that has only the tracks you like,
customized blue jeans, or a car manufactured (just in time) to your
specifications—personalized goods may become the norm, put-
ting the "joy" back into the economy and replacing the era of mass
production with an era of mass customization.

Some signs of this were visible even before the information
revolution: Lower costs of customization have already undermined
one of Scitovsky's examples as fresh-baked bread makes its come-
back at many supermarkets and specialty stores. And Alfred P.
Sloan created General Motors and the automobile industry of the
post-World War II era by piling different body styles, colors, and
option packages on top of the same Chevy drive train.

In either the "price gouging" or the "kindly service" story, the
advent of services such as BargainFinder and R-U-Sure presents
retailers of many goods with a dilemma: If they join in, they
contribute toward turning the market for CDs, books, consumer
electronics, and other, similar goods into a commodity market with
competition only on price. If they act "selflessly" and stay out, in
order to try to degrade the utility of shop-bots and meta-sites (and
preserve their higher average markup), they must hope that their
competitors will understand their long-run self-interest in the same
way.

But overt communication in which all sellers agreed to block
BargainFinder would, of course, violate the Sherman Act. And
without a means of retaliation to "punish" players that do not
pursue the collusive long-run strategy of blocking BargainFinder,
the collapse of the market into a commodity market with only price
competition, and with little provided in the way of ancillary shopping services, appears likely.

When we wrote the first draft of this chapter, we noted that if CD
retailers were trying to undermine BargainFinder by staying away,
their strategy appeared to be failing. Some CD retailers that initially
blocked BargainFinder later unblocked it, while others were clam-
oring to join. Since then, the rise of a new generation of meta-sites

and alternate means of creating price competition makes the question somewhat moot. The technological arms race, pitting meta-sites and shop-bots against merchants, will continue, but the attackers seem to have the advantage, if only because of their numbers.

Whether or not this is an occasion for joy depends on which of our explanations above is closer to the truth. The growth of the bookstore chain put the local bookshop out of business, just as the growth of supermarkets killed the corner grocer. Not everyone considers this trend to be a victory, despite the lower prices. A human element has been lost, and a "personal service" element that may have led to a better fit between purchaser and purchase has been lost as well.

So far, the discussion has operated on the basis of the assumption that merchants have an incentive to block comparison shopping services if they charge higher-than-normal prices. Strangely, some merchants may have an incentive to block it if they charge lower-than-normal prices. As we all know, merchants sometimes advertise a "loss leader," and offer to sell a particular good at an unprofitable price. Merchants do this in order to lure consumers into the store, either to try to sell them more profitable versions of the same good (leading, in the extreme case, to "bait-and-switch"), or in the hope that the consumer will spy other, more profitable, goods to round out the market basket.

You can explain this merchant behavior in different ways, by talking about the economics of information, locational utility, myopic consumers generalizing incorrectly on the basis of a small number of real bargains, or temporary monopolies caused by the consumer's presence in this store as opposed to another store far away.

It may be that merchants blocking BargainFinder did not want consumers to be able to exploit their "loss leaders" without having to be exposed to the other goods offered simultaneously. Without this exposure, the "loss-leaders" would not lure buyers to other, higher-profit, items, but would simply be losses. The merchant's ability to monopolize the consumer's attention for a period may be the essence of modern retailing; the reaction to BargainFinder and Auctionwatch, at least, suggests that this is what merchants believe.

The growing popularity of frequent-buyer and other loyalty programs also suggests that getting and keeping customer attention is important to sellers. Interestingly, this explanation works about equally well for the "kindly service" and "loss leader" explanations—the two stories that are consistent with the assumption that the CD market was relatively efficient before BargainFinder came along.

3.3 Browsing Is Our Business

More important, and perhaps more likely, is the possibility that BargainFinder and other shop-bots threaten merchants that are in the "browsing assistance" business. Some online merchants are enthusiastically attempting to fill the role of personal shopping assistant. Indeed, some of the most successful online stores have adapted to the new marketplace by inverting the information equation.

Retail stores in meatspace ("meatspace" being the part of life that is not cyberspace) provide information about available products— browsing and information acquisition services—that consumers find valuable and are willing to pay for, either in time and attention or in cash. Certainly meatspace shopping is conducive to unplanned (impulse) purchases, as any refrigerator groaning under the weight of kitchen magnets shows. Retail stores in cyberspace may exacerbate this tendency: What, after all, is a store in cyberspace but a collection of information?

CDNow, for example, tailors its virtual storefront to what it knows of a customer's tastes based on her past purchases. In addition to dynamically altering the storefront on each visit, CDNow also offers to send shoppers occasional email information about new releases that fit their past buying patterns.

One can imagine stores tailoring what they present to what they presume to be the customer's desires, based on demographic information that was available about the customer even before the first purchase. Tailoring might extend beyond showcasing different wares: Taken to the logical extreme, it would include some form of price discrimination based on facts known about the customer's preferences, or on demographic information thought to be correlated with preferences. (The U.S. and other legal systems impose constraints on the extent to which stores may generalize from demographic information: For example, stores that attempt race-based, sex-based, or other types of invidious price variation usually violate U.S. law.)

A critical microeconomic question in all this is how consumers and manufacturer/sellers exchange information in this market. Both consumers and sellers have an interest in encouraging the exchange of information: In order to provide what the consumer wants, the sellers need to know what is desired and how badly it is wanted. Consumers need to know what is offered where, and at what price. A shop-bot may solve the consumer's problem of price, but it will not tell him about an existing product of which he is unaware. Similarly, CDNow may reconfigure its store to fit customer profiles, but without some external source of information about customers, this takes time and requires repeat visitors. Indeed, it requires that customers come in through the front door: All the reconfiguration in the world will not help CDNow or E-bay if customers are unaware that they would enjoy its products, or if the customers' only relationship with CDNow is via a shop-bot or a meta-site.

The retail outlet in the average mall can plausibly be described as a mechanism for informing consumers about product attributes. The merchant gives away product information in the hope that consumers will make purchases. Physical stores, however, have fixed displays and thus must provide more or less identical information to every customer. Anyone who looks in the window, anyone who studies the product labels, or even the product catalogs, receives the same sales pitch.

Some of the more interesting recent writing on the microeconomics of virtual retailing suggests that what is really happening is a war for the customer's attention—a war for eyeballs.[25] Certainly the rush to create "portals" that, providers hope, will become the surfer-shopper's default home page on the Internet suggests that some large investors believe eyeballs are well worth having. So too does the tendency of successful early entrants in one product market to seek to leverage their brand into other markets.

It may be that the "dynamic storefront" story is the Internet's substitute for the "kindly service" story. If so, the rise of agent-based shopping may well be surprisingly destructive. It raises the possibility of a world in which retail shops providing valuable services are destroyed by an economic process that funnels a large percentage of consumer sales into what become commodity markets without middlemen: People use the high-priced premium cyberstore to browse, but then use BargainFinder to purchase.

To appreciate the problem, consider Bob, an online merchant who has invested a substantial amount in a large and easy-to-use "browsing" database that combines your past purchases, current news, new releases, and other information to present you with a series of choices and possible purchases that greatly increase your chances of coming across something interesting. After all, a customer enters seeking not a particular title, and not a random title, but a product that he or she would like. What is being sold is the process of search and information acquisition that leads to the judgment that this is something to buy. A good online merchant would make the service of "browsing" easy—and would in large part be selling that browsing assistance.

If this browsing is our business story, there is a potential problem: Browsing assistance is not an excludable commodity. Unless Bob charges for his services (which is likely to discourage most customers, and especially the impulse purchaser), there is nothing to stop Alice from browsing merchant Bob's Web site to determining the product she wants, and then using BargainFinder to find the cheapest source of supply. BargainFinder will surely find a competitor with lower prices, because Bob's competitor will not have to pay for the database and the software underlying the browsing assistance.

If so, projects such as BargainFinder will have a potentially destructive application, for many online stores will be easy to turn into commodity markets once the process of information acquisition and browsing is complete. It would be straightforward to run a market in kitchen gadgets along the lines of BargainFinder, even if much of the market for gadgets involves finding solutions to problems one was not consciously aware one had. First take a free ride on one of the sites that provide browsing assistance to discover what you want, then open another window and access BargainFinder to buy it.

Students and other people with more time than money have been using this strategy to purchase stereo components for decades:

Draw on the sales expertise offered at the premium store, then buy from the warehouse. But the scope and ease of this strategy is about to become much greater.

To merchants providing helpful shopping advice, the end result will be as if they spent all their time in their competitors' discount warehouse, pointing out goods that the competitors' customers ought to buy. The only people who will pay premium prices for the physical good—and thus pay for browsing and information services—will be those who feel under a gift-exchange moral obligation to do so: the "sponsors" of NPR. Thus, cyberstores that offer browsing assistance may find that they have many interests in common with the physical stores in the mall—which fear that consumers will browse in their stores, and then go home and buy products tax-free on the Internet.

3.4 Collaborative Filtering

Collaborative filtering provides part of the answer to the information exchange problem. It also provides another example of how information technology changes the way that consumer markets will operate. In their simplest form, collaborative filters such as FireFly[26] bring together consumers to exchange information about their preferences. The assumption is that if Alice finds that several other readers—each of whom, like her, likes Frisch, Kafka, Kundera, and Klima but gets impatient with James and Joyce—tend to like William Gass, the odds are good that Alice will enjoy Gass's *On Being Blue* as well.

In the process of entering sufficient information about her tastes to prime the pump, Alice adds to the database of linked preference information. In helping herself, Alice helps others. In this simplest form, the collaborative filter helps Alice find out about new books she might like. The technology is applicable to finding potentially desirable CDs, news, Web sites, software, travel, financial services, and restaurants, as well as to helping Alice find people who share her interests.

At the next level of complexity, the collaborative filter can be linked to a shop-bot. Once Alice has decided that she will try *On Being Blue,* she can find out who will sell it to her at the best price.

The truly interesting development, however, comes when Alice's personal preference data are available to every merchant Alice visits. (Leave aside for a moment who owns these data, and the terms on which they become available.) A shop such as CDNow becomes able to tailor its virtual storefront to a fairly good model of Alice's likely desires upon her first visit. CDNow may use this information to showcase its most enticing wares, or it may use it to fine-tune its prices to charge Alice all that she can afford—or both.

Whichever is the case, shopping will not be the same.

Once shops acquire the ability to engage in price discrimination, consumers will of course seek ways of fighting back. One way will be to shop anonymously, and see what price is quoted when no consumer data are proffered. Consumers can either attempt to prevent merchants and others from acquiring the transactional data that could form the basis of a consumer profile, or they can avail themselves of anonymizing intermediaries that will protect the consumer against the merchant's attempt to practice perfect price discrimination by aggregating data about the seller's prices and practices. In this model, a significant fraction of cyber commerce will be conducted by software agents that will carry accreditation demonstrating their creditworthiness, but will not be traceable back to those who use them.

Thus, potential legal constraints on online anonymity may have more far-reaching consequences than their obvious effect on unconstrained political speech.[27] In some cases, consumers may be able to use collaborative filtering techniques to form buying clubs and achieve quantity discounts, as in the case of Mercata.[28] Or consumers will construct shopping personas with false demographics and purchase patterns in the hope of getting access to discounts. Business fliers across America routinely purchase back-to-back round-trip tickets that bracket a Saturday night in an attempt to diminish the airlines' ability to charge business travelers premium prices. Airlines, meanwhile, have invested in computer techniques to catch and invalidate the second ticket.

Consumers will face difficult maximization problems. In the absence of price discrimination, and assuming privacy itself is only an intermediate good (i.e., that consumers do not value privacy in and of itself), the marginal value to the consumer of a given datum concerning her behavior is likely to be less than the average value to the merchant of each datum in an aggregated consumer profile. If markets are efficient, or if consumers suffer from a plausible myopia in which they value data at the short-run marginal value rather than the long-term average cost, merchants will purchase this information, leading to a world with little transactional privacy.[29]

Furthermore, the lost privacy is not without gain: Every time Alice visits a virtual storefront that has been customized to her preferences, her search time is reduced, and she is more likely to find what she wants—even if she didn't know she wanted it—and the more information the merchant has about her, the more true this will be.

The picture becomes even more complicated once one begins to treat privacy itself as a legitimate consumer preference rather than as merely an intermediate good. Once one accepts that consumers may have a taste for privacy, it is no longer obvious that the transparent consumer is an efficient solution for the management of customer data. Relaxing an economic assumption does not, however, change anything about actual behavior, and the same tendencies that push the market toward a world in which consumer data is a valuable and much-traded commodity persist.

Indeed, basic ideas of privacy are under assault. Data miners and consumer profilers are able to produce detailed pictures of the tastes and habits of increasing numbers of consumers. The spread of intelligent traffic management systems and video security and recognition systems, and the gradual integration of information systems built into every appliance, will eventually make it possible to track movement as well as purchases. Once one person has this information, there is, of course, almost no cost for making it available to all.

Unfortunately, it is difficult to measure the demand for privacy. Furthermore, the structure of the legal system does not tend to allow consumers to express this preference. Today, most consumer transactions are governed by standard-form contracts. The default rules may be constrained by state consumer law, or by portions of the Uniform Commercial Code, but they generally derive most of their content from boilerplate language written by a merchant's lawyer. If you are buying a dishwasher, you do not get to haggle over the terms of the contract, which (in the rare case that they are even read) are found in small print somewhere on the invoice.

Although it is possible to imagine a world in which the Internet allows for negotiation of contractual terms even in consumer sales, we have yet to hear of a single example of this phenomenon, and see little reason to expect it. On the contrary, to the extent that a trend can be discerned, it is in the other direction, toward the "Web-wrap" or "clip-wrap" contract (the neologisms derive from "shrink-wrap" contracts, in which the buyer of software is informed that she will agree to the terms by opening the wrapper), in which the consumer is asked to agree to the contract before being allowed to view the Web site's content. Indeed, the enforcement of these agreements is enshrined in law in the proposed, and very controversial, Uniform Computer Information Transactions Act <http://www.law.upenn.edu/bll/ulc/ucita/cita10st.htm>.

4. The Next Economics?

We have argued that assumptions that underlie the microeconomics of the *invisible hand* will fray when they are transported into tomorrow's information economy. Commodities that take the form of single physical objects are rivalrous and are excludable: There is only one of a given item, and if it is locked up in the seller's shop, no one else can use it. The structure of the distribution network delivered marketplace transparency as a cheap byproduct of getting the goods to their purchasers. All these assumptions did fail at the margin, but the match of the real to the ideal was reasonably good.

Modest as they may be in comparison to the issues we have left for another day, our observations about microfoundations do have some implications for economic theory and for policy. At some point soon, it will become practical to charge for everything on the World Wide Web. Whether it will become economically feasible, or common, remains to be seen. The outcome of this battle will have profound economic and social consequences.

Consider just two polar possibilities. On the one hand, one can envision a hybrid gift-exchange model, in which most people pay as much for access to Web content as they pay for NPR, and in which the few who value an in-depth information edge or speed-of-information acquisition pay more. At the other extreme, one can as easily foresee a world in which great efforts have been made to reproduce familiar aspects of the traditional model of profit maximization.

Which vision will dominate, absent government intervention, depends in part on the human motivation of programmers, authors, and other content providers. The *invisible hand* assumed a "rational economic man," a greedy human. The cybernetic human could be very greedy, for greed can be automated. But much progress in basic science and technology has always been based on other motivations than money. The thrill of the chase, the excitement of discovery, and the respect of one's peers have played a very large role as well, perhaps helped along by the occasional Nobel Prize, knighthood for services to science, or a distinguished chair; in the future, "Net.Fame" may join the list.

Government will surely be called upon to intervene. Adam Smith said that eighteenth-century "statesmen" could in most cases do the most good by sitting on their hands. The twenty-first-century "stateswomen" will have to decide whether this advice still applies after the fit between the institutions of market exchange and production and distribution technologies has decayed.

We suspect that policies that ensure diversity of providers will continue to have their place. One of the biggest benefits of a market economy is that it provides for sunset. When faced with competition, relatively inefficient organizations fail to take in revenue to cover their costs, and then they die. Competition is thus still a virtue, whether the governing framework is one of gift-exchange or buy-and-sell—unless competition destroys the ability to capture significant economies of scale.

The challenge for policy makers is likely to be particularly acute in the face of technological attempts to recreate familiar market relationships. That markets characterized by the properties of rivalry, excludability, and transparency are efficient does not mean that any effort to reintroduce these properties to a market lacking them necessarily increases social welfare. Furthermore, in some cases the new, improved, versions may provide more excludability or transparency than did the old model; this raises new problems.

Holders of intellectual property rights in digital information, be they producers or sellers, do have a strong incentive to reintroduce rivalry and excludability into the market for digital information.

4.1 Increasing Excludability

It appears increasingly likely that technological advances such as "digital watermarks" will allow each copy of a digital data set, be it a program or a poem, to be uniquely identified. If these are coupled with appropriate legal sanctions for unlicensed copying, a large measure of excludability can be restored to the market.[30] Policy makers will need to be particularly alert to three dangers:

• First, technologies that permit excludability risk introducing socially unjustified costs if the methods of policing excludability are themselves costly.

• Second, as the example of broadcast television demonstrates, imperfect substitutes for excludability can themselves have bad consequences that are sometimes difficult to anticipate.

• Third, over-perfect forms of excludability raise the possibility that traditional limits on excludability of information such as "fair use" might be changed by technical means without the political and social debate that should precede such a shift.

We counsel caution: In the absence of any clear indication of what the optimum would be, the burden of proof should be on those who argue that any level of excludability should be mandated. This applies particularly to information that is not the content being sold but that is instead about the current state of the market itself. There is a long tradition that information about the state of the marketplace should be as widely broadcast as possible.[31] We cannot see any economic arguments against this tradition.

In particular, reforming the law to give sellers a property right in information about the prices that they charge appears extremely dangerous. There has never in the past been a legal right to exclude competitors from access to bulk pricing data. It is hard to see what improvement in economic efficiency could follow from the creation of such a right in the future.

4.2 Increasing Rivalry

It is equally hard to imagine how rivalry might be re-created for digitized data without using an access system that relies on a hardware token of some sort or on continuing interaction between the seller and the buyer. Rivalry can be reintroduced if access to a program, a document, or other digital data can be conditioned on access to a particular "smart card" or other physical object. Or rivalry can be reintroduced by requiring the user to get permission every time the data are accessed, permitting the data provider to confirm, via IP lookup, caller ID, or some other means, that the data are being used by the credentialed user. Perhaps a crypto-graphically based software analog might be developed that relied on some secret that the purchaser would have a strong incentive to keep to herself. In each case, a form of rivalry results, since multiple users can be prevented from using the data simultaneously.

But imposing rivalry where it is not naturally found means imposing a socially unnecessary cost on someone. The result may look and feel like a traditional market, but it cannot, by definition, carry the "optimality" properties markets have possessed in the past. The artificial creation of rivalry ensures that many users whose willingness to pay for a good is greater than the (near-zero) marginal cost of producing another copy will not get one.

Policy makers should therefore be very suspicious of any market-based arguments for artificial rivalry.

4.3 Increasing Transparency

It might seem that anything that encourages transparency must be good. Indeed, all other things being equal, for consumers, for merchants selling products that can survive scrutiny, and for the economy as a whole, increases in the transparency of product markets are always a good thing. The issue, however, is to what extent this logic justifies a transparent consumer.

The answer is fundamentally political. It depends on the extent to which one is willing to recognize privacy as an end in itself. If information about consumers is just a means to an economic end, there is no reason for concern. If, on the other hand, citizens perceive maintaining control over facts about their economic actions as a good in itself, some sort of governmental intervention in the market may be needed to make it easier for this preference to express itself.

4.4 Policy Hazards in the New Economy

We have focused on the ways in which digital media undermine the assumptions of rivalry, excludability, and transparency, and have tried to suggest that the issue of transparency is at least as important, complicated, and interesting as the other two. In so doing, we have been forced to slight important microeconomic features of the next economy. We have not, for example, discussed the extent to which the replacement of human salespeople, travel agents, and shop assistants will affect the labor market.

The consequences may be earthshaking. For about two centuries starting in 1800, technological progress was the friend of the unskilled worker: It provided a greater relative boost to the demand for workers who were relatively unskilled (who could tighten bolts on the assembly line, or move things about so that the automated production process could use them, or watch largely self-running machines and call for help when they stopped) than for those who were skilled. The spread of industrial civilization was associated with a great leveling in the distribution of income. But there is nothing inscribed in the nature of reality to the effect that technological progress must always boost the relative wages of the unskilled.

Nor have we addressed potentially compensating factors such as the looming disaggregation of the university, a scenario in which "distance learning" bridges the gap between elite lecturers and mass audiences, turning many educational institutions into little more than degree-granting standards bodies, with financial aid and counseling functions next to a gym or (just maybe) a library. While this may benefit the mass audience, it has harmful effects on one elite: It risks creating an academic proletariat made up of those who would have been well-paid professors before the triumph of "distance learning" over the lecture hall.

Along a number of dimensions, there is good reason to fear that the enormous economies of scale found in the production of nonrivalrous commodities are pushing us in the direction of a winner-take-all economy. The long-run impact of the information revolution on the distribution of income and wealth is something that we have not even begun to analyze.

Similarly, we have completely ignored a number of interesting macroeconomic issues. Traditional ideas of the "open" and "closed" economy will have to be rethought on sectoral grounds. Once a nation becomes part of the global information infrastructure, its ability to raise either tariff or nontariff walls against certain foreign trade activities becomes vanishingly small. Nations will not, for example, be able to protect an "infant" software industry. It will be hard to enforce labor laws when the jobs are taken by telecommuters.

National accounts are already becoming increasingly inaccurate as it becomes harder and harder to track imports and exports. Governments are unable to distinguish the arrival of a personal letter, with a picture attached, from the electronic delivery of a $100,000 piece of software. Monetary and financial economics will also have to adapt.

Traditionally, the field of economics has always had some difficulty explaining money: There has been something "sociological" about the way tokens worthless in themselves get and keep their value that is hard to fit with economists' underlying explanatory strategies of rational agents playing games of exchange with one another. These problems will intensify as the nature and varieties of money change. The introduction of digital currencies suggests a possible return of private currencies. It threatens the end of seigneurage, and raises questions about who can control the national money supply.[32]

The market system may well prove to be tougher than its traditional defenders have thought, and to have more subtle and powerful advantages than those that defenders of the *invisible hand* have usually listed. At the very least, however, defenders will need new arguments. Economic theorists have enormous powers of resilience: Economists regularly try to spawn new theories—today, evolutionary economics, the economics of organizations and bureaucracies, public choice theory, and the economics of networks.

Experience suggests that the regulations for tomorrow's economy are likely to be written today. That means policy choices will be made in advance of both theory and practice, and with disproportionate input from those who have the most to lose from change, or who have garnered short-term first-mover advantages from the first stage of the transition now under way. If we are correct in believing that some of the basic assumptions that drive most thinking about the market (and most introductory economics classes) will not hold up well in the online economy, it is particularly important for those choices to be made with care.

Acknowledgments

This is a revised and updated version of "The Next Economy," posted on the World Wide Web in early 1997 at http://www. law.miami.edu/~froomkin/articles/newecon.htm and http://econ161.berkeley.edu/Econ_Articles/newecon.htm. DeLong would like to thank the National Science Foundation, the Alfred P. Sloan Foundation, and the Institute for Business and Economic Research of the University of California for financial support. We both would like to thank Francois Bar, Caroline Bradley, Steven Cohen, Joseph Froomkin, Brian Kahin, Tom Kalil, Ronald P. Loui, Paul Romer, Steven Cohen, Carl Shapiro, Andrei Shleifer, Lawrence H. Summers, Hal Varian, Janet Yellen, and John Zysman for helpful discussions.

Notes

1. Emphasis added. Adam Smith, *The Wealth of Nations* (London: 1776), Cannan edition, p. 423.

2. For estimates of growth in economic product and increases in material welfare over the past century, see Angus Maddison, *Monitoring the World Economy* (Paris: OECD, 1994).

3. Within national borders, that is. Migration across national borders is more restricted today than ever before.

4. See Gerard Debreu, *The Theory of Value* (New York: Wiley 1957).

5. In Britain at least. Inhabitants of West Africa or India in Adam Smith's day had very good reason to dispute such a claim.

6. See Jeffrey K. MacKie-Mason and Hal R. Varian, "Some Economic FAQs About the Internet," *Journal of Electronic Publishing* (June 1995) <http://www.press. umich.edu/jep/works/FAQs.html>; Lee McKnight and Joseph Bailey, "An In-

troduction to Internet Economics," *Journal of Electronic Publishing* (June 1995) <http://www.press.umich.edu/jep/works/McKniIntro.html>.

7. When the *Wall Street Journal* sells a Berkeley economics professor an annual subscription to its e-version, does it imagine that the same user's identification-and-password might be used in one day to access the e-version by the professor at work, by a research assistant working from home on the professor's behalf, and by the professor's spouse at another office? Probably not.

8. See George Akerlof, "Labor Contracts as Partial Gift Exchange," in George Akerlof, *An Economic Theorist's Book of Tales* (Berkeley: University of California Press, 1985).

9. See Brad Cox, *Superdistribution: Objects as Property on the Electronic Frontier* (New York: Addison-Wesley, 1996).

10. In large part because the government did not restructure property rights to help them. Had the government made the legal right to own a TV conditional on one's purchase of a program-viewing license, the development of the industry might well have been different. And such a conditioning of legal right would have been *technologically* enforceable. As British billboards used to say: "Beware! TV locator vans are in your neighborhood!"

11. Newton Minow, *Equal Time* 45, 52 (1964); Newton M. Minow and Craig L. LaMay. *Abandoned in the Wasteland: Children, Television, and the First Amendment* (New York: Hill & Wang, 1996).

12. It is worth noting that in the debate over Microsoft in the second half of the 1990s, virtually no one proposed a Federal Operating System Commission to regulate Microsoft as the FCC had regulated the Bell System. The dilemmas that had led to the Progressive-era proposed solution were stronger than ever. But there was no confidence in that solution to be found anywhere.

13. Andrei Shleifer, "Yardstick Competition," *Rand Journal of Economics* (1986).

14. See Charles Ferguson, *High Stakes, No Prisoners* (New York: Times Books, 1999).

15. See Jean Tirole, *The Theory of Industrial Organization* (Cambridge, MA: MIT Press, 1988).

16. See generally http://www.gnu.org/ (free software) and http://www.opensource.org/ (open source generally).

17. See http://www.gnu.org/copyleft/gpl.html.

18. See, e.g., http://www.gnu.org/philosophy/categories.html (categorizing types of licenses).

19. A useful corrective to some of the hype is Kathyrn Heilmann et al., "Intelligent Agents: A Technology and Business Application Analysis," http://haas.berkeley.edu/~heilmann/agents/#I

20. In January 1997, BargainFinder shopped at nine stores: CD Universe, CDNow!, NetMarket, GEMM, IMM, Music Connection, Tower Records, CD Land, CDworld, and Emusic. A sample search for the Beatles' White Album in

Speculative Microeconomics for Tomorrow's Economy

January 1997 produced this output:

> I couldn't find it at Emusic. You may want to try browsing there yourself.
> CD Universe is not responding. You may want to try browsing there yourself.
> $24.98 (new) GEMM (Broker service for independent sellers; many used CDs, imports, etc.)
> I couldn't find it at CDworld. You may want to try browsing there yourself.
> $24.76 Music Connection (Shipping from $3.25, free for 9 or more. 20 day returns.)
> CDNow is blocking out our agents. You may want to try browsing there yourself.
> NetMarkel is blocking out our agents. You may want to try browsing there yourself.
> CDLand was blocking out our agents, but decided not to. You'll see their prices here soon.
> IMM did not respond. You may want to try browsing there yourself.

21. See http://www.clickthebutton.com/nosite.html.

22. Interview with Tedd Kelly, executive director of e-college bid org, consultants for educational resources and research. 1 Nov 1999.

23. See http://www.auctionwatch.com/company/pr/pr5.html.

24. Tibor Scitovsky, *The Joyless Economy: An Inquiry Into Human Satisfaction and Consumer Dissatisfaction* (Oxford: Oxford University Press: 1976).

25. E.g. Michael H. Goldhaber, *The Attention Economy and the Net*, FIRST MONDAY, http://www.firstmonday.dk/issues/issue2_4/goldhaber/

26. http://www.firefly.com/.

27. A. Michael Froomkin, "Flood Control on the Information Ocean: Living With Anonymity, Digital Cash, and Distributed Databases," 15 *Pitt. J. L. & Com.* 395 (1996).

28. Nicholas Negroponte, "Electronic Word of Mouth," *Wired* 4.10 (Oct. 1996), http://www.hotwired.com/wired/4.10/negroponte.html.

29. Judge Posner suggests that this is the economically efficient result. See Richard A. Posner, "Privacy, Secrecy, and Reputation," 28 *Buffalo L. Rev.* 1 (1979); Richard A. Posner, "The Right of Privacy," 12 *Ga. L. Rev.* 393, 394 (1978). Compare, however, Kim Lane Scheppele, *Legal Secrets* 43-53, 111-126 (1988); see also James Boyle, "A Theory of Law and Information: Copyright, Spleens, Blackmail, and Insider Trading," 80 *Cal. L. Rev.* 1413 (1992) (arguing that most law and economic analysis of markets for information are based on fundamentally contradictory assumptions).

30. See Cox, *Superdistribution.*

31. For example, consider this: "Technology has set into motion dazzling challenges to market mechanisms whose free market dynamism is being impeded by anti-competitive handcuffs imposed by participants and sanctioned by regu-

lators. A free market is nurtured by a culture of disclosure and equal access to information that fuels rather than fetters the marketplace. The dangers are real and the opportunities abundant. The efficiency and expanse of an unburdened open market is limitless. Tear down the barriers to competition, remove the obstacles to greater innovation, spotlight all conflicts of interest, and unleash the flow of timely and accurate information, and our markets—like never before—will be driven by the power and the brilliance of the human spirit." SEC Chairman Arthur Levitt, "Quality Information: The Lifeblood of Our Markets," http://www.sec.gov/news/speeches/spch304.htm (delivered October 18, 1999).

32. See generally A. Michael Froomkin, "Flood Control on the Information Ocean," 15 *Pitt. J. L. & Com.* 395 (1996).

Advertising Pricing Models for the World Wide Web

Donna L. Hoffman and Thomas P. Novak

Introduction

The advertiser-supported Web site is one of several business models vying for legitimacy in the emerging medium of the World Wide Web on the Internet (Hoffman, Novak, and Chatterjee 1995). Advertising on the Web takes a number of forms. Currently, the two most dominant forms of advertiser-supported Web sites are *sponsored-content* sites, such as Hotwired, the Industry Standard, and Salon, and *entry-portal sites* (for example, Yahoo, MSN, and Altavista), which function as gateways to the Web and provide search and directory features to Web browsers.

The sponsorship model has attracted management attention because advertising is expected to be an increasingly significant source of revenues in the new medium of the World Wide Web.

Sponsored sites are of interest because they are well suited to the Web environment (Hoffman and Novak 1996), yet also retain important parallels to existing media in the physical world. In theory, institutional advertising practices and metaphors may be borrowed from traditional media environments to assist initial commercial efforts. In addition, although the "online storefront" model is now taking off, many Web managers are hedging their bets by relying on advertising revenue streams as an additional source of profit for online ventures.

Against this backdrop, firms are trying to understand the elements that make a sponsored site successful. As advertisers and marketers debate the best ways to measure and to track visits and use on commercial Web sites, most firms remain largely in the dark about the numbers of customers for their online offerings. The Web advertising industry currently lacks standards for measuring activities and use by potential customers on the Web. As a result, it is having difficulty envisioning the Web as an advertising medium. There is also no assurance that firms will be successful in generating significant revenues from Web advertising in the future, particularly as electronic commerce efforts continue to gain momentum. Ultimately, we believe that this lack of standardization is likely to limit the long-term viability of the Web advertising sponsorship model.

The lack of standardization exists on four fronts. First, there are no established principles for measuring traffic on commercial Web sites that seek to generate revenues from advertising sponsorship. Second, there is no standard way of measuring consumer response to advertisements. Third, there are no standards for optimal media pricing models. Finally, the complexity of the medium in general hinders the standardization process.

From an advertising perspective, the Web medium has some similarity to radio in that there are many different markets and they are clearly segmented theoretically. But the standardization of the radio media buy—that is, purchasing advertising time on a particular program on a particular radio station—considerably eases the process of advertising in that medium. In contrast, the Web presents a "nightmare buy" for agencies and their clients.

For example, Focalink's 1996 database of over 600 commercial Web sites (Focalink 1996) showed that there are more than 90 sizes for Web advertisement banners, that sites use many different metrics to price advertising, that there is no consistency in definitions even among the same or similar metrics, and that consumer demographic information is virtually nonexistent. In the two years that followed, the situation only increased in complexity as new advertising forms such as so-called rich media (involving, for example, streaming video or Java applets), animated banners, and other interactive banner ads evolved from static banner ads.

Despite the lack of information in this chaotic emerging environment, there is no dearth of activity. Total Internet advertising revenues approached $2 billion in 1998 (Forrester Research 1999) and the category appears to be growing faster than traditional mass-media advertising vehicles such as television and print. From a comparatively insignificant $550 million in 1997, the Internet advertising industry has now logged nearly three years of revenue growth.

According to forecasts, online advertising revenues are expected to reach nearly $13 billion by 2002 (Forrester Research 1999). At this rate, Internet advertising expenditures will exceed billboard advertising expenditures (estimated at over $2 billion as this chapter goes to press) by the end of 1999 and will have surpassed all forms of outdoor advertising (logging revenues of over $4 billion) by the turn of the century. For perspective, it is important to note that total United States advertising expenditures were expected to top $285 billion in 1998 (Competitive Media Reporting 1999).

As industry forces point toward advertising as an increasingly significant source of revenues in the new online medium, and with online shopping revenues expected to reach $184 billion by the year 2004 (Forrester Research 1999), it is no wonder that the advertising sponsorship business model is attracting ever greater management attention, especially in traditional circles.

Yet, despite these heady forecasts, there is still doubt among advertisers about advertising sponsorship as a business model. Their skepticism may be traced to the fact that few have specified conclusively the precise manner in which advertising on the Web might and should further a firm's strategic marketing objectives. Clearly, standardizing the Web measurement process is a critical first step on the path toward the successful commercial development of the Web. Without standardization, ad hoc Web advertising pricing models will continue to hinder the sponsorship model as a legitimate revenue stream.

This chapter examines current practice for advertising pricing models on the Web and proposes models based on constructs that are arguably more suited to the Web environment. The policy considerations that are likely to affect the development of Web advertising standards are then addressed. Finally, the chapter concludes with some thoughts on the best means to develop optimal Web advertising pricing models.

Current Web Advertising Pricing Models

There is considerable confusion regarding the terminology currently in use for Web advertising. The first step is the development of a common vocabulary. If terminology from traditional media is appropriate for use in the context of Web-based advertising, it should be employed to avoid confusion and to ease the process of adopting standards.

The currently dominant forms of Web-based advertising are banner advertisements and target communications. A *banner advertisement* is a small, typically rectangular, graphic image that is linked to a *target communication.* Banner advertisements typically provide little information beyond the identification of the sponsor and serve as an invitation for the visitor to click on the banner to learn more. Banner advertisements appear in various sizes; 90 percent of banner advertisements range from 120 to 500 pixels wide (with a median of 460 pixels) and from 45 to 120 pixels high (with a median of 60 pixels) (Focalink 1996). To minimize confusion, the Internet Advertising Bureau (Internet Advertising Bureau 1999) has proposed that online advertisers voluntarily adopt a small number of banner sizes.

Target communications, in contrast, may be fairly detailed, ranging from a single Web page with basic HTML to a Web page enhanced by technologies such as Java applets (programs written in the Java programming language that can be included in a Web page to enhance functionality), streaming media (real-time broadcasting of audio or video over the Internet), Shockwave (multimedia playback over the Internet), or Web fill-out forms, to a series of linked pages, or to a complete corporate "Internet presence," "content," or "online storefront" site (Hoffman, Novak, and Chatterjee 1995).

Banner advertisements are a primitive type of Web-based advertising and are not likely to ultimately be the most effective new media form. However, because they are the most prevalent form, it is appropriate to discuss Web pricing in relation to them. Although other Web-based advertising efforts will evolve, it is difficult to make general recommendations that can encompass online advertising forms that have yet to be developed.

Chatterjee (1998) considers banner ads to be a form of *passive advertising exposure,* in that the consumer does not consciously decide to view the banner advertisement. Rather, the banner advertisement is presented as an outcome of accessing a particular Web content page or of entering a series of keywords into a search engine. Conventional market segmentation theory would lead to the prediction that the more targeted the banner advertisement is, the higher the click rate will be.

Advertisements placed on home pages of general-interest sites or on the entry page of a portal would have lower click rates, therefore, than advertisements that are consistent with the content of a narrowly targeted Web site or banner advertisements that are presented by a search engine in response to specific keywords (e.g., ads for Lionel trains presented every time a visitor searches for "model railroad" or for "Neil Young").

Paid links are a different form of passive advertising, and may be most simply viewed as text versions of banner advertisements. Paid links are often incorporated into directories, which may contain large numbers of them.

Chatterjee (1998) considers target communications, on the other hand, to be a form of *active advertising exposure,* since the consumer actively decides to access the target communication by clicking on the banner advertisement after being passively exposed to the banner. *Active advertising exposure is under the consumer's control; passive advertising exposure is under the marketer's control.* The distinction between passive advertisements and active advertisements implies a crucial difference, therefore, between banner and target communications. Furthermore, the concept of an active advertisement is a feature that differentiates Web advertising from advertising in traditional media.

To date, most of the focus in Web advertising measurement has been on banner advertisements, most likely because banner advertisements, by their passive nature, have many more parallels with traditional media planning than do active advertisements. The factors that affect consumer attention to an advertisement—so-called perceptual selection—in print media should also influence perceptual selection of Web banner advertisements. These factors are closely tied to the creative function in advertising and include size, position, motion, color, and novelty (e.g., Wilkie 1990), all of which are considered relevant for predicting the likelihood that a visitor will click on a banner advertisement.

Currently, exposure models, based on CPMs (cost per thousand impressions) or flat fees applied to site exposure or banner advertisement exposure, are the dominant approach to Web media pricing. Fees based on actual *click-throughs* are also in use; with these, the advertiser pays only when individuals actually click on the banner advertisement with their mice. A click-through takes the viewer to the advertiser's target communication. The following sections consider exposure models, click-through models, and other possible pricing models. While it is premature to recommend any one media pricing model as optimal, it is important to understand the relative strengths and limitations of methods that are currently in use or that have been proposed.

Cost per Thousand and Flat Fee Exposure Models

Flat fee pricing consists of a fixed price for a given period of time. Flat fees were the earliest Web advertising pricing model. Flat fee pricing may be implemented with or without traffic (the number of individuals who visit a Web site) guarantees. Naturally, it would be advantageous to the advertiser to receive traffic guarantees. The earliest advertising pricing approaches on the Web simply used flat fees, such as advertisement cost per month, without clear specification of the traffic delivered in that period of time. At a minimum, accurate information on site traffic must be made available to the advertiser so that the advertiser can evaluate alternative Web media vehicles.

Assuming accurate traffic information, flat fee prices can be readily converted into a CPM model. CPMs may also be enhanced by providing "guarantees" of the number of impressions in a given period of time. The flat fee and CPM models are interchangeable if traffic information, specifying the number of (possibly unique) visitors to a Web site, is available. If traffic information is not available, flat fee pricing can still be used, although its value is then impossible to evaluate.

In 1996, 90% of CPMs for Web advertising (Focalink 1996) ranged from $10 to $150, with a median of $60. The average CPM online has dropped dramatically in the past three years. The average is currently $35 (Adknowledge 1999). In comparison, CPMs for advertising in traditional media range from $6 to $14 for national television, $8 to $20 for magazines, $18 to $20 for magazines, and $18 to $20 for newspapers (*Advertising Age* 1999).

The ultimate challenge will be the identification of the business models that will be effective in the new Web environment. At present, the advertiser-supported business model is driven largely by a broadcast paradigm, which has initially gravitated toward CPMs as the appropriate unit of measure. In this model, the belief is that exposure-based pricing takes into account different advertisers' response functions and represents a rational way to price advertising on the Web.

But in fact, impression/exposure models go only part of the way, because the Web is different from traditional broadcast media. The Web is based on a many-to-many communication model and traditional media are based on a one-to-many communication model. In addition to exposure metrics, therefore, interactivity metrics are also required. The CPM approach places too much emphasis on the banner advertisement and essentially no emphasis on the target communication, which is the real marketing communication that the advertiser wishes the visitor to read.

In the CPM model, larger numbers of online visitors translate into Web sites that are bigger winners because the one to-many model seeks a mass audience for its message. The danger of relying solely on exposure models is that interactive managers will be driven to scale their sites to larger, mass audiences, with more homogeneous tastes, in order to attract more advertising revenue. This goal conflicts with solving the more difficult problems of how to measure interactivity and how to price advertising according to the value of a consumer's interactive visit to the advertiser.

CPM and flat fee models do nothing more than simply count the number of visitors exposed to a particular banner advertisement on a particular site. But, since consumer behavior on the Web depends on a whole host of measurable factors, including the type of site and the consumer's motivation for visiting it (Hoffman and Novak 1996; Novak, Hoffman, and Yung 1999), a simple tally of visits is not sufficient to demonstrate to the advertiser the value of its advertising expenditures. It is meaningless to compare directly between

Web sites the number of visitors exposed to banner advertisements without also taking these other factors into account.

Models Based on Click-Throughs

Advertising pricing based on click-throughs is an attempt to develop a more accountable way of charging for Web advertising. The payment for a banner advertisement is based on the number of times visitors have actually clicked on it. In 1996, the fee was approximately $0.25 per click (I/PRO 1996). Because click-through rates have been dropping, owing to consumer boredom with the format, the fee now ranges from $0.04 to $0.20 per click (see, for example, ClickQuick 1999).

A relatively small proportion of those exposed to a banner advertisement actually click on the banner. Several years ago, DoubleClick (1996) reported that an average of 4% percent of Web site visitors who are exposed to a banner advertisement click on the advertisement the first time they see it. The top 25% performing ads in terms of click-through across all the sites in the DoubleClick Network had an average click rate of 8%, with some click rates as high as 12% to 15%. Click-through rates declined after the first exposure, falling to 2% for the second and third exposures, and to 1% or less at four exposures. The click-through rate has since plummeted and now averages around 0.58% (CyberAtlas 1999).

Payment based on click-throughs guarantees that the visitor not only was exposed to the banner advertisement, but also actively decided to click on the banner and to be exposed to the target communication. Click-through payment may be viewed as payment for target communication exposures. However, at current CPMs and click-through rates, such pricing is rapidly becoming prohibitive.

Click-through pricing is not without controversy, however. Procter & Gamble was the first to insist it would pay the Web site (Yahoo, in this case) only for the click-throughs by viewers rather than for gross impressions of the banner advertisements (Associated Press, 1996). Some Internet publishers continue to feel that this pricing strategy is unfair, arguing that the click-through is at least partially a function of the level of creativity of the advertisement and the level of interest generated in the viewer by it, which are not under the publisher's control.

On the other hand, as argued above, applying only traditional media exposure models to the Web does not take into account its unique, interactive nature. In addition, the Internet is the first commercial medium in which it is actually possible to measure consumer response, not just to assume it. Although the click-through model may not represent the optimal approach to measuring the value of interactivity, it offers a departure point from which to proceed.

Proposed Web Pricing Models

Interactivity

While payment based on a click-through guarantees that the advertiser knows that the visitor has been exposed to a target communication, it does not guarantee that the visitor liked the communication or even spent any substantial time viewing it. It is proposed that an additional measure of the value of an advertisement should be based on the degree to which the visitor interacts with the target communication. An interactivity metric might be based on the duration of time spent viewing the communication, the depth or number of pages of the target communication accessed, the number of repeat visits to the target communication, or some combination of these three elements.

Such a practice was announced for the first time in 1996, when a member of the Internet mailing list Online Advertising Discussion List (1996) posted to the list that Modem Media, the interactive advertising agency, had developed a pricing model in which its clients would pay, not for exposures or click-throughs, but only for activity at the client's Web site. This development raised anew the controversy about the best Web media pricing models. Web publishers argued that the problem with activity-based measures, such as click-throughs or interactivity, is that the Web publisher cannot be held responsible for the activity related to an advertisement. An analogy is drawn to print: The Web publisher argues that the print medium charges for advertisements whether or not they lead to sales.

Not surprisingly, advertisers and their agencies continue to argue that since the Web medium allows accountability, it is possible and desirable to develop models that measure consumer behavior. In the long run, the solution will probably be found through acceptance of the reality that the medium and the advertisement interact and all parties share responsibility for outcomes.

Outcomes

Ultimately, marketers are interested in outcomes, and the ultimate outcome is purchase. As Stephen Klein, former I/PRO manager, once stated, "One hundred thousand people going to a site is worth something, but a site that only five people visit can be worth more if they are the right five people" (Murphy 1996).

The metrics discussed above are related to early stages of the purchase process. Banner advertisements affect the consumer's awareness, and interaction with the target communication affects the consumer's comprehension and understanding. Beyond these initial stages are the marketing objectives of attitude change, purchase intention, and, ultimately, purchase.

An outcome-based approach to pricing Web advertising begins by specifying precisely the marketer's goal for the target communication. Examples of typical outcomes include influencing attitudes, motivating the consumer to provide personal information, and leading the consumer to purchase. Whatever the marketing objective, the Web provides a vehicle for integrated marketing campaigns, which allows the marketer to track the advertisement and to measure its effectiveness.

A current example is per-inquiry (PI) advertisements. PI advertisements pay royalties only on actual product sales and require no other payment. Consider the online affiliate programs offered by CDnow, Amazon.com, Dell Computers, and REI.com, among many other advertisers. In such programs, affiliates advertise products on their Web sites that are sold by the advertiser and that the affiliates feel are appropriate to the content of their Web sites. If a visitor accesses the advertiser through the affiliate's Web site and purchases the product advertised on the affiliate's site, the affiliate receives a referral fee or commission. Currently, referral fees range from $0.50 to $5.00 or more for each lead, while commissions usually range from 8% to 12% of the purchase price of the product. Some commissions are as high as 25%.

Affiliate programs are expected to be a dominant force in the near future. Forrester Research (1999) estimates that half of the projected $33 billion per year in worldwide online advertising spending will be performance-based by 2004. Jupiter Communications (1999) further estimates that fully 25% of Internet retail sales will be acquired through sites using the affiliate advertising model by 2002. In just the third quarter of 1998, the popular technology site CNET, for example, facilitated over $80 million in sales for dozens of its online advertisers, receiving a flat fee for every referral in the process.

Although the pricing models most frequently applied to the Web are based on traditional, mass-media models, it may make more sense to incorporate the direct-response paradigm when considering outcomes.

Consider the following definition of direct marketing (Direct Marketing Association 1996): *any direct communication to a consumer or business recipient that is intended to generate a response in the form of an order (direct order), a request for further information (lead generation), and/or a visit to a store or other place of business for purchase of a specific product(s) or service(s) (traffic generation).*[1]

The concepts of direct order, lead generation, and traffic generation are immediately and obviously applicable in the many-to-many environment underlying the Web. Outcome definitions and metrics developed from considering the Web as a unique hybrid of direct response and traditional communication media will lead to the optimal set of models for measurement and pricing.

Integrating Exposure, Interactivity, and Outcomes

Following the creation of measurement and pricing models, it will be necessary to develop a set of integrated response measures, over time and, possibly, over sites that relate exposure and interactivity metrics to consumer response. Exposure and interactivity metrics may take the form, for example, of purchase behavior in an online storefront, attitude change, and the number of visitors who request further information. The development of such metrics, however, requires two things: (1) identified visitors and (2) multi-site data on every Web site involved in the integrated marketing campaign. Until these data are available, the measurement of outcome remains elusive.

In addition to the metrics described above, several other behavioral and psychological measures should be considered in the context of Web advertising measurement. These additional measures include primary navigation patterns through the Web site; cross-site navigation patterns; demographic, psychographic, and behavioral characteristics of visitors to a Web site and to specific pages within a Web site; cognitive and attitudinal measures, including flow; and visitor loyalty and repeat visits. It is anticipated that innovative future pricing models will incorporate these measures in unique ways.

Policy Considerations

When Web measurement standards and pricing models are being developed, a number of policy issues must be considered, including privacy and ethics. The policy considerations are particularly important because consumer protection, fraud, and deceptive claims problems are potential points of entry for government regulators into the Web marketplace.

Privacy

Although a thorough analysis of privacy issues is beyond the scope of this chapter, it is important to raise these issues in the context of Web pricing models. A networked, distributed computing environment such as the Internet offers unprecedented opportunities for the invasion of privacy. Information about individuals is more accessible and more easily combined and integrated than in the physical world. It is not so much that it is possible to learn things about consumers that could not be learned before, but, rather, that gaining access to such information might previously have been too expensive, too time-consuming, or too difficult to gather.

In addition, it is not clear who would be able to gain access to such consumer information or what they might do with it. In a different context, serious privacy issues have arisen regarding patient mental-health information that has been entered into computer networks at the insistence of insurance companies (Lewin 1996; Scarf 1996). A class of "health information trustees" had access to this information; their inappropriate use of it in some cases has had serious and damaging consequences to consumers. A parallel class of "marketing information trustees" could potentially have access to vast databases of consumer transaction data.

In the context of Web measurement for marketing and advertising purposes, the specific issues are the information that is gathered from consumers, the awareness of consumers that it is being gathered, and the uses to which the information is put. There is a tension between the marketer's need to have information about individual consumers for the purpose of targeted marketing efforts and the consumer's right to privacy. In our opinion, the ultimate resolution of this tension is the establishment of a full partnership with consumers, in which they control ownership of their demographic and behavioral data and determine the manner in which it will be used, if at all. This solution respects the many-to-many model underlying the World Wide Web, which permits consumers also to be providers to the medium and allows consumers to remain active participants in the interactive communication process.

For one educational demonstration of the type of information available to marketers about visitors to Web sites, visit the Web site http://www.anonymizer.com/. The "Anonymizer" site demonstrates the sort of information about the visitor that is available to the Web sites that people visit. Depending on the platform from which the "Anonymizer" site is accessed, the information ranges from what domain you are coming from, to what kind of computer you have, to the Web browser you are using, to your name and other personal details. Obviously, when people register for Web site access, the amount of personal information that is collected and stored about them increases.

The advertisers whose approaches to privacy issues are most likely to attract the attention of government regulators are those that ignore consumers' rights and fail to enter into explicit agreements with consumers about their demographic and behavioral data.

A recent study (Hoffman, Novak, and Peralta 1999) found that Web users value their privacy, particularly as expressed by visiting sites anonymously or by adopting various aliases, depending on the circumstances of a given visit. Furthermore, users desire complete control over whether a particular Web site receives any information about them. While users recognize that marketers may desire demographic and behavioral data on visitors for business purposes, users do not feel that marketers have the right to sell these data to other firms. Web users seem willing to provide demographic information if marketers identify the information that is being collected and the uses that will be made of it.

These findings suggest that privacy policies in this emerging medium should be driven by the unique characteristics of the medium, such as interactivity, and the desires of its users—for control, for example—as they experience that medium (Hoffman and Novak 1996).

Ethics

Researchers are beginning to address the question of ethical behavior in the conduct of online research (Boehlefeld 1996; Duncan 1996; Thomas 1996). A key result of this research, that "informed consent" is a critical component of ethical research in many online environments, has general implications for the way marketers may approach gathering data from Web visitors. Much more specific consumer research is necessary, however, to determine the best ways to develop and to implement such policies in commercially oriented Web environments.

"Disguised advertisements" are another potential ethical concern. Suppose that an advertiser-supported search agent site presents links to an advertiser's Web site at the beginning of a list produced by a search request for a set of keywords. In this case, while the person performing the research may believe a link appears at the beginning of the list because it is the most *relevant* to the search request, the top position of the link may be the result of sponsor payments. Such practices must be made clear to users of the search agent, because they have the potential to deceive consumers and undermine trust in search agent sites.

Conclusion

The standardization of the Web measurement process is a necessary precursor to the development of optimal Web advertising pricing models. Indeed, without such efforts, the Web is not likely to achieve its full potential as a unique and revolutionary commercial many-to-many mass medium. Managers must now begin to address the question of what the appropriate standards for Web advertising pricing models should be. The distinction between passive advertisements that are under the marketer's control and active advertisements that are under the consumer's control has important implications for the measurement and pricing process.

We believe that the best pricing models will be based on interactivity metrics. The rationale behind this argument is that the degree to which the visitor interacts with the target communication is a better measure of the value and effectiveness of an advertisement than mere exposure.

Metrics based solely on impressions are necessary in the Web measurement process, but must not form the basis of Web advertising pricing efforts. Ultimately, what is required is a set of integrated response measures that relate exposure and interactivity metrics to consumer response. These "interactivity metrics" and "outcome metrics" must be included in any complete program for Web measurement and advertising pricing.

Further research will be necessary to identify those metrics that are most useful for judging the effectiveness of advertising, for determining the placement of advertisements, and for determining optimal pricing schemes for efficient media buys.

Our primary objective in writing this chapter is to stimulate further research and discussion and to help facilitate the process of developing optimal pricing models for the Web. Because of the unique nature of the Web medium, this process should proceed as a partnership among all stakeholders in the industry, including advertisers; Web publishers; measurement, placement, and auditing agencies; and consumers (Hoffman and Novak 1997). In particular, advertisers and commercial Web sites that sell advertising space must work together to measure consumer outcomes in the context of direct response rather than solely in terms of mass media exposure.

Only through cooperative effort among diverse constituents, whose needs often conflict, are we likely to make progress on the rough path toward profitable commercial development.

Note

1. *Direct Order* includes all direct response advertising communications, through any medium, that are specifically designed to solicit and close a sale. All of the information necessary for the prospective buyer to make a decision to purchase and complete the transaction is conveniently provided in the advertisement. *Lead Generation* includes all direct response advertising communications, through any medium, that are designed to generate interest in a product or service, and provide the prospective buyer with a means to request and receive additional information about the product or service. *Traffic Generation* includes all direct response advertising communication conducted, through any medium, that are designed to motivate the prospective buyer to visit a store, restaurant, or other business establishment to buy an advertised product or service.

References

Adknowledge, Inc. (1999), http://www.adknowledge.com.

Advertising Age (1999), Ad Age Dataplace, *Advertising Age* Web site, http://adage.com.

Advertising Age (1996), "Fall Prime-Time Pricing Survey," *Advertising Age*, September 16, 1996.

Associated Press (1996), "Procter & Gamble World Wide Web Ad Strategy Raises Online Ire," San Francisco, April 28, 1996, 1:17 p.m. EDT, http://www2.nando.net/newsroom/ntn/info/042896/info5_380.html.

Boehlefeld, Sharon Polancic (1996), "Doing the Right Thing: Ethical Cyberspace Research," *The Information Society*, 12, 141–152.

Chatterjee, Patrali (1998), "Modeling Consumer Network Navigation in World Wide Web Sites: Implications for Advertising," Doctoral Dissertation, Owen Graduate School of Management, Vanderbilt University, Nashville.

ClickQuick (1999), "In-Depth Reviews of Affiliate and Pay-Per-Click Programs," http://www.clickquick.com/

Competitive Media Reporting (1999), http://www.usadata.com/usadata/cmr.

CyberAtlas (1999), http://www.cyberatlas.com.

Direct Marketing Association (1996), "DMA Report—Economic Impact: U.S. Direct Marketing Today," http://www.the-dma.org.

DoubleClick (1996), http://www.doubleclick.com.

Duncan, George T. (1996), "Is My Research Ethical?" *Communications of the ACM*, Special Issue on Internet in the Home, 39 (December): 67–68.

Focalink (1996), MarketMatch Data Base.

Forrester Research (1999), http://www.forrester.com.

Hoffman, D. L., T. P. Novak, and Patrali Chatterjee (1995), "Commercial Scenarios for the Web: Opportunities and Challenges," *Journal of Computer-Mediated*

Communications, Special Issue on Electronic Commerce, 1 (December). http://shum.huji.ac.il/jcmc/vol1/issue3/vol1no3.html.

Hoffman, D. L. and T. P. Novak (1996), "Marketing in Hypermedia Computer-Mediated Environments: Conceptual Foundations," *Journal of Marketing*, 60 (July): 50–68.

Hoffman, Donna and Thomas P. Novak (1997), "A New Marketing Paradigm for Electronic Commerce," *The Information Society*, 13 (January–March): 43–54.

Hoffman, Donna L., Thomas P. Novak, and Marcos Peralta (1999), "Information Privacy in the Marketspace: Implications for the Commercial Uses of Anonymity on the Web," *The Information Society*, 15, Issue No. 2 (April–June): 129–139.

Internet Advertising Bureau (1999a), http://www.iab.net/advertise/adsource.html.

Internet Advertising Bureau (1999b), "IAB/CASIE PROPOSAL FOR VOLUNTARY MODEL BANNER SIZES," http://www.iab.net/advertise/adsource.html.

Lewin, Tamar (1996), "A Loss of Confidence: A Special Report. Questions of privacy roil arena of psychotherapy," *The New York Times*, May 22, Section A, p. 1, col. 1.

Murphy, Ian P. (1996), "On-line ads effective? Who knows for sure?" *Marketing News*, 30(20), September 23, 38.

Novak, Thomas P., Donna L. Hoffman, and Y. F. Yung (2000), "Measuring the Customer Experience in Online Environments: A Structural Modeling Approach," forthcoming, *Marketing Science*.

Online Advertising Discussion List (1996), 1(91), September 24, www.tenagra.com/online-ads.

Rebello, Kathy (1996), "Special Report: Making Money on the Net," *Business Week*, September 22, 104–118.

Scarf, Maggie (1996), "Keeping Secrets," *The New York Times*, June 16, Section 6, p. 38, col. 1.

Thomas, Jim (1996), "Introduction: A Debate about the Ethics of Fair Practices for Collecting Social Science Data in Cyberspace," *The Information Society*, 12, 107–117.

Wilkie, William L. (1990), *Consumer Behavior*, 2d ed., New York: John Wiley & Sons.

Profiting from Online News: The Search for Viable Business Models

Susan M. Mings and Peter B. White

Introduction

With the increasing popularity of the World Wide Web as a consumer-oriented mass medium (December, 1997, 11–12), the past several years have seen enormous interest in, and a documented explosion of, digital (or "online") newspapers published on the World Wide Web (WWW). Outing (1996, "Hold On (line) Tight"; 1996, "Newspapers Online") noted that 100 commercial newspapers existed online, worldwide, at the beginning of 1995, a number that, according to *Editor & Publisher*'s statistics, grew to 750 by early 1996, to over 1,500 by early 1997, to 2,764 in early 1998, and to 3,581 in June 1999.[1] Meyer (1998) charts a similar rapid growth trend in the numbers of newspapers establishing an online presence in the mid- to late 1990s.

The explosion in online news publishing has largely taken the form of newspapers based on the Internet or the WWW. Early commentators pointed to WWW publication as the fastest-growing trend in digital newspaper publishing (M. L. Fulton, managing editor, washingtonpost.com, personal email communications, November 25, 1996 and December 2, 1996; see also Cameron et al., 1995; Erlindson, 1995; Fulton, 1996; Lapham, 1995, 1996; and Meyer, 1995).

But can this explosion of interest result in economically sustainable online publications? This chapter examines the news industry's search for business models to make online newspapers economically viable. It documents the debate about appropriate business models that took place between 1995 and 1999.

Questions regarding the economic viability of these Internet newspaper efforts are a matter of ongoing industry interest and concern. Newspaper publishers' (and others') initial rush to the Internet vastly outstripped their understanding of how to profit from these endeavors (Hayter, 1996). As the president of the *Washington Post*'s Digital Ink online publishing effort put it, online newspaper publishers came to realize that "publishing on the Web is easy: making money is the hard part" (Lapham, 1996).

Outing (1996, "Net Profitability") noted that despite the rapid proliferation of Web newspapers, "profitability remains a niggling problem" (p. 22). Different commentators made different predictions about the problem of profitability. William Bass, a speaker at the newspaper industry conference Connections '96, told attendees to "plan on losing money until 1999" (Newspaper Association of America [NAA], 1996, "Postcards"). In 1997, most online newspapers continued to lose money (although nearly one-third of online newspapers did report no losses or some level of profitability) (PR Newswire, 1997, NAA Survey Indicates 36 Percent). Nevertheless, 80 percent of newspaper executives surveyed in 1997 expressed confidence in the Internet as "an important force in the [future of] the communications industry" (*New Media Week*, "Only 1 in 7 Newspapers," 1997).

Others emphasized issues of profitability not simply as problems, but as matters of survival. The Reuters Business Report, citing the Yankee Group (a Boston research firm) stated that "Darwin's theory of evolution will apply to online newspapers, and to guarantee survival major players must establish themselves within five years or risk extinction" (Newspage, "Online Newspaper Shakeup," 1996). The Yankee Group predicted that "there's going to be a lot of money lost in the next four years" (Newspage, "Overset/ Interactive," 1996).

Meyer (1996) also assigned life-or-death importance to the issue of profitability, and saw these concerns as an evolutionary stage in the development of the online news industry:

Online publishing has gone through a progression. At one time it was dominated by concerns about philosophical questions (haves vs. have nots, the liberation of technology, Rheingold and Handy and Negroponte stuff). It then went through a design phase and a technology phase—the era of the techno-designers, Java, CGI, bigger and better. Now we're in a very dollar-and-cents mode—the era of the publisher. . . .

The Web is now entering the era of economics. And that's a very dangerous era for it to enter. It means experimentation and learning are no longer enough. Dollars must follow, or most assuredly the termination notice will. (18 July 1996)

Our review of academic and industry online and print resources has identified four basic economic models to which online newspapers have turned in their effort to achieve profitability:

- The Subscription Model
- The Advertising Model
- The Transactional Model
- The Bundled Model

The Subscription Model

The Subscription Model is familiar to newspaper readers and to the print-based newspaper industry. A traditional revenue model for print newspapers has been roughly a split of 20% versus 80% (Meyer, 1995) or 30% versus 70% (Erlindson, 1995) between subscription and advertising income, respectively. Erlindson (1995) contended that a similar split would be difficult, if not impossible, to achieve online, because there's not much of a market for Web publication subscriptions. With "several hundred publications [available] at the touch of a URL button" (Erlindson, 1995, "Ads vs. Subscriptions" section), there's too much competition for Web subscription dollars.

Further, as noted by Outing (1996, "Where's the Money?"), Web users are reluctant to pay for online publications to begin with. Many Web users, who already pay connection fees of some sort, are unwilling to pay more to access specific content (Shaw, 1998).

Meyer (1995) made a similar point:

News, already hard to sell at anything near its true cost, may be especially hard to sell on the Internet. Directly charging Internet users for information has met with substantial resistance, particularly among early adopters of the "Internet culture." The Internet was created specifically to encourage free exchange of information among academic and government researchers.[2] Users steeped in this tradition tend to view any commercial activity as infringing and hold one credo above all others: "Information wants to be free."[3] . . . [These users] question why they should pay for one package of information when other packages, able to be searched and read any number of ways, are available without charge.[4] (p. 39)

Some contend that this reluctance to pay for Internet access and information consumption will fade as the pool of Internet users is transformed. Indeed, as evidenced by increasing numbers of paying subscribers to Internet service providers (ISPs) (see Wyman, 1996, "Re: Making the Jump"), reluctance to pay for Internet access is a declining trend. Dave Creagh, electronic publishing manager at the *Christian Science Monitor*'s Electronic Monitor[5] contended that "the people who make all the noise about how things have to be free on the Net are a shrinking minority" (quoted in Gipson, 1996, "*The Christian Science Monitor*"). According to Creagh, for consumers who paid high rates for early proprietary services like CompuServe and America Online, $20 per month for an unlimited Web connection may seem like a good deal.

Cameron et al. (1996) suggest the following subscription-based economic models:[6]

• The New Subscriber Model
• The Maturation Model
• The Multiple Subscriber Model

In the New Subscriber Model, electronic newspapers are seen as alternatives to, but not competitors of, print newspapers. Electronic papers may attract and hold an audience of younger readers, a demographic group that isn't reading print newspapers and that is seen as having vast potential for online newspapers. In this model, online papers are a product distinct from print newspapers, with a distinct readership; they are "self-supporting profit center[s]" (Cameron et al., 1996, "Electronic Newspapers' Business Models" section).

Outing (1996), however, concluded that even though college students "'found actual use of a full-featured electronic newspaper fun, easy and appealing' [citing Cameron et al., 1996] . . . they are not inclined to pay to subscribe to an electronic newspaper service" (1996, "E-Newspaper Business Models").

Cameron et al. address this point by proposing the Maturation Model, in which electronic newspapers are supplemental "loss leaders" for print papers. In this model, electronic newspapers may attract young readers to a newspaper, initiating a youthful habit of newspaper reading, and leading to an adult print newspaper subscription. Online papers wouldn't necessarily generate their own profit; rather, they'd be investments leading to print paper subscriptions down the road. In this model, "Electronic offerings could be marginally unprofitable, yet because of their net long-term benefit to the newspaper enterprise, represent a justifiable investment" (Cameron et al., 1996, "Electronic Newspapers' Business Models" section).

In Cameron et al.'s third model, the Multiple Subscriber Model, information that is available electronically is seen as a valuable addition to information that is available from the printed paper. That is, a newspaper's electronic edition is used to offer readers information not available in the print edition. Cameron et al. give some examples of the "unique content" electronic papers might offer, including

additional advertising content . . . [or] unique forms and features of [news and] editorial content . . . [such as] searchable classified ads and regional advertising not available in the local print paper[,] such as state-wide employment opportunities or display advertising for businesses in major cities near the reader's hometown. ("Electronic Newspapers' Business Models" section)

Both Meyer (1995) and Outing (1996) suggested addressing any reluctance to pay for Internet newspapers with a "tiered" or "teaser" strategy: that is, by "charging for access to [the] full content of a Web [newspaper] service," and giving some of the content away (Outing, "Where's the Money?" p. 8I).

Outing (1996, "Where's the Money?") cited Knight-Ridder's subscription policies as illustrative of this tiered strategy. The

Philadelphia Online Web's experiment with "Clipper" service provides an example of this strategy (Outing, 1996, "The Death"). While providing most information free of charge, the Online Web did charge $6.95 per month for unlimited access to the newspaper's electronic archive and a personalized news search-and-retrieval "Clipper" account. The experiment must have been successful, because in 1999 the philly.com news site still provided subscriptions to Knight-Ridder's personalized NewsHound‰ for $7.95 per month, or $59.95 per year.[7]

Meyer (1995) also contended that a successful online subscription model could not be flat-rate, but must be incrementally imposed. He predicted that viable online subscription strategies will incorporate teaser, or trial, elements. In one example of such a teaser approach, the bottom layer of information is available for free, but readers have to pay for more detailed or more in-depth information on the second or subsequent layers (p. 41). In another example, a paper provides free access for some startup period (such as a week or a month) before charging for continuation (pp. 43–44). This free trial period strategy is now widely used among Internet newspapers and services of all kinds, including such sites and providers as Wall Street Journal Interactive, America Online (AOL), and Microsoft's MSN.

Peterson (1996) also discussed the strategy of first attracting online readers with free information and charging for access once the online paper has a sufficient mass of readers. Peterson claimed that if papers do start charging, "finding the right balance between a subscriber model and a transaction, or 'clicks,' billing model, is part of the challenge" (p. 37I).

The *Christian Science Monitor*'s Electronic Monitor is an example of a paper searching for that balance. According to Dave Creagh, the Electronic Monitor's electronic publishing manager, the Electronic Monitor (initially available free of charge) planned a two-pronged strategy for pricing access. One prong is "a monthly all-you-can-eat package with access to the full site," which Creagh assumed would cost $6–$15 per month (Gipson, 1996, "*The Christian Science Monitor*"). The other option is

pay-as-you-go, where certain pages on the site are assigned a value to be determined, and that would be measured by . . . ClickShare.[8] [In this scheme], the day's news from the newspaper would always be free. [That is,] it's important to put a lot of valuable stuff on the front porch ... [and] it's the best way to get people coming in the door. (Gipson, 1996, "*The Christian Science Monitor*")

In 1999, the *Christian Science Monitor* charged only for access to its personalized news service, which includes access to the paper's archives back to 1980. The *Monitor*'s selection of this strategy indicates that it has had success with providing much information free of charge, then charging for an enhanced subscription.

Donatello's (1996) research validated the view that online readers may be more likely to pay for content after a free sample. According to Donatello, both the *Chicago Tribune* and the *Wall Street Journal* have conducted consumer research leading them to believe there is some financial promise in the subscription model. As a result, the *Tribune* considered (but rejected) fee-based access to its online paper, and the *Journal* began fee-based access in September 1996. To make online subscriptions attractive, prices for Wall Street Journal Interactive were set at $49 per year (and have since risen to $59 per year), much less than the $175 yearly print subscription price (Kirsner, 1997). (*Journal* print subscribers can get the online edition for an additional $29 per year.)

Owen Youngman, the *Tribune*'s director of interactive media, told Donatello, "In general, willingness to pay increased after people used [the Web edition of the paper]. Further, the research indicated that people are more likely to pay for content they specifically request than for what we serve up without asking" (Donatello, 1996). As Donatello summarized the situation, "People will pay more after sampling content, and if they ask for it first" ("The Kitchen Sink" section).

As of June 1998, Wall Street Journal Interactive had 150,000 paying customers (Stone, 1998). According to Mossberg (1997), 60%–65% of subscribers in 1997 were not print subscribers. This represented significant growth from the October 1996 figures of 30,000 subscribers to Wall Street Journal Interactive. (Compaine, 16 Oct. 1996, citing October AP report).

In mid–1998, Compaine estimated that Wall Street Journal Interactive was generating subscription revenues of $6 million and advertising revenues of $10 million annually. According to

Compaine, the profitability of the venture depended on how the joint and common costs were distributed between the print and online publications (cited in Stone, 1998). With 150,000 online subscribers compared with a print subscriber base of about 1.8 million, Wall Street Journal Interactive is the most successful of all online newspapers in generating reader revenue.

The fact that the *Journal* was still charging subscription fees in 1999 indicates that for the *Journal*, this model is working. This success shows that a subscription model may work not only for premium additional content at any newspaper's site, but also for branded, specialized information that is widely recognized as premium content—such as that provided by the *Wall Street Journal*.

Nevertheless, a recent review of forty-eight worldwide Internet newspapers (including publications from several different countries) found only eight that have adopted a subscription revenue model. Like Wall Street Journal Interactive, which in fact is one of these eight papers, "these . . . papers were very specialized either in content or in strong coverage of a particular geographic region" (Palmer and Eriksen, 1999).

Other newspapers' experience with subscription models has been cautionary. Moving from free information to subscription access does not necessarily bring the desired results. When the Colorado Springs *Gazette-Telegraph*'s GT-Online service implemented charges, the number of visitors to its site dropped from 300–500 per day to just 80 paying subscribers. GT-Online subsequently dropped subscription charges (Hipschman, 1995).

The *Los Angeles Times*[10] and the *Milwaukee Journal-Sentinel*[11] had similarly disappointing experiences with the subscription model. As Outing noted,

[these papers] learned the hard way on Prodigy that few online consumers will pay an extra fee on top of online access to view a newspaper's content online. They now operate Web services where all but truly premium services like archive access are free (1996, "The Death").

Microsoft's Michael Kinsley also learned the hard way how unsustainable using a subscription model to finance an online publication can be. Kinsley built a subscriber base for his online news magazine, Slate, before implementing subscription fees in early

1998. After the "inevitable drop-off in readership ensued" (Benning, 1999), Slate returned to free access in February 1999. The resulting steep rise in readership—"from nearly 225,000 unique monthly visitors in January [1999] to 916,000 in May" increased Slate's advertising revenues and, according to Kinsley, "[reaffirmed] the wisdom of dropping the subscription, or the stupidity of doing it in the first place" (Benning, 1999).

The Forrester Research Group[12] advised caution when online publications look to a subscription model, and even predicted that electronic publications won't survive if they depend solely on subscription revenues:

Electronic publications supported solely by subscriptions . . . will face even greater hurdles [than sites supported by advertising] and can expect nearly $1.5 million a year in losses until the turn of the century. . . . Even online publications with advertising can expect little but red ink for the next five years. . . . Forrester predicts Web site publishers can only make up 40% of their costs from online subscriptions, which, unlike advertising, will show scant improvement by the year 2000. In order for an online publication to post a profit in the next two years, it would have to exceed 95,000 subscribers or charge a $77 average sub price. Neither scenario is likely, Forrester says. ("Sub Fees Won't Pay Rent," 1996)

Another subscription model that some papers are experimenting with is to charge for access to personalized news services—services that provide readers with only those news and information subjects that they preselect.

Wall Street Journal Interactive incorporates the personalized subscription model by offering a Personal Journal to Interactive Edition subscribers. A subscription to the Personal Journal is included with online subscriptions. The Personal Journal allows readers to specify their interests—by topic, feature, or column—and subsequently displays an Interactive Edition tailored to those interests.[13] The Interactive Edition's business director, Thomas Baker, noted that it's important, in the personalized subscription model, for newspapers to provide consumers with only the information they want, sparing them an overload of news and information (Gipson, 1996, "Web Subscriptions").

Individual Inc.'s Newspage[14] personalized email news service originally implemented a three-pronged subscription strategy:

• Providing free access to "Basic" news summaries and stories for anyone who registers with the site

• Charging $3.95 per month for expanded access to both "Basic" and "Premium" news

• Charging $6.95 per month for a service that emails subscribers abstracts of news stories of interest, which can be viewed in their entirety on the Web site[15]

Harper (1996, "The Daily Me") provided a useful overview and review of several personalized news services. Harper reviewed twenty-three personal news services, and noted that five of these charge subscription fees. It is interesting to note that all five for-fee sites are among Harper's highest-rated sites. (Two subscription sites receive a four-star rating, the highest; two subscription sites receive three stars; and one site draws the only two-star rating that goes to a subscription service. No for-fee sites are placed in the one-star category.) This clustering of subscription sites near the upper end of Harper's quality-based rankings may provide some support for the contention that online readers are willing to pay for personalized or quality content.

In their survey of the revenue models of forty-eight Internet newspapers, Palmer and Eriksen found only four papers generating revenue "through the development of customized products, ranging from research services and archiving to specialty items such as crossword puzzles" (1999, p. 37).

To summarize, offering subscriptions for online newspapers is an economic model that has drawn industry interest and attention, and has been the subject of considerable industry experimentation. Several variations of a subscription model have been implemented or considered, including Cameron et al.'s New Subscriber Model, Maturation Model, and Multiple Subscriber Model; a flat access fee; a tiered or teaser scheme; and subscriptions for specialized content or personalized news. Although there are some indications that providing quality, specialized, or personalized content can boost online subscriptions, it is not yet possible to make definitive pronouncements about the success of a subscription model, or of different implementations of it, or of models that include subscriptions in a mix of revenue strategies. It is useful, then, to explore the application of another familiar revenue model from print to online publications: the Advertising Model.

The Advertising Model

According to Erlindson, "the subscription versus advertising debate is the most important issue facing online newspapers" (Erlindson, 1995, "Ads vs. Subscriptions" section). Erlindson was pessimistic about the subscription model; he doubted that online subscriptions could match the 30% of total revenues print papers achieve with subscriptions. Despite this bleak outlook, Erlindson found online publishers "fixated" on selling subscriptions "because this is what . . . worked in the past." Erlindson's comment here refers not only to the 30%-subscriptions-versus-70%-advertising-revenue split that is familiar from print papers' traditional economic model; he also refers to online newspapers' early agreements with proprietary online services.

Electronic newspapers were first offered via these proprietary services. In this situation, the online papers had, in effect, a captive audience, and were also among the most interesting of the limited choice of sites available to the services' subscribers (Erlindson, 1995, "The Pull Factor," "Money Talks," and "Ads vs. Subscriptions" sections; Liebman, 1994). As we have mentioned, the situation has changed in that many newspapers now provide direct WWW access, a change that according to Erlindson (1995) further limits the efficacy of a subscription model.

Erlindson (1995) suggests that online papers look to advertising for more of the revenue mix. Several online publications adopted this strategy. As of February 1996, 71% of daily Web newspapers and 78% of weekly Web papers included display ads (Garneau, 1996). At that time, too, 70% of Web dailies and 81% of Web weeklies included classified ads (Garneau, 1996). Palmer and Eriksen's review of forty-eight Internet newspapers found only five that "did not carry some sort of advertisements" (1999, p. 38).

Early online manifestations of display advertising included sponsorships and banner ads, in which information about the advertiser or their product is displayed on the Web page. Laura Porto, editorial supervisor at Times Information Services, Inc., and a member of the team that established the Seattle Times Northwest Online[16] Web site, indicated in early 1996 that banner advertising was a widespread, and promising, revenue source for online publications (personal communication, January 8, 1996). She cited HotWired,[17] boston.com[18] (a media conglomerate site that includes the *Boston Globe* newspaper among its listings), the San Jose Mercury Center online, and the Nando News Network (another composite media site, including the online *Nando Times* newspaper in its listings) as sites making good use of banner advertising.

Erlindson (1995) articulated some reasons for this belief in advertising as a promising revenue model:

Advertising on the Internet and on the WWW has many benefits. The primary benefit, aside from exposure, is the low cost of a Web page. They range anywhere from $80 to $500 a page depending on the complexity. It is also easy to audit the performance of an advertising Web page.[19] Firstly, the advertiser can determine the number of hits or the number of times the ad has been read. If the Web page contains a response feature, such as a form asking for browser information—sometimes in the form of a contest—the advertiser can find out the user's name and address. The postal code, for example, could then be used to determine the demographics of who uses the Web site. In addition, the Web page can contain product order forms. One florist in the [Midwest] takes 2,000 orders a day over their Web page. Kim Komando writes, "You don't have to be a Wall Street wizard to see this is a pretty good return on investment."[20] (1995, "Ads vs. Subscriptions" section)

Outing, too, claimed that advertising may be the most promising economic model for "general interest publications like newspapers operating a Web site" (1996, "The Death"). Outing maintained this position in the face of what might seem contradictory evidence, the folding of the Web Review, an esteemed online publication that relied on an advertising model.

The Web Review's experience was widely interpreted as a demonstration that the Advertising Model doesn't work for Web publications. After four months online, the Web Review was forced to suspend publication because advertising revenues didn't cover its expenses. In an online letter announcing the suspension of publication in May 1996, Web Review editors asked readers if they would be willing to pay $19.95 for six months' access to the publication

(Allen, 1996; Sims, 1996). Out of roughly 1,100 responses, 700 readers were willing to pay (Allen, 1996; Sims, 1996). Though this response was encouraging, 700 subscriptions would not cover expenses (Sims, 1996) any more than advertising revenues had, and the magazine stopped publication.

As this scenario unfolded, it seemed to demonstrate that neither a display advertising model nor a subscription model was viable for the Web Review. As Allen (1996) notes, "[the] Web Review's fate demonstrate[s] the peculiar economics of Internet publishing[:] 'The barriers to entry are relatively few, but the barriers to success are enormous.'"[21] In the Web Review's own words, "We were a good publication, but we weren't a good business" (Sims, 1996, "Web Review Teams").[22]

Meyer (1995) pointed out that advertising may be a more difficult sell online than it is on paper, for several reasons. First, advertisers don't really buy an advertisement, or even space for one, in a print paper; what they actually buy is the production and door-to-door distribution of the advertisement. The paper cannot reproduce these services online. In addition, online news services face the challenge of a "narrowcast" audience, with "exceedingly high costs per thousand reached" (p. 26). Another potential weakness of online advertisements is that they are easily ignored. Finally, there is currently no consensus on rates for online advertising displays. In sum, said Meyer, "given [the] unresolved variables, it seems ill-advised for an online newspaper to expect to generate substantial revenue through [display] advertising" (1995, p. 33).[23]

Meyer did not deny, however, that there are possibilities in other advertising models for financing online publications. After all, the Web's demographics are desirable to advertisers. Web consumer demographics have consistently reflected a rapidly expanding high-income, high-education audience (see Meyer, 1995, and December, 1997).

First, newspapers can offer services to design and create advertising sites (Meyer, 1995, p. 34). The Norfolk *Virginian-Pilot*, for example "[brought] in $100,000 [in 1994–95] from designing Web pages for advertisers and secondarily linking them to its Pilot Online newspaper" (p. 34).[24] Meyer mentioned that this might be a particularly appropriate revenue strategy for papers in "medium-size markets" such as Raleigh, North Carolina (p. 34).

Interactive advertising is another possibility:

There are other advertising services [rather than display or banner ads] that an online newspaper can provide [to this desirable demographic group]. Interactive advertising allows advertisers to institute direct order-taking and to generate highly personalized follow-up ads online and by electronic or traditional mail. (Meyer, 1995, pp. 33–34)[25]

The New Century Network (NCN) newspaper consortium made a similar point about the promise of online targeted advertising, contending that "[t]he Net, by its very nature, is a direct marketing medium. It enables very efficient, targeted and measurable reach into segmented audiences" (NCN, 1996, "So How Are You Going To"). Cameron et al. (1995) also discussed the beneficial possibilities of targeting advertisements to receptive online consumers, pointing out that "advertisement inquiries, ordering history, and other database information volunteered or garnered about the user can be used to deliver highly personalized follow-up ads online as well as online direct mail customized to the user's profile (Bender, 1993)" ("Commercial Messages" section).[26]

One example of the interactive approach is the InfoSeek Personal[27] news service, which, in addition to offering customized news, also takes advantage of interactive marketing, "retriev[ing] advertisements . . . meant to fit [the consumer's] preferences, . . . based on things [the consumer] disclosed in registration" (Williams, 1996, p. F21).

Revenues from classified advertising are another possibility for online papers that wish to implement an advertising model. Classified ads are crucial to the survival of traditional newspapers. For example, in the United States, about 37% of all print-based newspaper income is derived from classified advertising (Levins, 1996) and in the United Kingdom, classified advertising represents 12% of national newspapers' revenues and 51% of regional newspapers' revenues (*The Economist*, "Caught in the Web," 1999).

However, transferring this revenue stream to online endeavors was initially virtually ignored by newspaper organizations—a missed opportunity of disastrous proportions, some say. In June 1996, Wyman warned that

...the newspaper industry held a virtual monopoly over the public posting of open jobs. Today, the industry finds that it is only one of many players [that] use the Internet as a means of posting and gathering employment-related information.

Oddly, while most of the companies that have entered the business in the last few months are either generating or seeking to generate revenues from their efforts, few newspapers have even attempted to use online postings as anything other than a "freebie" which is included in the base price of their paper-based listings ("The Last Link").

As a result, said Wyman, "The help wanted market is only one of many examples of franchises that were once held by the newspaper industry that are currently being cherry-picked and plundered by a vast number of new businesses" (1996, "The Last Link").

Six months later, according to excerpts from a report focused specifically on newspaper revenues and online classified advertising, Wyman's warnings seemed eerily prescient. Specifically, the *Online Classifieds Report* (authored by Steve Outing, Colin Brannigan, and Heidi Anderson, and available from *Editor & Publisher*) [28] found that as of late 1996, "although many newspapers have set up Web sites that include classified advertising sections, the strategies and functions of those sections are generally weak and ineffectual in comparison to the innovative systems deployed by the leading non-newspaper cyber-classifieds companies" (Levins, 1996, "Cyber Classifieds Companies Do It Better" section).

Marsha A. Stoltman, vice president of marketing relations and research at *Editor & Publisher*, made a similar point. She noted that even those daily newspapers publishing their classified ads online have yet to decide how to generate significant amounts of money from their online ventures. She reported on interviews with classified advertising managers at twenty-five daily newspapers that, on average, have had their classifieds online for 3.5 years. She said that while they might be considered industry pioneers, they have all been hesitant about charging extra for this service, often asking as little as one dollar more for each classified advertisement (Stone, 1999).

Research suggests that classified advertising is of particular significance for online newspapers because it generates both revenue and readership. As far as revenue is concerned, a survey conducted by the Newspaper Association of America revealed that online newspaper classified advertising generated approximately $92 million in revenue in 1998. This represented about 42% of all online newspaper advertising revenue (Gilbert, 1999, "Newspapers Carve Slice Out of Auction Pie"). And from a readership perspective, a 1999 *Editor & Publisher* survey of online newspaper readers showed that classified advertising was the target destination for 38% of readers. Classified advertising was only marginally less popular than national news (39%) (PR Newswire, August 16, 1999, "Classified Advertising Accounts for 38% of Online Newspaper Traffic, E&P Survey Reveals").

The contestability of online classified advertising creates problems for online news publishers whose business models are based on the revenue generated from online classified advertising. While classified advertising revenue may be draining from print-based operations, the revenue generated by online classified advertising is both limited in scale and a highly contested commodity online.

The advantages that nonnewspaper online classifieds have had over their print and online-newspaper counterparts include better functionality; more "timely and effective connection[s] between buyers and sellers, employers and job-seekers" (Levins, 1996, "Cyber Classifieds May Just Work Better" section); immediacy; customizability; and special functions such as keyword search and retrieval (Levins, 1996, summarizing *The Online Classifieds Report*). Toner (1996) and Levins (1996) mention nonnewspaper classified advertising services that regularly email pertinent ads to consumers. Levins (1996), citing *The Online Classifieds Report*, notes that "only a small number of newspaper companies" have been competitive with nonnewspaper cyber classifieds in areas such as these ("Cyber Classifieds May Just Work Better" section).

Currently, online news publishers seeking to generate revenues from classified advertising are being challenged on two fronts, by specialist online classified operations and by mass-market online auction sites such as eBay.[29]

Specialist online classified sites, such as monster.com and hotjobs.com, are drawing readers and revenues away from both traditional and online newspaper-based classified recruitment sections. For example, in 1999, monster.com had 1.5 million resumes in its database, and a growing number of employers paid to search the database. The percentage of monster.com's revenue derived from employer searches—a measure of corporate America's willingness to change its recruiting habits—rose from 8% in 1998 to a projected 25% in 1999, with revenues of $92 million being predicted for 1999 (Walker, 1999). While newspaper organizations are unable to provide a clear explanation, there was a significant drop in newspapers' help-wanted advertising during 1998–99 in at least five major advertising markets—San Jose, Dallas, Boston, New York, and Los Angeles (Barringer, 1999). It is possible that online classified advertising on specialist job sites contributed to this slump.

Real estate advertising is under challenge from specialist portals such as Microsoft's HomeAdvisor[30] and Yahoo! Real Estate.[31] And Microsoft's Carpoint[32] may be challenging auto advertising revenues by providing services that go beyond the functionality of traditional advertising. In addition to the proliferation of advertising sites, the proliferation of online auction sites threatens other revenue streams that would have been derived from classified advertising, whether paper-based or online.

Predictions of future revenue from online classified advertising suggest that a very large market will emerge. In 1999, Jupiter Communications estimated that the traditional newspapers will lose $3.2 billion of classified advertising to their online competitors in 2003. Forrester arrived at parallel conclusions, estimating that traditional newspapers stand to lose $11 billion in total advertising revenues (including display ads) by 2004 (Stone, 1999).

The publishers of traditional newspapers, which are often the publishers of online newspapers accompanied by classified advertising, have attempted to meet the challenge of online classified advertising in a number of ways. While developing an online presence for their existing papers, they have entered strategic partnerships with, or made investments in, competitive online services. The *Boston Globe* has launched its own online auction site on the grounds that many people wish to buy goods and services at auction locally (Sullivan, 1999).

Mass-market online auction sites are growing quickly (Barrett, 1999) and they are being positioned as competitors for print-based classified advertising. As Margaret Whitman, from eBay, has noted:

For 25 cents to $2 a week, people can buy unlimited space on eBay to describe their product. They can show pictures. And they can find the most efficient price. Instead of listing a used Toyota Corolla at $1,100, they can set a reserve price, and then see how much buyers might want to pay in an auction (Anders, 1999).

In an attempt to compete with mass-market auction sites such as eBay and uBid, newspaper companies have partnered two online auction companies, PowerAdz.com, with its Auction Hill site, and Classified Ventures, which runs Auction Universe. These two organizations represent more than 800 newspapers in the United States. Both companies offer their member newspapers a combination of co-branded online classified ads and access to local and national auctions (Zarert, 1999). Classified Ventures offers classified advertising sites (Apartments.com, cars.com, and NewHomeNetwork.com), and these sites are linked to local sites provided by newspaper affiliates. The local sites include local editorial material, advertising, and classifieds as well as national editorial material, advertising, and classifieds from Classified Ventures. Users can choose to browse through local or national classified advertising (Levins, 1998).

In turn, mass-market online auction providers such as eBay are developing regional and metropolitan auction sites designed for the sale of bulky items that are not easily transported over long distances after sale (Anders, 1999).

Traditional newspapers are attempting to maintain and leverage brand awareness by forming partnerships with their erstwhile competitors. Eighteen Texas newspapers, representing diverse owners, have created Texas4U.com, an online classified advertising site that capitalizes on their existing brand names (PR Newswire, 1999, "Four Texas Newspaper Groups Create Online Classified Alliance"). Following a similar strategy, the Newspaper Association of America (NAA) has created the Bona Fide Classified program, which is designed to emphasize the quality, reliability, and trustworthiness of online classifieds originating from traditional newspapers (Business Wire, 1999, "PowerAdz.com First to Participate in NAA's Bona Fide Classified Internet Initiative").

Another implementation of an advertising model online is to offer online personal ads. Outing (1996, "How the Web Is Changing") discussed changes in the personal ad model as it moved online. As with other functions that were once limited to print newspapers, competition for personal ad revenue springs from nonnewspaper cyber companies. Andy Sutcliffe, president of Telepublishing, Inc., which runs an online personal advertising network for alternative weekly newspapers, described online users as "a fundamentally different group of people," better educated and younger (by an average of four years) than readers of print personal ads (McMenzie, 1998). If this analysis is accurate, online personal ads could draw this new demographic to newspaper viewership.

In sum, it can be seen that as far as advertising models are concerned, predictions are both positive and negative, and experiences are mixed. Advertising models that have been considered or tried include sponsorships, banner or display advertising, advertisement design and development, targeted ads, classified and personal advertisements, and auctions. Online, any of these advertising models can take advantage of the medium's interactivity, though perhaps newspaper sites have been slower than their competitors to see and make use of this advantage. Online, advertisers have opportunities not simply to promote products, but also to facilitate consumer research and purchases. The opportunities for publishers and advertisers to engage consumers in online transactions have received enough attention to be considered an economic model in their own right.

The Transactional Model

Some commentators see a promising economic model for online publications based on the electronic media's provision of a "transactional space" where advertisers and consumers can meet. White (1996) defined transactional space as follows:

We are all familiar with conventional transactional spaces in our everyday lives. Shops are where merchants display goods, shoppers make purchasing decisions and . . . funds and goods are exchanged. Courts are associated with legal transactions and schools with educational transactions. We are used to the idea that transactions occur in specialized, often purpose-built physical spaces. But the new media and communications systems are leading to the development of equivalent electronic transactional spaces. (p. 5)

Kresser (1996), specifically considering merchandising transactions, defined the online market similarly:

In this new model, information or content is not merely transmitted from a sender to a receiver, but instead, mediated environments are created by participants and then experienced.

The role of companies on the Web, then, becomes to create such a mediated environment or "marketspace" in which consumers can interact with the firm and each other, receive and contribute information and content, and buy and sell products and services. (introductory section)

Palmer and Eriksen (1999) describe an emerging role for digital newspapers as "market intermediaries . . . bringing buyers and sellers together" in an electronic market (p. 38).

Cameron et al. (1995) directly addressed the potential of transactional advertising for generating newspaper revenues, making two points. First, they suggested that newspaper readers specifically selecting particular ads could be considered "information seekers," and advertisers could provide "copy-heavy" advertisements to meet these viewers' information needs. Second, they pointed out that "once an ad is viewed, electronic papers offer the advertiser a marketing advantage by making direct response/ordering features available" Cameron et al. also noted that the newspapers can serve as their audience's gateway to "commercially sponsored electronic places. Like a McDonald's playground or a Nike World, analysts envision these sponsored places as enjoyable, informative locations for exposure to and information about products provided by the sponsor and by other users" ("Commercial Messages" section).[33]

Besides providing a gateway to advertisers' electronic locations, online newspapers can establish electronic locations of their own. ZDNet's AnchorDesk site[34] is an example of this, providing a place where consumers can subscribe to any of several Ziff-Davis publications, view ZDNet's reviews of companies and products, read technology-related articles, and email ZDNet columnists and other readers.

Conaghan saw much promise for newspaper revenue in the Transactional Model:

Microtransacations/payments impact newspaper-operated Websites in three respects: as a possible payment mechanism for online subscriptions, as a "pay-per-view" option for information products from electronic archives or for new premium services, and as a method of paying for goods and services offered by advertisers through the newspaper Website. (1996)

In fact, said Conaghan (1996), "Many—if not most—Web seers and soothsayers view [microtransactions] as the eventual salvation for Web profitability." However, Conaghan also pointed out that serious concerns needed to be addressed before the "transactional approach . . . as a revenue model" could really "take off." These concerns include security, ease of use, accounting for taxes and import duties, and price combinations (that is, dividing the trans-action revenues among all parties that facilitate the transaction: the newspaper, the advertiser, the bank, etc.). Conaghan briefly re-viewed several companies that were addressing these concerns, including Clickshare,[35] CyberCash,[36] FTT Inc.'s NetGAINS,[37] First Virtual's Internet Payment System,[38] IBM's InfoMarket[39] and Cryptolope,[40] Open Market's OM-Transact[41] and other products, and Visa's and MasterCard's work on Secure Electronic Transmis-sion (SET) standards.[42]

Like subscription and advertising models—and especially like the very similar interactive advertising model discussed above—the Transactional Model has been considered and tried by various online publishing interests, and both optimistic and pessimistic projections for its success can be found.

The Bundled Model

One final revenue model to consider is the Bundled, or Partner-ship, model. Some online newspapers have established, or consid-ered establishing, partnerships with other publishing and/or Internet entities as a means of gaining revenue. These Bundled revenue models may take the form of online newspapers partnering with online proprietary services, with Internet access providers, with Web browsers, with other newspapers, or with other content providers.

Partnerships between online newspapers and proprietary ser-vices were the earliest Bundled Model. Erlindson (1995) labeled this kind of partnership the Information Provider Model. According to Erlindson, in the Information Provider Model, information providers such as America Online (AOL), Prodigy, and CompuServe allowed their subscribers to access newspapers for a fee paid in addition to the online service's basic subscription fee. Different providers and newspapers have different pricing scales. In this model, the newspapers gain the benefits of low startup costs and the online service's technical expertise. But there are also significant drawbacks: The newspaper must share revenue with the access provider, and the newspaper's potential audience is limited to the number of subscribers to the proprietary service.

Cameron et al. (1995) noted that online newspaper efforts in the early 1990s developed partnerships with "established online services" (such as Prodigy, Genie, Delphi, AOL, and CompuServe) to take advantage of the services' "market penetration, . . . relative ease of use, [and] . . . information service infrastructure" ("The History of Electronic Newspapers" section). However, like Erlindson (1995), Cameron et al. noted that online newspapers had moved away from such partnerships with proprietary services to direct Internet access:

A number of newspapers have opted for delivery on the Internet's World Wide Web.[43] . . . The Internet's appeal to newspaper publishers is partly economic: while commercial services often get up to 80% or more of connect-time revenue, only modest costs are associated with establishing an information server on the Internet. ("Management and Economic Issues" section)

Others have noted that papers that once had partnership agreements with service providers have been abandoning them for direct WWW sites. Outing (1996, "Hold On (line)") noted that "the World Wide Web is the online publishing platform of choice" (p. 5I). Newspaper partnerships with online proprietary services were established only in the United States, said Outing, and after initial partnerships were established, the number of these arrangements remained "flat" (p. 5I), while the number of WWW newspapers grew exponentially.

In another Internet partnership model, a newspaper offers Internet access bundled with its online newspaper subscription.

Some newspapers offer Internet access independently (for example, the Tucson, Arizona *Daily Star*'s StarNet service) (Outing, 1996, "Where's the Money?").[44] Other newspapers partner with an already established Internet service provider (ISP). Meyer (1995) noted that this is a "popular" though "roundabout" way for newspapers to gain revenue (p. 53), whose promise is based on the fact that "providing consumer access to the Internet is one of the fastest growing segments of the U.S. economy" (p. 53). Meyer further contended that this model is most promising in markets where reasonably priced Internet (and/or proprietary service) access is not already available, most probably somewhat small or remote areas (pp. 53, 56).

Some commentators claimed that it is more promising for a newspaper to partner with an ISP than to establish itself as an ISP:

Providing your own ISP is a good idea if you have the resources to manage it, and if there's no strong local competition. My paper was in an area with no reliable local Internet provider 15 months ago. We heard an aggressive, professional provider was coming in, so we cut a deal for revenue sharing. They get promotion in our paper. We get some revenue, and subscribers log on to our home page first. If we'd had the expertise (or hired it) to set up our own ISP, we would have had to commit systems and customer service support, as well as a capital investment. That's not to say you can't do this. . . . But you have to weigh these costs versus what will come in and for how long. (Roiter, 23 June 1996)

Another newspaper had a similar experience:

Our decision-making followed a similar path. We considered becoming an ISP. The combination of costs (customer service, tech support staff, equipment, etc.) and uncertainty (we could see AT&T et al. coming) backed us off. We became an InfiNet affiliate and thus earn revenue via that ISP relationship as well as from our online advertising. Thus we concentrated our resources on publishing and marketing, businesses we know well, rather than on becoming an ISP. I think we all agree that it was the right path for us to take. (Frink, 23 June 1996)

Outing (1996, "Where's the Money?") also cautioned, however, that there are risks for newspapers that adopt an ISP partnership model. Cable television and telephone companies offering Internet access may prove to offer too much competition for newspapers,

says Outing. Meyer (1995) made a similar point about the drawbacks of this bundled strategy, stating that any ISP is "quite vulnerable to competition in terms of prices and level of service,"
particularly "in larger communities, [where] the Internet access
market may already be glutted" (p. 56).[45] And Wyman (1996)
contended that newspapers essentially missed the opportunity to
maximize revenue from this model:

It is a real pity that more newspapers didn't get seriously into the ISP
business [in the early to mid-1990s,] when the opportunity existed. Had
the papers done so, they would be paying for operations out of connection fees rather than being forced to offer most of their product for free
and relying on advertising. . . .
  The newspapers have lost more than an opportunity to make money
off connection fees. They have also lost much of the opportunity to
position themselves as the number 1 information providers in their
communities. (19 June 1996 [*])

Another partnership model that could hold promise for online
newspaper publishers is the establishment of newspaper consortiums. Meyer (1995) contended that these consortiums may "hold
the key to how well newspapers can compete for online readers and
advertisers against franchise-interlopers such as Time-Warner, CNN
and ESPN" (p. 155), because they "[devise] mechanisms to pool
news and advertising," and thus "free each member from having to
duplicate efforts and allow specialized coverage from one region to
be available in any other region at any time" (p. 155).

Meyer cited the Associated Press (AP) and the New Century
Network (NCN) as examples of such consortiums (though he
points out problems with AP's business model) (1995, pp. 155–
156). Also, it should be noted that NCN disbanded in early 1998,
perhaps because of competing interests among the individual
papers, or because the organization was quite cumbersome, or
because of competition from other nonnewspaper ventures (Dugan,
1998).

Another example of a partnership revenue model is the *Los
Angeles Times* and *Washington Post*'s joint News Service,[46] available to
"corporations, government agencies, educational institutions and
newspapers for a monthly site fee" (*Los Angeles Times–Washington*

Post, 1996). Subscribers to the service get information from all Times Mirror- and *Washington Post*-owned companies. (These include several contributing newspapers—the *Los Angeles Times,* the *Washington Post, Newsday,* the *Baltimore Sun,* the *Hartford Courant,* and others—the Ski Web site, *Yachting Magazine, Newsweek,* the Legi-Slate Web News Service, and *Virtual City* magazine.)[47] The information available includes international news from foreign correspondents; U.S. political and legislative news from Washington, D.C., correspondents; regional coverage from ten contributing newspapers; finance and business news; sports news and commentary; and access and republication rights.[48]

Outing quoted Lincoln Millstein, the *Boston Globe*'s vice president of new media, as contending that it's only through such partnerships that newspapers, whose "'content is really quite thin,' when you consider that what fills a printed newspaper often originates from freelancers, third-party content providers (e.g., weather), and wire services" can provide information "deep . . . and compelling enough to succeed online" ("Connections 96," 1996). Further, Outing quotes Tony Marsella, an NAA executive, as pointing out that similar alliances are "the key" to protecting newspapers' classified advertising market online ("Connections 96," 1996).

As this discussion indicates, not only is the Bundled (or Partnerships) Model another possible revenue strategy for online newspapers, but the lines between various revenue models can become blurred. Partnerships might be established to provide specialty content or to share advertising or subscription fees, for example. This realization leads us to some concluding thoughts about online newspaper economic models.

Conclusion

This chapter reviewed industry thinking about and experience with revenue models for online newspapers between 1995 and 1999. These revenue models have been suggested for newspapers making the transition from print to online media. The economic models examined here include variations on four basic models: subscription, advertising, transactional, and bundled. This discussion is not meant to indicate that any one of these revenue models, or even any particular mix of them (for instance, the roughly 30%-subscription-versus-70%-advertising mix familiar from print newspapers) is guaranteed to be successful.

In fact, there seems to be a general consensus that, given the complex challenges for online newspaper publishers trying to turn a profit, no single economic model, or particular mix of models, can be entirely suitable. A successful revenue model for online newspapers will be some mix of revenue models. According to Outing,

As I've said before . . . you can't live on advertising alone. . . . Multiple revenue streams are necessary for your financial health. For some papers that means being an Internet access provider; for some, it means designing and constructing Web sites for local businesses; it means figuring out a classified ads online strategy; etc. (1996, "The Death")

Meyer (1995), too, saw online newspaper publishers' paths to prosperity as diverse:

Publishers should keep in mind that they possess huge cost advantages in entering the online market. . . . Advertising sales in large markets, advertising site design in medium markets and sales of Internet access in smaller markets can make online ventures profitable today for newspapers that already have recovered most costs of operation. In addition, online editions have tremendous potential to serve as promotional tools for newsprint editions. (p. 153)

Finer makes the same point, and summarizes it succinctly:

Look for a moment at the big dailies . . . WP, NYT [*Washington Post, New York Times*], etc. . . . their Web sites are open at the moment, and they are analyzing usage, improving content, navigation, performance, tracking, etc. They want to charge, yes? YES. But they are not convinced that subscriptions are the best, or only way to go. They need an analog to newsstand sales . . . and maybe more. They need to charge for new types of services . . . like archive searches, or book review searches. Obviously they cannot charge much for these, but a quarter a search could generate meaningful sums.

The model is not advertising OR subscriptions OR microcharges . . . it is all of them, in combinations that suit the customer's needs. (19 July 1996)

Palmer and Eriksen (1999), too, point out that "the current picture is that digital newspapers are utilizing multiple marketing approaches" (p. 40). Palmer and Eriksen see these diverse marketing approaches as experiments with both technology- and content-based profit-making strategies. And they contend that this mix of strategies is reflective of, and suitable for, a communication phenomenon that is a hybrid of digital technology and traditional newspapers.

Palmer and Eriksen's point about the diversity of revenue strategies being adopted by online newspapers echoes that of Resnick's earlier reflections on the unique, hybrid, and fluid qualities of online newspapers. Resnick pointed out that not only different and diverse revenue strategies, but also new and creative ones, will be necessary for profitable online newspaper publishing:

... there are plenty of ... creative ways that online publishers can [make] and are making money. ... Publishers need to do more than simply adapt existing business models for use in cyberspace; they need to pioneer new models that fit the medium. (18 July 1996)

Acknowledgment

This chapter is based on research funded by the Telstra Fund for Social and Policy Research. The full report, *Making Money on the Web? Business Models for Online Newspapers,* is published by, and available from, the La Trobe University Online Media Program, Bundoora, Victoria, 3083 Australia. http://teloz.latrobe.edu.au/teloz.

Notes

1. For the most current statistics regarding online newspaper count, see the online media statistics started by Outing and now maintained by *Editor & Publisher,* available online at http://www.mediainfo.com/ephome/npaper/nphtm/statistics.htm.

2. J. December and N. Randall (1994). *The World Wide Web Unleashed.* Indianapolis, IN: Sams Publishing. [Meyer's citation.]

3. K. Cooke and D. Lehrer (1993, July 12). The whole world is talking. *The Nation,* 60–64. [Meyer's citation.]

4. December and Randall (1994). [Meyer's citation.]

Profiting from Online News

5. http://www.csmonitor.com/.

6. Cameron et al. (1996) also discuss a fourth, non-subscription-based economic model. A full consideration of this model is not included in this paper, as its focus is more on containing costs than on generating revenue. Briefly, this fourth model, labeled the Economic Efficiency Model, "justifies electronic newspapers in terms of the economic efficiencies associated with electronic delivery" (Cameron et al., 1996, "Electronic Newspapers Business Models" section). Electronic newspapers are seen as economically efficient in that material already gathered for the print edition can be included online with minimal time and effort. There need not be additional investments in news gathering. According to Cameron et al., electronic distribution is also inexpensive when compared to the costs of print paper distribution. And electronic newspapers can be sold to advertisers as an efficient medium for providing consumers with opportunities not only to learn about products, but also to purchase them. In addition, this advertising efficiency can provide the newspaper industry with the opportunity to regain advertising revenue lost to direct marketing and telemarketing.

7. For details see http://www.philly.com and http://www.newshound.com.

8. Creagh notes that ClickShare is an application that can track what screens users access and how long they stay on each screen (Gipson, 1996, "*The Christian Science Monitor*").

9. http://www.tribune/com/.

10. http://www.newsservice.com/.

11. http://www.onwis.com/.

12. See http://www.forrester.com/.

13. See http://www.wsj.com/tour.htm for more about the *WSJ*'s Personal Journal.

14. http://www.newspage.com/.

15. See http://www.newspage.com/NEWSPAGE/nptb-subsinfo.html.

16. http://www.seattletimes.com/.

17. http://www.hotwired.com/frontdoor/.

18. http://www.boston.com/.

19. Kim Komando (1995, February 16). "Marketing on Internet doesn't have to tangle web." *Arizona Business Gazette*. High Technology section, p. 7. [Erlindson's citation.]

20. Ibid. [Erlindson's citation.]

21. Allen is quoting from an interview with Betty J. Lyter, senior research analyst with Montgomery Securities in San Francisco.

22. Citing Dale Dougherty, Web Review publisher.

23. For further discussion of the problems with banner advertising, and pessimistic projections for this model, see Resnick (1996, July 1) "AdTech 96," and the

online-news list discussion thread "Is banner advertising dead?" available online starting at http://www.social.com/social/hypermail/news/online_news/ Jun_30_Jul_6_1996/0039.html.

24. http://www.pilotonline.com/.

25. W. Bender (1993, May), "Riding the Digital Highway," *Presstime*, pp. 54–55. [Meyer's citation.]

26. Ibid. [Cameron et al.'s citation.]

27. http://personal.infoseek.com/.

28. See http://www.mediainfo.com/ephome/store/storehtm/contents.htm for the Online Classifieds Report's Table of Contents, and ordering and additional information.

29. http://www.ebay.com.

30. http://carpoint.msn.com.

31. http://realestate.yahoo.com/.

32. http://homeadvisor.msn.com.

33. Personal communication, Dennis DuBé, Apple e-World, 1994. [Cameron et al.'s citation.]

34. http://www5.zdnet.com/anchordesk/.

35. http://remington.clickshare.com/.

36. http://www.cybercash.com/.

37. http://www.fttnet.com/netgains.htm.

38. http://www.fv.com/.

39. http://www.infomkt.ibm.com/.

40. http://www.infomkt.ibm.com/.

41. http://www.openmarket.com/.

42. See http://www.visa.com/cgi-bin/vee/sf/standard.html.

43. R. Resnick (1994 , July). Newspapers on the Net. *Internet World*, 5(5): 68–73, and J. Rosenberg (1993, September). "Virus attacks: Are newspaper PC systems susceptible?" *Editor & Publisher*, 121(36): 19, 40–41pc. (Cameron et al.'s [1995] citations.)

44. http://www.azstarnet.com/.

45. R. Resnick (1995, July). Should you be an Internet access provider? *Interactive Publishing Alert*. Highlights available online (July 1995): http://www.netcreations. com/ipa/. [Meyer's citation.]

46. See http://www.newsservice.com/.

47. See http://www.newsservice.com/links.html.

48. See http://www.newsservice.com/info.html.

References

Allen, M., 1996, May 28. Web Review suspends publication. *The New York Times:* CyberTimes [Online]. Available: http://www.nytimes.com/web/docsroot/library/cyber/week/0528zine.html [1997, January].

Anders, G., 1999, October 1. eBay opens 50 regional centers. *WSJ Interactive Edition* [Online]. Available: http://www.zdnet.com/zdnn/stories/news/0,4586,2345609,00.html [1999, November].

Barrett, L., 1999, October 27. eBay tumbles despite beating 3Q estimates. Inter@ctive Investor [Online]. Available: http://www.zdnet.com/zdnn/stories/news/0,4586,1017869,00.html [1999, November 12].

Barringer, F., 1999, August 30. Newspapers Seek Partners to Fight Challenges in Online Ad Market. *New York Times* [Online]. Available: http://www.nytimes.com/library/tech/99/08/biztech/articles/30help.html [1999, October 19].

Benning, J., 1999, September 28. From the drawing board to Slate . . . and beyond. *Online Journalism Review* [Online] (4 pp). Available: http://ojr.usc.edu [1999, October 19].

Business Wire, 1999, June 14. (vol. 13, no. 11) PowerAdz.com First to Participate in NAA's Bona Fide Classified Internet Initiative. [Online]. Available: Lexis-Nexis http://www.lexis-nexis.com/lncc/ [1999, October 1].

Cameron, G. T., P. A. Curtin, B. Hollander, G. Nowak, and S. A. Shamp, 1995, June 15. Electronic newspapers: Toward a research agenda [Online]. Available: http://www.grady.uga.edu./protopapers/reports/CoxMono/CoxMono.html [1996, June].

Cameron, G. T., B. A. Hollander, G. J. Nowak, and S. A. Shamp, 1996, February 20. Assessing the potential of a full-featured electronic newspaper for the young adult market [Online]. Available: http://www.grady.uga.edu./protopapers/reports/assessingprotopapers/tableof content.html [1996, June].

Cameron, G. T., Nowak, G. J., and Krugman, D. M., 1993. The competitive position of newspapers in the local/retail market. *Newspaper Research Journal,* 14(3): 70–81.

Caught in the Web, 1999, July 17. *The Economist* (U.S. edition) [Online]. Available: Lexis-Nexis http://www.lexis-nexis.com/lncc/ [1999, October 1].

Compaine, B. [bcompaine@usa.net], 1996, October 15. Early financial results of WSJ Interactive [Posting to online-news discussion list]. Available: http://www.social.com/social/hypermail/news/index.html [1997, June].

Conaghan, J., 1996. *Christian Science Monitor* mini-summit on measurement and microtransactions. Newspaper Association of America: The Digital Edge [Online]. Available: http://www.naa.org/edge/csm.html [1998, March].

December, J., 1997. *World Wide Web 1997 Unleashed* (4th ed.). Indianapolis, IN: Sams.net Publishing.

Donatello, M., 1996, September. For some, pricing research pays dividends; Others "Just do it": "How much would you be willing to pay for —?" Newspaper Association of America: The Digital Edge [Online]. Available: http://www.naa.org/edge/csm.html [1998, March].

Dugan, I. J., 1998. New-media meltdown at new century: How a big online newspaper venture bit the dust. *BusinessWeek* [Online]. Available: http://www.businessweek.com/1998/12/b3570103.htm [1999, November 12].

Editor & Publisher, 1996, April 18. Publications and research papers on online newspaper services [Online]. Available: http://www.mediainfo.com/ephome/research/researchhtm/public.htm [1998, March].

Erlindson, M., 1995, April. Online newspapers: The newspaper industry's dive into cyberspace [Online]. Available: http://ourworld.compuserve.com/homepages/MErlindson/paper1.htm [1998, March].

Finer, S. [xerxes@clark.net], 1996, July 19. Re: Profiting Indirectly (was Is [Au: Is "was Is" correct?] banner advertising dead?) [Posting to online-news discussion list]. Available online: http://www.social.com/social/hypermail/news/index.html [1997, July].

Frink, G. [dmgf@foto.infi.net], 1996, June 23. Re: making the jump to ISP [Posting to online-news discussion list]. Available online: http://www.social.com/social/hypermail/news/index.html [1997, July].

Fulton, K., 1996, March/April. http://www.journalism.now: A tour of our uncertain future. *Columbia Journalism Review* [Online]. Available: http://www.cjr.org/kfulton/contents.html [1998, March].

Garneau, G., 1996, February 17. Online services top interactive agenda. *Editor & Publisher*, 12(7): 40I.

Gilbert, J., 1999, June 21. Newspapers carve slice out of auction pie. *Advertising Age*, 32.

Gipson, M., 1996, June. The Christian Science Monitor (Internet). Excerpt from Interactive Publishing Alert[colon?] "Testlab: The Christian Science Monitor," 6/15/96. Newspaper Association of America: The Digital Edge [Online]. Available: http://www.naa.org/edge/csm.html [1998, March].

Gipson, M., 1996, September. Web subscriptions? The answer's in your e-mail. Newspaper Association of America: The Digital Edge [Online]. Available: http://www.naa.org/edge/csm.html [1998, March].

Harper, C., 1996, November. The Daily Me: We rate the services that try to tailor the news to your interests [Online]. Available: http://www.bnet.att.com/news/dailyme.htm [1996, November].

Hayter, S., 1996, May. Newspapers and new media: A *Newspaper Focus* special report. *Newspaper Focus*, 8(4): 19–29.

Hipschman, D., 1995, August 1. Online news: Would you subscribe? *Web Review* [Online]. Available: http://webreview.com/reviews/newsrev/index.html [1996, November].

Kassel, A., 1996, February/March. Current news on CompuServe: Fast and affordable. *Database*, 19(1), 21–30.

Kirsner, S., 1997, December 1. Profits in site? (Newspapers hoping for profits from their Web sites). *American Journalism Review*, 41ff.

Kresser, C., 1996, June. Building "Webcentricity." CMC Magazine [Online]. Available: http://www.december.com/cmc/mag/1996/jun/kresser.html [1999, November 8].

Lapham, C., 1995, July. The evolution of the newspaper of the future. [Online]. Available: http://sunsite.unc.edu/cmc/mag/1995/jul/lapham.html [1999, November 8].

Lapham, C., 1996, June. The evolution of the revolution. CMC Magazine [Online]. Available: http://www.december.com/cmc/mag/1996/jun/lapham.html [1999, November 8].

Levins, H., 1996, Nov. 21. The online classifieds report: New cyberspace advertising technologies to impact newpaper revenues in 3 years. Editor & Publisher Interactive [Online]. Available: http://www.mediainfo.com/ [1996, December].

Levins, H., 1998, August 8. *New York Times* joins Classified Ventures. Editor & Publisher Interactive [Online]. Available: Lexis-Nexis http://www.lexis-nexis.com/lncc/ [1999, October 1].

Liebman, H., 1994, April 25. Newspapers hit the highway. *Mediaweek*, 4(17): 16–17.

Matson, E., 1995, November/December. The *Wall Street Journal* delivered to your virtual doorstep. *Online*, 19(6): 54–58.

McMenzie, M., 1998, March. Online newspapers forge ahead. *The Seybold Report on Internet Publishing*. Available: Lexis-Nexis http://www.lexis-nexis.com/lncc/ [1999, October 1].

Meyer, E. K., 1995. *Tomorrow's News Today* (research report). Pewaukee, WI: News Link Associates.

Meyer, E. K. [meyer@newslink.org], 1996, July 18. Re: Free Mercury Center trial this month [Posting to online-news discussion list]. Available: http://www.social.com/social/hypermail/news/index.html [1997, March].

Meyer, E. K. [meyer@newslink.org], 1998, March 17. An unexpectedly wider web for the world's newspapers. *American Journalism Review (AJR) Newslink* [Online] (743 words). Available: http://www.newslink.org/emcol10.html [1998, March 23].

Morris, P., 1996, February. Newspapers and the new information media. *Media International Australia*, 79: 10–21.

Mossberg, W., 1997, April 17. Major newspapers try to adapt personals to new Web format. *The Wall Street Journal*, p. B1.

New Century Network (NCN), 1996. So, how are you going to pay for all this? [Online]. Available: http://www.newcentury.net/about/how2ad.htm [1997, March].

Newspaper Association of America (NAA), 1996. Postcards from Connections 96: Get set for Web profits . . . in 1999. Newspaper Association of America: The Digital Edge [Online]. Available: http://www.naa.org/edge/connex1.html [1998, March].

Online newspaper shake-up within five years. 1996, August 23. Newspage [Online]. Available: http://www.newspage.com/ [1996, August].

Only 1 in 7 online newspapers are showing profit. 1997, June 9. *New Media Week* 3(18) [Online]. Available: Lexis-Nexis http://www.lexis-nexis.com/lncc/ [1999, January 10].

Outing, S., 1996, June 17. Connections 96: New media meets old under the desert sun [Online]. "Stop the Presses" column. Available: http://www.mediainfo.com/ephome/news/newshtm/stop/stop617.htm [1996, December].

Outing, S., 1996, May 22. The death of the advertising model? Nah! [Online]. "Stop the Presses" column. Available: http://www.mediainfo.com/ephome/news/newshtm/stop/stop522.htm [1996, December].

Outing, S., 1996, March 7. E-newspaper business models for attracting younger readers [Online]. "Stop the Presses" column. Available: http://www.mediainfo.com:4900/ephome/news/newshtm/stop/stop307.htm [1996, December].

Outing, S., 1996, February 17. Hold on (line) tight. *Editor & Publisher*, 12(7): 4I–6I.

Outing, S., 1996, June 7. How the Web is changing the personal ads business [Online]. "Stop the Presses" column. Available: http://www.mediainfo.com:4900/ephome/news/newshtm/stop/stop607.htm [1996, December].

Outing, S., 1996, May. Net profitability. *Newspaper Focus*, 8(4): 22.

Outing, S., 1996, May 13. Newspapers online: The latest statistics [Online]. "Stop the Presses" column. Available: http://www.mediainfo.com/ephome/news/newshtm/stop/stop513.htm [1996, December].

Outing, S., 1996, February 17. Where's the money? *Editor & Publisher*, 12(7): 8I, 34I.

Overset/Interactive [Online], 1996, August 26. Newspage [Online]. Available: http://www.newspage.com/ [1996, August].

Palmer, J. W., and L. B. Eriksen, 1999, September. Digital newspapers explore marketing on the Internet. *Communications of the ACM*, 42(9): 33–40.

Peterson, R. S., 1996, February 17. Multimedia possibilities. *Editor & Publisher*, 12(7): 23I–26I, 36I–37I.

PR Newswire, 1997, February 7. NAA Survey Indicates 36 Percent of Online Newspapers Made Money in 1996; 24 Percent Indicate They Will be Profitable in Four Years. Available: Dow-Jones Interactive http://www.djinteractive.com [1999, November 18].

PR Newswire, 1999, August 16. "Classified Advertising Accounts for 38% of Online Newspaper Traffic, E&P Survey Reveals" [Online]. Available: Lexis-Nexis http://www.lexis-nexis.com/lncc/ [1999, October 1].

PR Newswire, 1999, February 19. Four Texas Newspaper Groups Create Online Classified Alliance. Available: Lexis-Nexis http://www.lexis-nexis.com/lncc/ [1999, October 1].

Resnick, R. [rosalind@netcreations.com], 1996, July 18. Re: Free Mercury Center trial this month [Posting to online-news discussion list]. Available: http://www. social.com/social/hypermail/news/index.html [1996, December].

Roiter, N. [nroiter@ultranet.com], 1996, June 23. Re: making the jump to ISP [Posting to online-news discussion list]. Available: http://www.social.com/social/hypermail/news/index.html [1996, December].

Shaw, R., 1998, March 16. New media: Bandwidth, ads make Web TV-like. *Electronic Media* [Online] (2 pp.). Available: Lexis-Nexis Universe http://web.lexis-nexis.com [1999, January 10].

Sims, D. 1996, August 14. Personal email communication. Re: Web review subscriptions.

Sims, D. 1996, September 20. Web Review teams with Miller Freeman [Online]. Available: http://webreview.com/96/09/20/feature/index.html [1996, December].

Sims, D. 1996, September 27. Personal email communication. Re: Web Review Rides Again.

Stone, M., 1998, June 17. Online newspaper sites not profitable quite yet. ZDNet News [Online]. Available: http://www.zdnet.com/zdnn/stories/news/0,4586,2113048,00.html [1999, October 4].

Stone, M., 1999, September. The classifieds conundrum. *Editor & Publisher*, 6–8.

Sub fees won't pay rent for electronic publishers. 1996, August 23. Newspage [Online]. Available: http://www.newspage.com [1996, August].

Sullivan, C., 1999, September 18. Newspapers make strides with online classifieds. Editor & Publisher [Online]. Available: Lexis-Nexis http://www.lexis-nexis.com/lncc/ [1999, October 1].

Toner, M., 1996. Online classifieds: Promise and peril. Newspaper Association of America: The Digital Edge [Online]. Available: http://www.naa.org/edge/conclass.html [1996, December].

Walker, L., 1999, July 8. A job seekers' auction. The Washington Post [Online]. Available: Lexis-Nexis http://www.lexis-nexis.com/lncc/ [1999, January 10].

Walston, John N. [walston1@voicenet.com], 1996, June 5. Re: Models [Posting to online-news discussion list]. Available: http://www.social.com/social/hypermail/news/index.html [1996, December].

White, P. B., 1996, February. On-line services: The emerging battle for transactional space. *Media International Australia*, 79: 3–9.

Williams, M., 1996, August 12. Counts on the Internet. *The Washington Post*, p. F21.

Wyman, B., 1996, June. Employment listings are another forfeited franchise. CMC Magazine [Online]. Available: http://www.december.com/cmc/mag/1996/jun/last.html [1999, November 8].

Wyman, B. [bobwyman@healthgate.com], 1996, June 19. Re: making the jump to ISP [Posting to online-news discussion list]. Available online: http://www.social.com/social/hypermail/news/index.html.

Zaret, E., 1999, May 13. Are Web auctions classified killers? ZDNet News [Online]. Available: http://www.zdnet.com/zdnn/stories/news/0,4586,2258398,00.htm [1999, October 10].

The Economics of Copy Protection in Software and Other Media

Oz Shy

1. Introduction

Information and know-how are perfect examples of what economists call public goods. A public good is a commodity or a service whose "consumption" by one agent does not preclude its use by other agents; the term *agents* here refers to consumers and firms. See Kindleberger (1983) for a discussion of public goods in this context.

As a result of the public-good nature of information, consumers can gain access to information without having to pay for obtaining it as long as some consumers initially obtain it and then distribute it free of charge to others. Consequently, information providers have been forced to design information-transmitting media that can, at least partially, exclude nonpaying consumers from easily accessing the information purchased by one agent. Examples of such hardware devices include decoders for cable TV, plugs which users must attach to the parallel port of the computer, and software-protection algorithms for preventing software duplications, watermarks on paper, and printing with blue ink on blue paper to prevent photocopying of originals. It is interesting to note that these devices generally produce side effects that reduce the quality of originals and copies and therefore their value for consumers.

The natural questions to ask now are (i) why photocopying in the printed media has become more legally acceptable in the past few years and (ii) why copy protection in the software industry has declined (it has been virtually eliminated in the market for word processors and spreadsheets). These questions constitute the major motivation for the present chapter.

This chapter is organized as follows: Section 2 classifies the information-reproduction copying patterns. Section 3 analyzes the technology and the economics of print photocopying. Section 4 compares print photocopying and audio/video reproduction with reproduction of digital information (software in particular). Section 5 provides the core of this chapter, showing that software providers may find it profitable to unprotect software, especially when there is competition from other providers of similar software. Section 6 concludes the chapter.

2. Classification of Information-Reproduction Patterns

Pricing of information depends on how information is reproduced and copied. Before analyzing how rents are distributed in various copying technologies, we therefore need to understand how information is diffused. I now define three extreme patterns in which information can be reproduced or copied by users who may not have acquired permission from the original provider (Figure 1).

We say that information is *vertically reproduced* if each agent (the provider and each consumer) reproduces one copy for the benefit of the next consumer, *horizontally reproduced* if each consumer makes a copy of the original directly from the provider, and *mixed-reproduced* if information is copied in "horizontal" and then in "vertical" layers.

Clearly, it is hard to show how information is copied in general. However, some information cannot be copied vertically a large number of times. For example, photocopying and audio and video (analog) dubbing distort the product when it is reproduced vertically more than once or twice. Thus, a library photocopying model cannot assume vertical information copying. In fact, only digital-information technology allows vertical copying a large (potentially infinite) number of times.

The horizontal information-copying model describes how journal photocopying is provided by libraries. Each library subscriber makes one photocopy of a journal article, generally for private use.

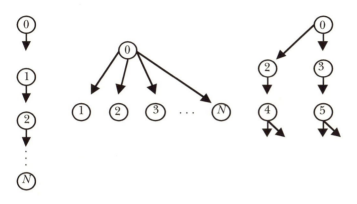

Figure 1   Left: Vertical information reproduction. Middle: Horizontal reproduction. Right: Mixed reproduction. Agent 0 is the information provider.

The mixed information pattern describes how journal-article copying is currently done in the academic sector. First, photocopying enterprises (e.g., Kinko's) make a photocopy of a document from a nearby university library. Then these enterprises photocopy the photocopy for an entire class in the form of "course packs." Further reproduction of these "course packs" is generally not feasible because of the reduced quality that characterizes the photocopying technology.

3. Photocopying: Reproduction of Printed Media

3.1 The Library Model

The economics literature on information reproduction focuses mainly on journal, book, and music copying and less on software copying. See Novos and Waldman (1984), Johnson (1985), Liebowitz (1985), Besen (1986), and Besen and Kirby (1989). These papers model the market for legal subscribers and model photocopying as similar to a secondary market for used durable goods.

This literature shows that publishers may earn higher profits when photocopying of originals is allowed, as compared with the case in which information is protected, and as a result, restrictions on photocopying may reduce the total welfare. These results were obtained under the assumption that publishers can price-discrimi-

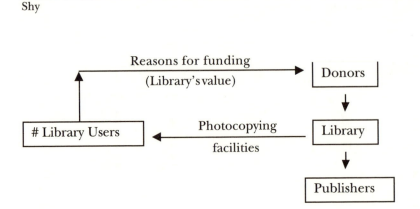

Figure 2 The library model: An increase in journal photocopying increases a library's value and hence its funding, which in turn allows journal publishers to increase subscription fees.

nate between individual subscribers and libraries (or other types of dealers), charging the libraries higher subscription rates that take into account the number of photocopies normally made from these journals. More precisely, the argument relies on the assumption that a library's willingness to pay for journals should increase when photocopying is done on the premises because the availability of photocopying causes a library's users to value the library's journal holdings more highly and library funding will increase as a result (Figure 2).

Section 5 of this chapter provides an alternative approach to the literature on the economics of photocopying by ignoring the issue of appropriability of value from copies and focusing instead on network effects generated by users' compatibility needs.

3.2 The Built-in Copy Protection of Printed Media

As I remarked in section 2, pure vertical photocopying is technically infeasible in the printed media. Thus, unlike producers of digital media, publishers of printed matter are protected by the fact that one original is insufficient to produce a large number of copies, unless copying switches to a horizontal form at one stage of the information-reproduction chain.

Enforcement of copyright laws ensures that reproduction centers are restricted to photocopying which limits the quality com-

Table 1 Surplus obtained by consumers from vertical photocopying (as compared with digital information copying)

Information format	1	2	3	4	5	Total surplus
Printed	$1.00	$0.50	$0.25	$0.125	$0.06	$1.93
Digital	$1.00	$1.00	$1.00	$1.00	$1.00	$5.00

pared to that of the original. Paradoxically, the fact that the quality of photocopies is lower than the quality of originals motivates agents to purchase originals rather than engage in photocopying. Thus, even if individual users are engaged in vertical reproduction of printed material, the publishers should be able to appropriate the rents from all the users by charging a higher price for originals. This is in contrast to digital-information copying, in which the quality remains unchanged if the copying is properly done, in which case the publishers will not be able to capture all the rents from copying.

To see this, consider the following example. Each information consumer is willing to pay $1 for an original journal article. However, since the quality is reduced with each instance of photocopying, a consumer is willing to pay 50% less for a photocopy, 50% of 50% for a copy of a copy, and so on. The first consumer buys an original, makes a photocopy, and sells it to the second consumer, who also makes a photocopy and sells it to a third consumer, and so on. Table 1 demonstrates the willingness to pay of five consumers who are engaged in vertical photocopying.

Table 1 shows that if the publisher raises the price of originals from $1 to $1.93, it can successfully capture the entire surplus associated with vertical copying. The only consumer to purchase the original may be inclined to pay the higher price. Notice, however, that if this information is digital, the entire surplus sums to five times the valuation of each consumer, so it is unlikely that any consumer will be willing to pay this price. Thus, my point here is that printed-information providers are better protected, in the sense that they tend to capture a higher percentage of total surplus than digital-information providers. Appendix A shows how to calculate the surplus generated from copying made by an arbitrary number of information users under vertical and horizontal copying patterns.

The above argument may imply that copy protection is more profitable to digital-information providers than to printed-information providers. However, it turns out that this is not always the case. In section 5, I show that the exact opposite holds, at least in the software industry.

4. A Comparison of Copy Protection among the Different Information-Providing Media

In this section, I argue that the economic effects of copy protection vary significantly among the different types of information-providing media. Besen and Kirby (1989) argue that the differences in conclusions regarding the effects of private copying on social welfare result from differences in (i) the extent to which the sellers of originals can appropriate the value placed on them by all users, (ii) the relative market sizes for used and new copies, and (iii) the degree to which copies can be substituted for originals.

A natural question to ask is how software piracy differ from journal and book photocopying, or even from the reproduction of audio and video cassettes. Pirating software differs from journal and book photocopying in several ways:

1. When software is not protected, any copy (or copy of a copy) is identical to the original. In contrast, paper and cassette copies are not equivalent to the originals, and copies of copies tend to become unreadable (or hard to hear). Moreover, paper copying always loses information such as fine lines, fine print, and color images (even in color copying); therefore,

2. In the case of photocopying, the number of copies made depends on the number of originals purchased in the market, whereas software piracy can theoretically originate from a single diskette. However, there is also a limit on the number of copies that can be made from a single diskette because of the rising costs of identifying a large number of additional users.

3. Journal and book publishers find it difficult and costly to physically protect their goods against illegal photocopying, whereas

software developers can install protective devices that make piracy very difficult and sometimes impossible.

4. Software users depend on services and documentation provided by developers, whereas copied journal articles and books can be read without any need for contact with the original publishers. Similarly, listening to and viewing audio and video cassettes does not require the use of any operating instructions from the manufacturer.

Because of these differences, the law treats photocopying and software piracy in different ways. For example, Section 170 of the Copyright Act states that "the fair use of copyrighted work . . . for purposes such as criticism, comment, news reporting, teaching (including multiple copies for classroom use), scholarship, or research, is not an infringement of copyright." In contrast, the Computer Software Copyright Act does not have a fair-use doctrine equivalent to that for photocopying. In fact, on February 12, 1996, the U.S. Court of Appeals for the Sixth Circuit handed down a landmark ruling [Princeton University v. Michigan Document Service, Inc., 74 F.3d 1512 (6th Cir. 1996)] that the Copyright Act does not prohibit professors and students who may make copies themselves from using the photoreproduction services of a third party in order to obtain those same copies at a lower cost. Thus, this ruling allows third parties to produce "course packs" based on copyrighted material. Note that (i) this ruling has been overturned by the same court, and (ii) a different finding was reached under a somewhat different set of facts, in American Geophysical Union v. Texaco Inc., 60 F.3d 913 (2d Cir. 1995).

Thus, the law recognizes that photocopying has different market consequences for journal and book publishers as compared with the market consequences of software piracy. Therefore, we limit the scope of the remainder of this chapter to analyzing only the software industry. In section 3, we presented an argument, found in the literature, that photocopying of printed matter may increase the value (profit) of a library if the producers of originals can capture the value of copies from the users of copied material. Can we have a similar situation in which copying increases profit in the software industry? An argument (similar to the library-photocopying model) can be made that if software firms start discriminating between individual buyers and business buyers, it may happen that copying will also increase software firms' profits, since business buyers will pay for the software and then employees will copy the software for home use. Businesses will be motivated to pay high software prices, since doing so will enable their employees to work at home during the evenings and weekends. In fact, site licenses giving business and university employees the right to copy in return for higher software prices can be viewed precisely in this manner.

The next section develops an argument as to why a software firm will refrain from protecting its software even if it cannot price-discriminate between business and private users.

5. Software Protection

There are two reasons that the software industry is of particular interest: (i) Software is digitally stored and digitally transmitted, and (ii) this industry has removed copy protection from most of its products. Thus, the products of this industry have characteristics similar to those of other types of digital information provided by the private sector.

Over the past decade, software protection has gradually been removed (and virtually eliminated from word processors and spreadsheets). This is partly the result of pressure from frustrated consumers who could not fully utilize protected software. However, this chapter demonstrates that there is also a strategic reason that software firms responded to the consumers' desire for elimination of software protection.

The following analysis departs from the literature by focusing on the network effects associated with consumers' desire for software compatibility, instead of focusing on the appropriability aspect. That is, we assume that consumers' willingness to pay for software increases with the total number of consumers who use (legally or illegally) the same software. This assumption is known as the network externalities assumption; it reflects the fact that software users (and perhaps users of other types of information) place a high value on compatibility and file sharing. See, for example, Rohlfs (1974), Katz and Shapiro (1985), and Shy (1996, Ch. 10) for theoretical models, and Greenstein (1993), Gandal (1994, 1995), and Brynjolfsson and Kemerer (1996) for empirical verifications.

Suppose now that software is protected, and let us assume that installed protective devices make it prohibitively costly for any consumer to pirate software. In this case, some consumers buy the software, whereas all others simply do not use it. Notice that if firms keep prices fixed, legal users have all the incentives in the world to give this software free of charge to nonusers, thereby increasing the compatibility value of the software. However, legal users are prevented from sharing their software by the protective devices installed in the software. If, however, the developers removed the protection from the software, some consumers might be willing to pay a higher price, since the value of the software increases with the total number of legal and illegal users. This is the core of the argument developed in this section.

Therefore, the reason that some software developers may gain by not protecting their software is as follows: Producing unprotected software increases the total number of users, since all consumers who were excluded from the market by not wanting to pay for the software now become users, thereby increasing the value of the software. On the other hand, if protection is removed, some consumers who buy the software may switch to pirating software. Thus, removing software protection generates two opposing effects on the demand for purchased software: a valuation effect, which boosts demand because of the increase in the software's popularity, and a loss-of-consumers effect because software can be obtained free of charge. The net effect on demand depends on how many legal users become illegal users when protection is removed. This number depends on how the support provided by the software firms to their legal users is valued by consumers. Those consumers who are heavily dependent on support will continue purchasing software even when protection is removed. Companies and schools, which must keep their reputations, will also continue to purchase software in order to avoid being sued by software companies.

The next two subsections demonstrate the above argument in two extremely simple examples. The first involves a monopoly software seller; the second describes a multifirm software industry.

Table 2 Network effects: Each (support-oriented) consumer's willingness to pay increases with the total number of legal and illegal software users

Number of users ($n = n^B + n^P$)	1	2	3	4
Willingness to pay	$200	$300	$450	$525

5.1 Effects of Copy Protection: The Monopoly Case

The effects of copy protection on the software market have been analyzed in Conner and Rumelt (1991) in a monopoly setting. They found out that, absent any network externality, a monopoly software developer increases its price and profit when the exogenously chosen protection technology increases software protection. In contrast, when network externalities are present, profit can rise or fall as the level of piracy protection is increased. We now demonstrate their result, using a very simple example.

Suppose that there are four potential software users. Two users are called support-oriented consumers. They are heavily dependent on support offered by software firms to their legal users; hence, they will always buy software as long as the price does not exceed a certain threshold level.

The remaining two users are called support-independent. These users are skilled at operating software without any help and without the manuals provided by software firms. Thus, these users are likely to pirate software rather than buying it. For the present example, assume that the support-independent consumers are willing to pay a very low price for the software, so that in practice they will never buy the software.

Suppose that there is only one software firm selling one piece of software. Let n^B denote the number of consumers buying this software, n^P the number of users who pirate the software (use it without paying), and $n = n^B + n^P$ the total number of users. Table 2 shows the support-oriented consumers' willingness to pay as a function of the total number of users.

The monopoly software seller has two options: It can protect the software, thereby preventing its unauthorized use, or it can sell the software unprotected, thereby increasing the total number of users from two to four.

Software is protected: In this case, the monopoly sells to $n^B = 2$ consumers, and no consumer pirates the software, i.e., $n^P = 0$. The total network size is therefore $n = 2$. Hence, in view of Table 2, the maximum price that the monopoly can charge is $300, so that it earns a profit of $2 \times \$300 = \$600$.

Software is unprotected: In this case, the monopoly also sells to $n^B = 2$ consumers, but now the support-independent consumers pirate the software, i.e., $n^P = 2$. The total number of users is therefore $n = 4$. Hence, in view of Table 2, the maximum price that the monopoly can charge is now $525, so that it earns a profit of $2 \times \$525 = \$1050 > \$600$.

The above example illustrates the argument, proposed in Conner and Rumelt (1991), showing that piracy may increase profit as long as the increase in the number of illegal users increases what they call the legitimate demand for software.

5.2 Effects of Copy Protection: The Duopoly Case

A natural question to ask now is whether the above example can be extended to a multifirm software industry with price competition. Shy and Thisse (1999) model a two-firm industry competing in prices over heterogeneous consumers differentiated in two aspects: their willingness to pay for service and their preference for one of the software brands. In what follows, I demonstrate their results using a very simple example.

Suppose now that there are two software firms, named Artichoke Software and Banana Software, each producing one piece of spreadsheet software. These are called A and B, respectively. Also, assume that one support-oriented consumer always buys software A, whereas the other support-oriented consumer buys only software B (assuming that prices do not exceed the threshold levels given in Table 2).

Each software firm decides what price to charge and whether to sell the software protected or unprotected. We now compare two cases: First, we compute prices and profit levels when both software firms protect their software. Second, we compute prices and profit levels when firm A sells its software unprotected while firm B continues to protect its software.

Table 3 Profit levels of the two software firms as a function of their prices

| | Software A (unprotected) | | | | | | | |
	$p_A = \$200$		$p_A = \$300$		$p_A = \$450$		$p_A = \$525$	
Software B (protected)								
$p_B = \$200$	200	200	200	300	200	450	200	0
$p_B = \$300$	0	200	0	300	0	450	0	0
$p_B = \$450$	0	200	0	300	0	450	0	0

Both firms protect their software: In this case, each firm sells to one consumer and, because of the protection installed in each piece of software, there are no other users. In view of Table 2, each firm can charge a maximum price of $200 and therefore each earns a profit of $1 \times \$200 = \$200$.

Artichoke Software does not protect, whereas Banana Software protects: In this equilibrium, the two support-independent consumers pirate software A, since neither of them can pirate software B. Hence, the total number of A-users is three, whereas the number of B-users is at most one (this is the service-oriented consumer who buys software B).

Table 3 shows the profit level of each software firm as a function of both firms' prices. Since Banana Software can sell to at most one consumer, and since the software is protected, software B is sold to at most one consumer. Therefore, Table 2 implies that Banana Software cannot charge a price above $p_B = \$200$. In contrast, although Artichoke Software can sell to at most one consumer, it has a larger network of users, since the two support-independent consumers pirate and use its software. With a network size of three users, Table 2 and Table 3 demonstrate that Artichoke can charge a maximum price of $p_A = \$450$ and earn a profit of $450. Hence, when software A is unprotected and software B is protected, the profit of Artichoke Software is $450, whereas the profit of Banana Software is only $200. Comparing this case to the one in which both firms protect their software (and therefore they earn $200 each), we can state the following: *In a software industry in which all firms*

protect their software, a software firm can increase its profit by removing the
copy protection from its software.

6. Concluding Remarks and a Look toward the Future

This chapter has described the economic approach to information copying. We first classified copying into horizontal and vertical types. Then we analyzed the literature on photocopying and video/audio cassette dubbing. The chapter concluded with an analysis of the software industry, in which we demonstrated that software firms may be able to increase profit by selling unprotected software. Thus, this paper introduced a strategic reason for the decrease in software protection in the mid-1980s. Whereas software protection was removed partly because of the pressure from frustrated consumers who could not fully utilize protected software, this paper has provided a strategic reason why software firms bothered to respond to consumers' pressure to drop software protection.

Most widely used software for personal computers is machine-specific. This means that an office must purchase as many copies of a software package as it has PCs so that workers can coordinate their output. Workers then need more copies to make their home machines compatible with their office machines. Thus, the current technology requires that users make legal or illegal copies of software.

It is possible that 10 years from now, most software will run on servers that support many machines. For example, effective this year, phone and cable companies in the U.S. are allowed to sell computer services via the phone and cable lines. This means that users will be able to use software shared by hundreds of thousands of other users without the necessity of installing software on each machine. If this technology dominates in the future, and since file servers can track who owes how much to whom for the use of a particular piece of information or software (Varian 1995), software companies will be able to rent software for the length of time it is used, thereby making piracy impossible.

Table 4 Surplus obtained by consumers from reproduced information

| | Information format | | | | | Total surplus |
	1	2	3	...	N	
Vertical Information Copying						
Printed	ρ	ρ^2	ρ^3	...	ρN	$\dfrac{\rho(1-\rho^N)}{1-\rho}$
Digital	1	1	1	...	1	N
Horizontal Information Copying						
Printed	ρ	ρ	ρ	...	ρ	$N \times \rho$
Digital	1	1	1	...	1	N

Appendix A. Captured and Uncaptured Surplus from Copying

This appendix proposes a method to calculate total surplus associated with copied information. This surplus can be interpreted as the maximum profit an information-providing firm can extract from each original if it can appropriate the rents from all users.

Appendix A.1 Calculating Total Surplus from Copying

Without specifying how and whether consumers pay for the information, we now calculate how much surplus consumers get from digital and nondigital copied information under the two extreme information-copying patterns illustrated in Figure 1.

First, since digitally stored information does not deteriorate during reproduction, each consumer always gains a surplus of $1 no matter who is the provider of this information. Therefore, total surplus is always N, which is the number of consumers multiplied by $1.

Second, for nondigitally stored and reproduced information, the total surplus to consumers depends on how the information is transmitted.

Digital information yields a uniform surplus of $1 to each consumer, and hence a total surplus of N. In contrast, printed information yields different surpluses to different consumers depending on how the information is reproduced. Let $0 < \rho < 1$. Under vertical reproduction, the consumer who copies the original gets a surplus of ρ. The consumer who copies directly from the first-reproduced copy gets a surplus of ρ^2, and so on. For example, if $\rho = 1/2$, the surplus of the consumer who copies the original is 50 cents, the consumer who copies from the first copy gets a surplus of 25 cents, and so on.

Table 4 shows the surplus obtained by each consumer, and by the entire group, under the two types of information; it shows that under both vertical- and horizontal-information reproduction patterns, total surplus generated by transmitted digital technology exceeds total surplus generated from photocopying of printed information.

From Table 4, we can conclude that *under either vertical or horizontal information reproduction, the total surplus enjoyed by the N consumers is higher when information is digital than when it is printed.* This result is not surprising, considering the fact that the average quality of digitally reproduced information exceeds the average quality of nondigitally reproduced information.

Appendix A.2 Surplus That Is Uncaptured by Information Providers

We focus our analysis here on situations in which consumers share information with other consumers without charging them. In this case, the provider can charge $1 for digital information and $\rho < 1$ for a copy of printed information. Therefore, the amount of consumer surplus that is uncaptured by a digital information provider is UCD $= N - 1$. The amount of surplus that is uncaptured by a provider of printed information is

$$\text{UCP} = \frac{\rho\left(1 - \rho^N\right)}{1 - \rho} - \rho = \frac{\rho\left(\rho - \rho^N\right)}{1 - \rho}.$$

Since UCD > UCP, we can conclude that the amount of uncaptured consumer surplus when information is digital exceeds the amount of uncaptured consumer surplus when information is printed.

Thus, despite the fact that digital information is preferred over printed information by all consumers, digital-information providers earn proportionally less relative to the potential surplus compared with providers of printed information. Therefore, despite the fact that digital information is priced higher ($1 compared with ρ), the amount of uncaptured surplus is higher when information is digital.

Acknowledgment

I thank Hal Varian and Brian Kahin for their valuable comments on an earlier draft.

References

Besen, S. 1986. "Private Copying, Reproduction Costs, and the Supply of Intellectual Property." *Information Economics and Policy* 2: 5–22.

Besen, S., and Kirby, S. 1989. "Private Copying, Appropriability, and Optimal Copying Royalties." *Journal of Law and Economics* 32: 255–280.

Brynjolfsson, E., and Kemerer, C. 1996. "Network Externalities in the Microcomputer Software: An Econometric Analysis of the Spreadsheet Market." *Management Science* 42, 1627–1647.

Conner, K., and Rumelt, R. 1991. "Software Piracy: An Analysis of Protection Strategies." *Management Science* 37: 125–139.

Gandal, N. 1994. "Hedonic Price Indexes for Spreadsheets and an Empirical Test of the Network Externalities Hypothesis." *Rand Journal of Economics* 25: 160–170.

Gandal, N. 1995. "Competing Compatibility Standards and Network Externalities in the PC Software Market." *Review of Economics and Statistics* 599–608.

Greenstein, S. 1993. "Did Installed Base Give an Incumbent Any (Measurable) Advantages in Federal Computer Procurement?" *Rand Journal of Economics* 24: 19–39.

Johnson, W. 1985. "The Economics of Copying." *Journal of Political Economy* 93: 158–174.

Katz, M., and Shapiro, C. 1985. "Network Externalities, Competition, and Compatibility." *American Economic Review* 75: 424–440.

Kindleberger, C. 1983. "Standards as Public, Collective and Private Goods." *KYKLOS* 36: 377–396.

Liebowitz, S. 1985. "Copying and Indirect Appropriability: Photocopying of Journals." *Journal of Political Economy* 93: 945–957.

Novos, I., and Waldman, M. 1984. "The Effects of Increased Copyright Protection: An Analytical Approach." *Journal of Political Economy* 92: 236–246.

Rohlfs, J. 1974. "A Theory of Interdependent Demand for a Communication Service." *Bell Journal of Economics* 5: 16–37.

Shy, O. 1996. *Industrial Organization: Theory and Applications.* Cambridge, MA: MIT Press.

Shy, O., and Thisse, J.-F. 1999. "A Strategic Approach to Software Protection." *Journal of Economics and Management Strategy* 8: 163–190.

Varian, H. 1995. "The Information Economy." *Scientific American* (September): 200–201.

Aggregation and Disaggregation of Information Goods: Implications for Bundling, Site Licensing, and Micropayment Systems

Yannis Bakos and Erik Brynjolfsson

1. Introduction

The emergence of the Internet as a way to distribute digital information, such as software, news stories, stock quotes, music, photographs, video clips, and research reports, has created new opportunities for the pricing of information goods. Providers of digital information goods are not sure how to price them and are struggling with a variety of revenue models. Because perfect copies of these goods can be created and distributed almost costlessly, some of the old rules, such as "price should equal marginal cost," are not applicable (Varian, 1995).

As noted by Varian (1995), Bakos and Brynjolfsson (1996, 1999a), Odlyzko (1996), Chuang and Sirbu (2000), and others, the Internet has also created new opportunities for repackaging content through bundling, site licensing, subscriptions, rentals, differential pricing, per-use fees, and various other mechanisms; others may yet be invented. All these schemes can be thought of as either aggregating or disaggregating information goods along some dimension. For instance, aggregation can be done across products, as in the case of bundling digital goods for sale in an applications software "suite" or providing access to an online service for a fixed fee. Aggregation can also be done across consumers, as with the provision of a site license to multiple users for a fixed fee, or over time, as with subscriptions (Odlyzko, 1996; Varian, 1995, 1996). Fishburn, Odlyzko, and Siders (1997) argue that the choice between aggregation and disaggregation cannot be made based on utility maximization, and ultimately rely on noneconomic arguments to predict that aggregation will dominate when marginal production and distribution costs become negligible.

In this chapter, we generalize the model of bundling introduced in Bakos and Brynjolfsson (1996, 1999a) by including a parameter that indexes the cost of distributing goods over a network. This, in addition to the parameter for the marginal cost of production introduced in our earlier work, allows us to compare pricing strategies based on aggregation and disaggregation. We find that lower transaction and distribution costs tend to make unbundling (disaggregation) more attractive for sellers, while lower marginal costs of production tend to make bundling (aggregation) more attractive. We then demonstrate how some of our earlier results on bundling can be generalized to other types of aggregation, such as site licensing and subscriptions. We find that, as with bundling, aggregating information goods across consumers or across time is often an effective strategy that maximizes societal welfare and the sellers' profits; however, aggregation is less attractive when marginal costs are high or when consumers are very heterogeneous.

In section 2, we present the basic argument for the impact of aggregation on profits and efficiency. In section 3, we present a simple mathematical model demonstrating how changes in production and transaction costs affect the profitability of bundling and unbundling goods. In section 4, we show how the formal results can be applied to questions of site licensing, subscriptions, and micropayments. Section 5 discusses some implications for practice and suggests questions for further research.

2. Aggregation Changes Demand

Most goods can be thought of as aggregations, or bundles of smaller goods (Lancaster, 1966). For instance, a spreadsheet program is a bundle of components—the ability to calculate sums, to produce charts, to print in various fonts, and so on (Brynjolfsson and Kemerer, 1996). Similarly, the purchase of a durable good is equivalent to a series of rental contracts (Christensen and Jorgenson, 1966), and sharing of books or videocassettes can be seen as multiple separate transactions (Varian and Roehl, 1996).

Why Aggregate?

There are two main reasons that sellers may wish to use aggregation when selling information goods. First, aggregation can directly increase the value available from a set of goods, because of technological complementarities in production, distribution, or consumption. For instance, it is more cost-effective to deliver a few hundred pages of news articles in the form of a Sunday newspaper than to separately deliver each of the individual components only to the people who read it, even if most of the Sunday bundle ends up in the recycle bin without ever being read. Likewise, having a consumer purchase a movie on videocassette may be cheaper than repeatedly renting it, or for the seller to attempt charging members of the household separately for viewing it. These cost savings increase the surplus available to be divided between the buyer and the seller, although they may also affect the way the surplus is divided.

Second, aggregation can make it easier for the seller to extract value from a given set of goods by enabling a form of price discrimination. This effect of aggregation is subtler and, in the case of bundling, has been studied in a number of articles in the economics literature (Adams and Yellen, 1976; McAfee, McMillan, and Whinston, 1989; Schmalensee, 1984). While the benefits of aggregation due to cost savings are relatively easy to see, the price discrimination effect does not seem to be as widely recognized, although it can dramatically affect both efficiency and profits (Bakos and Brynjolfsson, 1996, 1999a).

The Effects of the Internet and Digitization

Ubiquitous low-cost networking, low-cost digital processing, and low-cost storage of information will profoundly affect the incentives for sellers to aggregate goods that can be delivered in digital form, whether to take advantage of cost savings or to price-discriminate. For example, the Internet is making it feasible to disaggregate news stories that were formerly aggregated in a newspaper simply to economize on transaction and distribution costs. The Internet has also made detailed monitoring and micropayment systems feasible, making it more attractive to sell small units of information, perhaps for use within a limited period of time, by a limited number of people or in a limited set of situations. As a result, many observers have predicted that software and other types of content will increasingly be disaggregated and metered, for instance as on-demand software "applets" or as individual news stories and stock quotes. For instance, Bob Metcalfe writes, "When the Internet finally gets micromoney systems, we'll rent tiny bits of software for seconds at a time. Imagine renting a French spelling checker for one document once" (Metcalfe 1997).

On the other hand, the near-zero marginal costs of reproduction for digital goods make many types of aggregation more attractive. While it is uneconomical to provide goods to users who value them at less than the marginal cost of production, when the marginal cost is zero and users can freely dispose of goods they do not like, then *no* users will value the goods at less than their marginal cost. As a result, economic efficiency and, often, profitability are maximized by providing the maximum number of such goods to the maximum number of people for the maximum amount of time. In this chapter, we show that selling goods in large aggregates will often achieve this goal.

Thus, goods that were previously aggregated to save on transaction or distribution costs may be disaggregated, but new aggregations of goods will emerge to exploit the potential for price discrimination, creating new efficiencies and profit opportunities. We show that strategies involving bundling, site licensing, and subscriptions can each be understood as a response to the radical declines in production, distribution, and transaction costs for digital information goods, while micropayments can be seen as both a consequence and a cause of radically lower transaction and distribution costs.

Graphical Intuition: The Case of Bundling

The possibility of extracting more value from consumers by aggregating information goods can be illustrated by graphically analyzing the effect of bundling on the demand for information goods. Consider a simple linear demand curve for all goods, and assume that the initial fixed costs of producing a good are significant, but

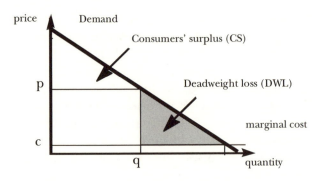

Figure 1 Deadweight loss from sales of a zero-marginal-cost information good.

that after the first unit, marginal production costs, denoted by c, are close to zero. At price p, the number of units purchased will be q, resulting in profits of pq. However, as long as $p > c$, some consumers who value the good at more than its production costs will not be willing to pay as much as p. As a result, these consumers do not get access to the good, creating a deadweight loss, denoted by the shaded region in Figure 1. In addition, there are consumers who would have been willing to pay more than p for access to the good, but who have to pay only p to receive it. These consumers enjoy a consumers' surplus, as indicated in Figure 1.

If the seller is able to price-discriminate, charging a different price to every consumer based on his or her willingness to pay, it will be able to increase its profits. Perfect price discrimination will maximize the seller's profits and will eliminate both the consumers' surplus and the deadweight loss (Varian 1995). If the seller cannot price-discriminate, however, the only single price that would eliminate the inefficiency from the deadweight loss would be a price equal to the marginal cost, which is close to zero. Such a low price would not generate sufficient revenues to cover the fixed cost of production and is unlikely to be the profit-maximizing price. Yet any significant positive price will inefficiently exclude some consumers.

Aggregation can sometimes overcome this dilemma. Consider two information goods, say a journal article and a music video, and suppose that each is valued between zero and one dollar by some consumers, generating linear demand curves such as the one in Figure 1. Suppose further that a consumer's valuation of one good

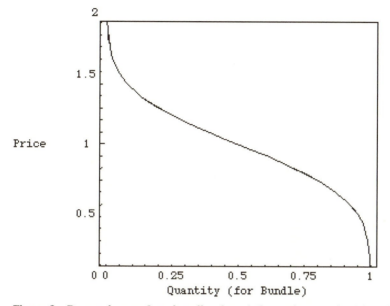

Figure 2 Demand curve for a bundle of two information goods with independently distributed uniform valuations.

is not correlated with his or her valuation of the other, and that access to one good does not make the other more or less attractive.

What happens if the seller aggregates the two goods and sells them as a bundle? Some consumers—those who valued both goods at one dollar—will be willing to pay two dollars for the bundle, while others—those who valued both goods at almost zero—will not be willing to pay even a penny. The total area under the demand curve for the bundle, and hence the total potential surplus, is exactly equal to the sum of the areas under the separate demand curves. However, most interestingly, bundling changes the shape of the demand curve, making it flatter (more elastic) in the neighborhood of one dollar and steeper (less elastic) near either extreme, as shown in Figure 2.[1]

As more goods are added, this effect becomes more pronounced. For instance, the demand for a bundle of 20 goods, each of which has an independent, linear demand ranging from zero to one dollar, is shown in Figure 3.

A profit-maximizing firm selling a bundle of 20 goods will set the price slightly below the $10 mean value of the bundle, and almost

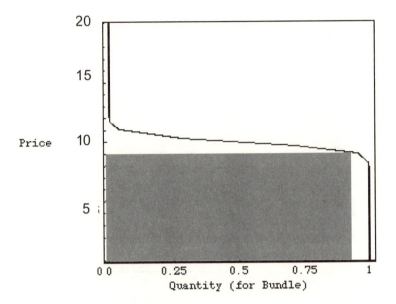

Figure 3 Demand curve for a bundle of 20 information goods with independently distributed uniform valuations

all consumers will find it worthwhile to purchase the bundle. In contrast, only half the consumers would have purchased the goods if they had been individually sold at the profit-maximizing price of 50 cents, so selling the goods as a bundle leads to a smaller deadweight loss and greater economic efficiency. Furthermore, the seller will earn higher profits by selling a single bundle of 20 goods than by selling each of the 20 goods separately. Thus, the shape of the bundle's demand curve is far more favorable both for the seller and for overall economic efficiency.

Why Does the Shape of the Demand Curve Change as Goods Are Added to a Bundle?

The law of large numbers implies that the average valuation for a bundle of goods with valuations drawn from the same distribution will be increasingly concentrated near the mean valuation as more goods are added to the bundle. For example, Figure 4 shows the uniformly distributed probability of a consumer's valuation for a good with the linear demand shown in Figure 1.

Figure 4   Uniform probability density function for a good's valuation.

If a second good is bundled with the first, the probability density function for the consumer's valuation for the bundle of two goods is the convolution of the two uniform distributions, which will be shaped like an inverted *V* (Figure 5).

As more and more goods are added to the bundle, the sum of valuations becomes more concentrated around the mean, reflecting the law of large numbers (Figure 6). That is, the high and low values for individual goods tend to "average out" so that consumers' valuations for the bundle include proportionately more moderate valuations. For example, some people subscribe to America Online for the news, some for stock quotes, and some for horoscopes. It is unlikely that a single person has a very high value for every single good offered; instead, most consumers will have high values for some goods and low values for others, leading to moderate values overall.

Sellers can take advantage of the fact that demand for the bundle (adjusted for the number of goods) will be more concentrated around the mean valuation than in the case of individual goods. The distribution of valuations for the bundle of 20 goods shown in Figure 6 corresponds to the demand curve shown in Figure 3.

Thus, bundling can be thought of as a type of price discrimination, except that instead of increasing the menu of prices to better match the heterogeneous distribution of consumers, bundling reduces the effective heterogeneity of the consumers so that a single price can effectively and efficiently allocate goods to them. Like the Procrustean bed, bundling changes consumers' demands so that a single price fits them all.

If consumers' demands remain heterogeneous even after bundling, then a mixed bundling strategy, which offers a menu of different bundles at different prices, will dominate pure bundling (which is simply a special case of mixed bundling). However, when

Bakos and Brynjolfsson

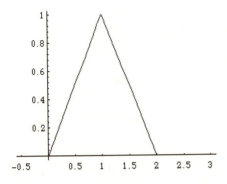

Figure 5 Convolution of two uniform probability density functions.

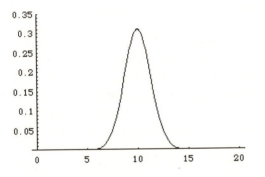

Figure 6 Convolution of 20 uniform probability density functions.

consumers' valuations for the goods in the bundle are not correlated, the profit advantage of mixed bundling over pure bundling
diminishes as the number of goods in the bundle increases.

Similar effects result in other types of aggregation, such as
aggregation across consumers, as in the case of selling a single site
license for use by multiple consumers. This analogy is explored
more fully in section 4. The law of large numbers, which underlies
these aggregation effects, is remarkably general. For instance, it
holds for almost any initial distribution, not just the linear one
shown graphically above.[2] Furthermore, the law does not require
that the valuations be independent of each other or even that the
valuations be drawn from the same distribution.

The desirability of bundling as a device for price discrimination
can break down when consumers' valuations are correlated with

one or more common variables. Similarly, applying the same type of analysis to study the impact of marginal costs, we find that when marginal costs are high, unbundling may be more profitable than bundling.

3. A Model for Aggregation and Disaggregation

The above insights can be modeled more formally. In particular, the aggregation of information goods into bundles entails several types of costs:

• *Production cost:* the cost of producing additional units for inclusion in the bundle. For instance, storage, processing, or communications costs incurred in the process.

• *Distribution cost:* the cost of distributing a bundle of information goods.

• *Transaction cost:* the cost of administering transactions, such as arranging for payment.

• *Binding cost:* the cost of binding the component goods together for distribution as a bundle. For example, formatting changes necessary to include a good in the bundle.

• *Menu cost:* the cost of administering multiple prices for a bundle. If a mixed bundling strategy for n goods is pursued, as many as 2^n prices (one for each separate sub-bundle of one or more goods) may be required.

We now focus on the impact of production costs and distribution/transaction costs, which seem to be most important for determining the desirability of aggregation; similar reasoning can be applied to the binding and price administration costs.

Consider a setting with a single seller providing n information goods.[3] Let p_n^*, q_n^*, and π_n^* denote the profit-maximizing price per good for a bundle of n goods, the corresponding sales as a fraction of the population, and the seller's resulting profits per good. Assume that

A1: The marginal cost of producing copies of all information goods and the marginal distribution and transaction cost for all information goods are zero.

A2: Each buyer can consume either 0 or 1 unit of each information good and resale is not permitted.

A3: For all n, buyer valuations are independent, identically distributed (i.i.d.) with continuous density functions, nonnegative support, finite mean μ, and finite variance σ^2.

By applying the law of large numbers to the above setting, we derived the following proposition and the corresponding corollary in Bakos and Brynjolfsson (1996, 1999a):

Proposition 1 (minimum profits from bundling zero-marginal-cost i.i.d. goods): Given assumptions A1, A2, and A3, bundling n goods allows the seller to capture as profits at least a fraction

$$1 - 2\left(\frac{(\sigma/\mu)^2}{n}\right)^{1/3} + \left(\frac{(\sigma/\mu)^2}{n}\right)^{2/3}$$

of the area under the demand curve.

Corollary 1 (bundling with symmetric distribution of valuations): Given assumptions A1, A2, and A3, if the distribution of valuations is symmetric around the mean, a fraction of the area under the demand curve of at least

$$1 - \frac{3}{2}\left(\frac{(\sigma/\mu)^2}{n}\right)^{1/3} + \frac{1}{2}\left(\frac{(\sigma/\mu)^2}{n}\right)^{2/3}$$

can be captured by bundling n goods.[4]

We now extend the original model by substituting Assumption A4 for Assumption A1:

A4: The marginal cost for producing each information good is c, and the sum of distribution and transaction costs for any individual good or bundle is d.

Assumption A4 implies that the total incremental cost of supplying a bundle of n information goods is $nc + d$.

Corollary 2 (bundling with production, distribution, and transaction costs): Given assumptions A2, A3, and A4, bundling n goods results in profits of π_B^* for the seller, where

$$\pi_B^* \geq \left(\mu - c - \frac{d}{n}\right)\left[1 - 2\left(\frac{(\sigma/\mu)^2}{n}\right)^{1/3} + \left(\frac{(\sigma/\mu)^2}{n}\right)^{2/3}\right].$$

Selling the goods individually, the seller faces a downward-sloping demand curve $q_i(p_i) = \int_p^\infty f(x)dx$ for each individual good, and will select the optimal price p_i^* and corresponding quantity q_i^* that will maximize profits $\pi_i(p_i) = (p_i - c - d) \cdot q_i(p_i)$, resulting in profits of π_i^*.

When the number of goods is large, bundling will be superior to unbundled sales in the limit as long as $\pi_B^* \approx \mu - c > \pi_i^*$. Furthermore, if there is no consumer with a valuation greater than v_{max}, unbundled sales will be profitable only as long as $c + d \leq v_{max}$.

Figure 7 depicts the impact of c and d on the desirability of bundling large numbers of goods. In Area I, unbundled sales dominate bundling. In Area II, bundling is more profitable than unbundled sales. Finally, in Area III, the marginal production, distribution, and transaction costs are high enough to make both bundled and unbundled sales unprofitable.[5]

A reduction in distribution or transaction costs can make unbundling more attractive than bundling (a move from A to A'). For example, it is often argued that as micropayment technologies and electronic distribution reduce d, there will be a move toward "atomic" pricing, that is, price per use (Metcalfe 1996, 1997). However, as soon as the marginal cost falls below a certain threshold c_0, bundling becomes more profitable than unbundling, even if distribution and transaction costs are zero, as demonstrated by the move from A' to A". While bundling is optimal in the neighborhood of A mainly as a way to economize on distribution and transaction costs, the benefits of bundling in the neighborhood of A" derive from its ability to enable the seller to extract more profits from consumers. Therefore, the types of bundles observed in a world of high production, distribution, and transaction costs (near A) may differ substantially from the types of bundles observed in a world with very low production, distribution, and transaction costs.

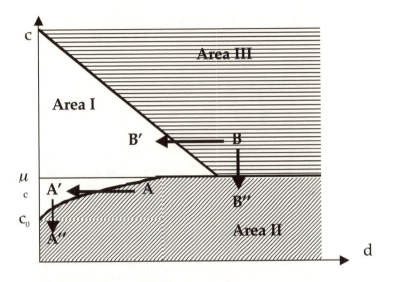

Figure 7 Phase diagram for bundling and unbundling strategies as a function of marginal cost and transaction/distribution cost.

A reduction in c, d, or both can move a good from Area III (no trade) to either Area I (unbundled sales, if the primary reduction is in the distribution and transaction costs) or Area II (bundled sales, if the primary reduction is in the marginal cost of production).

The threshold level c_0 below which bundling becomes unambiguously more profitable than unbundling depends on the distribution of the underlying valuations. For example, consider consumer valuations that are uniformly distributed in $[0, v_{max}]$, which corresponds to a linear demand function. Selling the goods individually, the seller faces a downward-sloping demand curve

$$q_i = \frac{v_{max} - p_i}{v_{max}}$$

for each individual good, resulting in a monopolistic equilibrium price of

$$p_i^* = \frac{v_{max} + c + d}{2}$$

for each good, and corresponding profit of

$$\pi_i^* = \frac{\left(v_{max} - c - d\right)^2}{4v_{max}}$$

as long as $c + d \le v_{max}$. Selling the information goods in bundles of n goods results in profits $\pi_B^*(n)$, where

$$\pi_B^*(n) \ge \left(\frac{v_{max}}{2} - c - \frac{d}{n}\right)\left[1 - 2\left(\frac{1}{3n}\right)^{1/3} + \left(\frac{1}{3n}\right)^{2/3}\right].$$

When the number of goods is large, bundling will be superior to unbundled sales in the limit as long as

$$\frac{v_{max}}{2} - c > \frac{\left(v_{max} - c - d\right)^2}{4v_{max}} \quad c \le \frac{v_{max}}{2} \text{ and } c + d \le v_{max}.$$

If $c + d > v_{max}$, unbundled sales will be unprofitable, while bundled sales will be unprofitable if $c > v_{max} / 2$. In this case, c_0 is approximately $0.41v_{max}$. Figure 8 shows a "phase diagram" of the corresponding profitability areas.

It can be argued that linear demand functions and the corresponding uniform distribution of valuations are not appropriate for information goods. For example, most consumers may have exactly zero valuation for 90% of the news stories provided by a news service, and a linear demand for the remaining 10%. The resulting piecewise linear demand curve would be similar to the one used by Chuang and Sirbu (2000) and to several numerical examples presented in Odlyzko (1996).

When many consumers have zero valuations for any given good, the effects of any marginal costs will be amplified and the region in which bundling is profitable will be reduced. This is because any bundle will likely include numerous goods with no value to any given consumer; if these goods are costly to provide, they will tend to reduce the value created by providing the bundle to that consumer. For instance, when consumers have nonzero valuations for only 10% of the goods, the threshold value, $c0$, at which bundling becomes unprofitable relative to bundled sales declines by a factor of 10 to $0.041v_{max}$.

As another example, when valuations are distributed exponentially—so that only a small number of people have high valuations

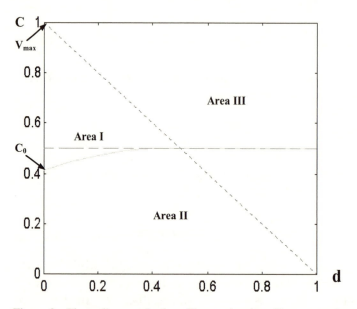

Figure 8 Phase diagram for bundling and unbundling strategies as a function of marginal production cost and distribution/transaction cost when valuations are uniformly distributed

and a long tail of people have low valuations but no one quite has a zero valuation—and marginal costs are near zero, bundling can allow sellers to profitably provide the goods to the long tail of people who have relatively low valuations for the good. Because the number of such people may be very large, the efficiency and profit effects can be substantial: One could grow quite rich by selling a joke per day to 10 million people, even if most of them valued the joke at only a penny or less. However, as soon as marginal costs begin to approach the average consumer's valuation, bundling becomes unprofitable. In contrast, because the exponential distribution assumes there is always a positive probability that someone will have a valuation equal to or greater than any finite number, unbundled sales are never completely unprofitable; they simply require a price greater than the sum of production, distribution, and transaction costs. Figure 9 shows the "phase diagram" with the corresponding two areas of profitability.

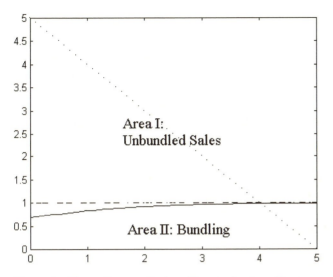

Figure 9 Phase diagram for bundling and unbundling strategies as a function of marginal production cost and distribution/transaction cost when valuations are exponentially distributed

4. Site Licensing and Subscriptions

The preceding section focused on the benefits of aggregation in the context of bundling. As has been noted in two examples by Odlyzko (1996) and several analytical models by Bakos and Brynjolfsson (1999c) and Bakos, Brynjolfsson, and Lichtman (1999), parallel arguments can be made for aggregation in other dimensions, such as site licensing (aggregation across users) and subscriptions (aggregation over time).

Site Licensing

As with bundling, there are many reasons that a firm may choose to sell its products through a site license instead of selling them to individual users. For instance, site licensing can reduce administrative costs and transaction costs; reduce or eliminate the need to check for piracy at a given customer's site; facilitate interoperability and foster positive network externalities; and reduce maintenance costs through standardization of software configurations. Many of these costs can be modeled as creating a fixed transaction cost, t, per sale, analogous to the distribution/transaction cost parameter, d, in section 3. When this cost is sufficiently high, aggregation (site licensing) will be more profitable than disaggregation (individual sales).[6]

As shown by Bakos and Brynjolfsson (1999c), an analysis similar to that for bundling shows that site licensing can also be seen as a mechanism for aggregation that increases seller profits and reduces the inefficiency of withholding a good from consumers who value it at more than its marginal cost. Where bundling aggregates a single consumer's valuations for many products, site licensing aggregates many consumers' valuations for a single product. As with bundling, the law of large numbers will lead to a distribution of valuations for the site license that, after adjusting for the number of users, is less dispersed and more predictable than the distribution of individuals' valuations for the same good.

For instance, some researchers at a university may have high valuations for Mathematica and be willing to pay $500 for access to it; other users might value it only at $50; and still others might be willing to pay $5 or $10 to have easy access to the program in case it is needed in the future. Wolfram Research, the publisher of Mathematica, could set a high price and exclude potential users with low valuations, or set a low price that fails to extract most of the surplus from the high-valuation users.[7] Alternatively, Wolfram could offer a site license to the university that gives all potential users access to Mathematica. The value of such a site license to the university is equal to the sum of all potential users' individual valuations. This amount is larger than the profits that can be obtained through individual sales. Thus, both profits and efficiency may be increased if the seller pursues a site license.

If the seller does not offer the goods for sale to individual users, then in principle it could offer the site license for a price just slightly less than the expected sum of individual valuations (i.e., at a price $p \approx m\mu$, where m is the number of individuals at the site and μ is the average valuation for the good in this population). Almost all sites would find this price acceptable, and thus almost all users would get access to the good.[8] As with bundling, in the limit, aggregation virtually eliminates inefficiency and maximizes profits, at the expense of consumers' surplus.

One important difference between site licensing and bundling is that the site-licensing strategy requires an agent who has authority to purchase information goods on behalf of their ultimate consumers. An agent may not have perfect information about the preferences of end users, and his or her incentives may not be perfectly aligned with those of the end users; this may reduce the benefits of a site-licensing strategy.

Subscriptions

Our model of aggregation can also be applied to dimensions such as time and space. For example, when the good can be costlessly provided over time, it may be more profitable to sell it as a long-term subscription than to sell individual uses in short periods of time. Since a given user may sometimes have high valuations for the good and sometimes low valuations, per-use (or short-term) pricing might inefficiently exclude use during low-valuation periods, even when the cost of provision is zero. Greater efficiency and profits can result from charging a single subscription fee and giving the user long-term access to the good, by an argument corresponding to those for bundling and site licensing.[9]

Similarly, allowing the user to access the good from multiple locations may also provide some of the benefits of aggregation; a requirement that the good be used only on a specific machine or in a specific location would undermine these benefits. Without aggregation, some users might forgo access to the good in places where their valuations were low; when the costs of providing additional access are even lower (or zero), this would create an inefficiency.

There are many other ways to "disaggregate" goods. Technologies such as micropayment systems, cryptolopes, autonomous agents, and software objects are enabling sellers to charge different prices when information goods are disaggregated in various ways. For instance, a seller of software, in principle, could charge users a price for each time a function of its product is invoked on a particular machine. Although such "atomic" pricing may become feasible, it would reduce or eliminate the benefits of aggregation and thus it might reduce efficiency and profits.

When to Use Micropayments: "Mixed Aggregation" Can Dominate Pure Aggregation

Our analysis in this chapter indicates that complete disaggregation and "mixed aggregation" (simultaneously selling both an aggregate and disaggregated components) can be more profitable than aggregation strategies in three specific circumstances.

First, if marginal costs are nontrivial, disaggregation can economize on these costs by allowing users to "opt out" of components with a marginal cost greater than their marginal benefit. For example, if the marginal cost of providing an additional component or servicing an additional user is c, a seller that charges a fixed price p plus an additional price of c per component or user will avoid the inefficiency of including too many components in the sale or servicing too many users. If c is very low, micropayment technology may be required to enable the seller to profitably pursue such a strategy.

Second, if some consumers are willing to pay more for all goods, mixed aggregation may be beneficial if it can help sort consumers. For instance, if consumers with high valuations tend to prefer to use more goods or use the goods more often, a mixed-aggregation strategy can induce them to self-select and pay higher prices for larger aggregations.

Third, even when marginal costs are negligible and consumers are homogeneous, large aggregations of goods (or users) may be required to fully extract profits and to maximize efficiency. Therefore, if the seller can feasibly aggregate over only a small number of goods, consumers, or time periods, it may be optimal to also offer some goods outside the bundle, site license, or subscription.

Aggregation and Disaggregation on Multiple Dimensions

Aggregation can also be practiced on multiple dimensions simultaneously. For instance, bundles of goods can be offered on a site-license basis to multiple users for an extended period of time. This strategy may enable the seller to get closer to full efficiency and earn higher profits, since aggregation along one dimension will not generally exhaust the benefits of aggregation in other dimensions. Indeed, when the valuations of the goods are independently distributed and these goods have zero marginal cost, the optimal strategy will be to offer the largest possible bundle of goods through the largest possible site license for the broadest possible set of conditions, and to charge a price low enough to get almost all users to participate. This strategy captures as profits nearly the entire possible surplus from the goods.

In practice, it might make sense to aggregate in some dimensions while disaggregating in other dimensions. For instance, if marginal costs are not negligible, it may be appropriate to offer only subsets of the goods in each of several bundles so that users can choose the sets of goods they find most valuable and avoid the production cost for the ones they do not. Similarly, the seller could choose to disaggregate (or avoid aggregating) in those dimensions that are most effective in getting users to reveal their valuations while aggregating in other dimensions.

5. Conclusion

The Internet is precipitating a dramatic reduction in the marginal costs of production and distribution for digital information goods, while reducing the transaction costs for their commercial exchange. These developments are creating the potential to use pricing strategies for information goods based on aggregation and disaggregation. Because of the ability to cost-effectively aggregate very large numbers of information goods, or, at the other end of the spectrum, offer small components for individual sale, these strategies have implications for information goods that are not common in the world of physical goods.

In particular, aggregation can be a powerful strategy for providers of information goods. It can result in higher profits for sellers as well as a socially desirable wider distribution of the goods, but it is less effective when the marginal production costs are high or when consumers are heterogeneous. Aggregation strategies can take a variety of forms, including bundling (aggregation across different goods), site licensing (aggregation across different users), and subscriptions (aggregation over time). These strategies can reduce buyer heterogeneity by aggregating a large number of goods, users, or time periods, and can also reduce distribution and transaction costs. Therefore, a decision to aggregate information goods should be based on the trade-off between the benefits of aggregation and the marginal costs of production and distribution. Low distribution costs make aggregation less attractive, while low marginal production costs make aggregation more attractive.

On the other hand, the low distribution and transaction costs offered by ubiquitous networking and micropayment technologies enable the use of disaggregation strategies such as per-use fees, rentals, and sale of small components. Disaggregation strategies enable sellers to maximize their profits by price discriminating when consumers are heterogeneous. For example, the number of goods desired by individual consumers may be correlated with their valuations for these goods, as when a professional stock trader demands more financial news stories and has higher valuation for these stories than an individual investor. The seller can take advantage of this correlation by incorporating the signal that reveals the consumer's valuation, that is, the number of news stories purchased, in the pricing of the goods, resulting in some type of pay-per-use pricing. In general, the pricing scheme used should incorporate all signals that may reveal a consumer's willingness to pay, and micropayment technologies can enable the implementation of such schemes.

The optimal pricing strategy will often involve mixed aggregation, that is, the simultaneous availability of information goods in aggregates of different sizes and compositions as well as individually. Mixed aggregation will be more desirable in three cases: first, when consumers are very heterogeneous, as it provides a device for price discrimination; second, when the marginal production costs are significant, as this increases the cost of offering goods to consumers who do not value them; and finally, when the number of goods for sale is relatively small, as the aggregation benefits of the law of large numbers will not be as powerful and the menu costs of administering the prices for all bundles offered will not be as high.

Our analysis of aggregation provides a framework in which to understand the pricing strategies of online content providers such as America Online and the Microsoft Network, the widespread use of site licensing of software and data access by companies such as Wolfram Research and Reuters, and subscription pricing in the sale of information goods by companies such as Consumer Reports Online and *The Wall Street Journal.* It can also explain how the dramatic reduction in marginal production, distribution, and transaction costs precipitated by the Internet is leading to pricing strategies based on both aggregation and disaggregation. Because the reasons for aggregating information goods when production and distribution costs are very low differ substantially from the reasons for aggregating goods when these costs are high, the content and nature of the aggregations (e.g., bundles) may differ substantially in these two situations.

In the models presented in this paper, we have focused on the demand-reshaping effects of aggregation and disaggregation, and have ignored their strategic aspects. In a related paper (Bakos and Brynjolfsson 1999b), we find that the profit-enhancing potential of bundling will often be increased when competitors are forced to respond.[10] The analysis in this chapter suggests that there may be similar competitive benefits in site licensing and subscription strategies.

Finally, aggregation also has significant effects on social welfare. Specifically, aggregation strategies can substantially reduce the deadweight loss from monopoly, but they can also lower the surplus left to consumers.

Notes

1. See Salinger (1995) for a detailed graphical analysis of the two-goods scenario.

2. There are several versions of the law of large numbers, but in general the random variables being combined must have only finite variance.

3. This setting, the assumptions, and the main result for bundling information goods are derived from Bakos and Brynjolfsson (1996).

4. For example, if consumer valuations are i.i.d. with a distribution symmetric around the mean and a coefficient of variation $\mu/\sigma = 1/\sqrt{3}$ (e.g., uniformly distributed in $[0, 2\mu]$), the seller can realize profits of at least 80% of the total area under the demand curve with a bundle of 100 goods. For most common distributions of independent valuations, this corollary provides a conservative lower bound; for instance, with valuations uniformly distributed in $[0, 2\mu]$, this level of profits can actually be achieved by bundling eight goods.

5. A similar diagram can be drawn to show when bundling or unbundling is economically efficient from a social-welfare standpoint. Unfortunately, the

regions in which bundling and unbundling are socially efficient are not identical to the regions in which each is profitable. In particular, bundling is socially inefficient in a substantial portion of Area II near the frontier with Area I.

6. Varian (1997) develops a model for sharing information goods that can be applied to site licensing; however, his analysis is driven by transaction cost considerations rather than the aggregation effects.

7. If Wolfram Research can identify the users who have high and low values, it can also price-discriminate by charging different prices to different users. However, because users can often disguise their true valuations, price discrimination typically leaves some rents in the hands of high-value users and excludes some low-value users from access to the good.

8. When individual copies are also available at a price that would leave some surplus in the hands of some consumers, the seller cannot extract the full value of the product through a site-licensing strategy. If the seller attempted to do so, the buyers would be collectively better off by individually buying or not buying the product.

9. A subscription may provide the user with different goods over time; in such cases, the logic of bundling applies directly. However, even when a subscription provides the *same* good in different time periods, the aggregation effects may still be important, since consumer valuations for the good may vary with time. If these valuations are serially correlated, however, the benefits of aggregation will tend to be lower (Bakos and Brynjolfsson, 1996).

10. Specifically, in the presence of fixed production costs (and low or zero marginal costs), aggregation can drive competitors out of the market, even when their products are qualitatively superior. Such a response will often increase the profitability of aggregation.

References

Adams, W. J., and Yellen, J. L. 1976. "Commodity bundling and the burden of monopoly," *Quarterly Journal of Economics* 90 (August): 475–498.

Armstrong, M. 1996. "Multiproduct nonlinear pricing," *Econometrica* 64, no. 1 (January):51–75.

Bakos, Y., and Brynjolfsson, E. 1996. "Bundling information goods: Pricing, profits and efficiency." *Working Paper*, MIT Sloan School.

Bakos, Y., and Brynjolfsson, E. 1999a. "Bundling information goods: Pricing, profits and efficiency." *Management Science* 45, 12 (December) Available at http://www.stern.nyu.edu/~bakos.

Bakos, Y., and Brynjolfsson, E. 1999b. "Bundling and competition on the Internet," *Marketing Science*, 2000. In press. Available at http://www.stern.nyu.edu/~bakos

Bakos, Y., and Brynjolfsson, E. 1999c. "Site licensing." *Working Paper*.

Bakos, Y., Brynjolfsson, E., and Lichtman, D. G, 1999. "Shared information goods," *Journal of Law and Economics* 42 (April):117–155.

Brynjolfsson, E., and Kemerer, C. F. 1996. "Network externalities in microcomputer software: An econometric analysis of the spreadsheet market," *Management Science* 42, 12 (December): 1627–1647. Available at http://ccs.mit.edu/erik.

Chuang, J. C.-I, and Sirbu, M. A. 2000. "Network delivery of information goods: Optimal pricing of articles and subscriptions." In this volume.

Christensen, L. R., and Jorgenson, D. W. 1969. "The measurement of U.S. real capital input, 1929-1967," *Review of Income and Wealth* 15 (4): 293–320.

Fishburn, P. C., Odlyzko, A. M., and Siders, R. C. 1997. "Fixed-fee versus unit pricing for information goods: Competition, equilibria, and price wars."In this volume.

Hanson, W., and Martin, K. 1990. "Optimal bundle pricing," *Management Science* 36, no. 2 (February): 155–174.

Lancaster, K.J. 1966. "A new approach to consumer theory," *The Journal of Political Economy* 74, no. 2 (April): 132–157.

McAfee, R. P., McMillan, J., and Whinston, M. D. 1989. "Multiproduct monopoly, commodity bundling, and correlation of values," *Quarterly Journal of Economics* 114 (May): 371–384.

Metcalfe, R. 1996. "It's all in the scrip—Millicent makes possible subpenny 'net commerce'," *Infoworld*, January 29, 1996.

Metcalfe, R. 1997. "Pollinate lets you rent the software you need for just the right amount of time," *Infoworld*, June 9, 1997.

Odlyzko, A. M. 1996. "The bumpy road of electronic commerce," *WebNet 96— World Conf. Web Soc. Proc.*, H. Maurer, ed., AACE, 1996, 378–389.

Odlyzko, A. M.1996. "On the road to electronic publishing," *Euromath Bulletin* 2 (1): 49–60.

Salinger, M. A. 1995. "A graphical analysis of bundling," *Journal of Business* 68 (1): 85–98.

Schmalensee, R. L. 1984. "Gaussian demand and commodity bundling," *Journal of Business* 57 (1): S211–S230.

Stigler, G. J. 1963. "United States v. Loew's, Inc.: A note on block booking," *Supreme Court Review*, 1963: 152–157. Reprinted in G. J. Stigler, *The Organization of Industry.* Homewood, IL: Richard D. Irwin, 1968.

Varian, H. R. 1995. "Pricing information goods," *Proceedings of Scholarship in the New Information Environment Symposium,* Harvard Law School, May 1995.

Varian, H. R. 1997. "Buying, sharing and renting information goods." *Working Paper,* School of Information Management and Systems, University of California at Berkeley, May 1997. Available at http://www.sims.berkeley.edu/~hal.

Varian , H. R., and Roehl, R. 1996. "Circulating libraries and video rental stores." Available at http://www.sims.berkeley.edu/~hal

Network Delivery of Information Goods: Optimal Pricing of Articles and Subscriptions

John Chung-I Chuang and Marvin A. Sirbu

1. Introduction

Academic journals have traditionally been sold in the form of subscriptions: Individual articles are bundled into journal issues; issues are bundled into subscriptions. This aggregation approach has worked well in the paper-based environment, because there exist strong economies of scale in the production, distribution, and sale of the journals.

Yet the demand for scholarly information is diverse, unique, and sometimes whimsical. Scholars are often willing to expend a great deal of effort to secure a copy of a specific article that is unavailable from their personal collection of journal subscriptions. Given the proliferation of journal titles, it is impossible for every scholar to subscribe to all journals that are relevant to his/her work. Libraries, through their institutional subscriptions to the journals, serve to satisfy the scholars' demand for individual articles. Ordover and Willig (1978) treat journals as "sometimes shared goods" in the study of their optimal provision. Under the fair-use provision of the Copyright Act,[1] a scholar is permitted to reproduce single copies of individual articles from the library subscription copy for noncommercial purposes. Frequently, however, the scholar's information needs go beyond the scope of the library's journal collection. In such circumstances, the library is permitted to duplicate articles and share them with other member libraries in an interlibrary loan (ILL) consortium, as long as such sharing does not lead to copying "in such aggregate quantities as to substitute for a subscription."[2] Empirical studies have found that libraries are incurring costs of up to $20 per ILL item obtained. This suggests that a potential market does exist for unbundled articles at both the individual and institutional levels.

The publishers, unable to directly appropriate charges for these forms of shared use, compensate for their loss of potential revenue by charging libraries an institutional subscription rate higher than that for individuals. This form of indirect appropriation constitutes price discrimination of the third degree.[3] While the legality of such practices is seldom questioned,[4] effective third-degree price discrimination requires clear demarcation of market segments and minimal leakage across the segments. Both the segmentation of the market and the preclusion of effective resale channels are fairly easy to enforce in the academic journal market, since institutions cannot easily disguise themselves as individual subscribers. Furthermore the subscribing institutions exhibit strong demand inelasticity for journals. Therefore we have seen an escalation of journal prices in recent years.[5]

With the global expansion and rapid commercialization of the Internet, the economics of journal publishing is quickly changing. Many publishers are experimenting with various forms of online access to their journals. It is now technically feasible for the publisher to electronically deliver, and charge for, individual journal articles requested by a scholar sitting at his/her desk. The establishment of a ubiquitous electronic payment infrastructure, and the deployment of micropayment services in particular, will dramatically lower the cost of purchasing digital information goods over the Internet. From the scholars' perspective, this form of access is instantaneous, is on-demand, and avoids the costs associated with traditional library access, such as travel to the library, physical duplication of the article, and congestion owing to shared use of journals.

Given the market demand for individual journal articles, it appears to be in the publishers' interest to unbundle their journals. This goes against the findings of several recent and independent works (Bakos and Brynjolfsson 2000; Fishburn et al. 2000) that argue for the bundling of information goods. This apparent contradiction can be resolved only by acknowledging that bundling (or unbundling) can exist in pure or mixed forms. By identifying the different "flavors" of bundling and quantifying their relative performances under different supply and demand conditions, this chapter demonstrates that not all forms of bundling are profit-maximizing strategies for information goods.

Specifically, by developing an N-good bundling model with multidimensional consumer preferences, this chapter shows that mixed bundling is the dominant strategy, outperforming pure bundling and pure unbundling in maximizing producer surplus. Pure unbundling is also shown to outperform pure bundling, even in the presence of some degree of economies of scale, if consumers positively value only a subset of the bundle components, which is the predominant case in the academic-journal context. These results provide strong incentives for academic journal publishers to engage in mixed bundling (by "unbundling" the previously "bundled" product) so that they can offer both individual articles and journal subscriptions. By extension, a publisher with multiple journal titles should also offer site licenses that are effectively "super-bundles" in addition to single-title subscriptions and individual articles. The model also provides solutions for the optimal pricing and resulting revenue mix for a profit-maximizing publisher.

The remainder of this chapter is organized as follows: Following a short survey of the product-bundling literature, we develop the N-good bundling model, first on the demand side, then on the supply side. The model is then applied to the academic journal industry for empirical results and analysis. Specifically, we look at how technology trends in distribution and transaction may change the supply side of the model without changing the fundamental results. Indeed, cost characterizations of the document delivery technologies indicate a shift toward a revenue mix that is well balanced between subscription and article sales.

2. Economics of Bundling

A multiproduct monopolist may choose to bundle its goods for a variety of reasons. On the supply side, commodity bundling can result in cost savings due to the presence of economies of scale. On the demand side, bundling can be used as an effective tool for extracting consumer surplus. Both factors must be taken into account in the design of optimal bundle prices. In addition, producers in imperfectly competitive markets may choose to bundle their products for strategic reasons. However, bundling for strategic leverage has no direct implications for pricing design and is outside the scope of this chapter.[6]

Burnstein (1960) and Stigler (1963) are generally credited with the first references to the bundling phenomenon in the economics literature. Adams and Yellen (1976) operationalize the model for a bundle consisting of two goods, and identify three modes of bundling strategies, namely pure bundling, mixed bundling, and component selling (or pure unbundling). In pure bundling, consumers are restricted to purchasing either the entire bundle or nothing at all. In pure unbundling, no bundle is offered but the consumer can put together his/her own bundle by buying both the component goods. Finally, a monopolist who chooses to engage in mixed bundling will allow consumers to purchase the bundle or either one of the individual components. Consumers who choose to purchase the bundle will usually pay less than if they had purchased both component goods separately.

Figure 1 illustrates the consumer choice regions under each of the three bundling strategies. The axes in each plot represent the consumers' valuation for each of the two component goods, G_1 and G_2. An individual consumer who is willing to pay w_1 for G_1 and w_2 for G_2 can thus be represented as a point (w_1, w_2) in this consumer space. Depending on the type of bundling strategy employed by the producer, the consumer will make the appropriate purchasing decision based on his/her position in this two-dimensional $\{W_1, W_2\}$ space. For example, consumer Alice at (a_1, a_2) will purchase only G_1 in Figure 1(a) because her willingness-to-pay (WTP) for G_1, a_1, is greater than its offer price P_1, but her WTP for G_2, a_2, is less than the offer price P_2. Bob, on the other hand, purchases nothing under this pure unbundling scenario because both b_1 and b_2 are less than P_1 and P_2, respectively. Interestingly, the situation almost reverses itself if the producer switches to pure bundling instead, as in Figure 1(b). Alice rationally chooses to purchase nothing because her aggregate WTP $(a_1 + a_2)$ is less than the price of the bundle, P_B. Bob

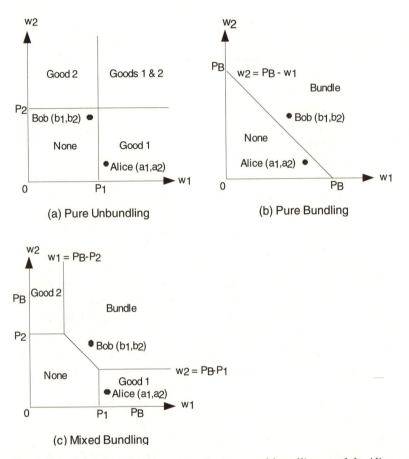

Figure 1 Consumer choice regions for two-good bundling model. Alice and Bob will choose different product offerings under different bundling regimes.

now purchases the bundle because the sum of b_1 and b_2 is greater than P_B. Using similar logic, Alice consumes G_1 and Bob consumes the bundle in the mixed-bundling case, as illustrated in Figure 1(c). This simple yet powerful illustration shows that the choice of the optimal bundling strategy and the selection of the optimal prices are strongly dependent on the distribution of the consumer population in this $\{W_1, W_2\}$ space.

Schmalensee (1982) and McAfee, McMillan, and Whinston (1989) build on the Adams/Yellen framework, with careful treatment of the consumers' correlation of value between the two components.

Among other results, they show that both pure bundling and pure unbundling are boundary cases of mixed bundling and are weakly dominated by the latter strategy in general. Chae (1992) applies the commodity-bundling model to information goods in his study of the subscription TV market. He concludes that the bundling of CATV channels is practiced not to extract consumer surplus, but simply because there are economies of scope in the distribution technology.

3. *N*-Good Bundling Model

All the abovementioned works are limited to bundles consisting of only two components. A typical academic journal, on the other hand, has between 80 and 100 articles per subscription period. An appropriate N-good bundling model is needed for this context. Unfortunately, a complete N-good model with 2^N bundle combinations and N-dimensional consumer preferences quickly becomes computationally unwieldy as N gets large. Hanson and Martin (1990), by formulating the model as a mixed-integer linear programming problem, manage to attack a bundle pricing problem with $N = 21$.[7]

Recognizing the need to balance profit-maximization and consumer rejection of a complex pricing schedule, we opt for a simpler model in which no sub-bundles are available. The consumer purchases either the journal subscription for a price P_J or individual articles at a price of P_A apiece. This simplifies the model from setting 2^N optimal prices to setting only two prices, P_A and P_J. This is reminiscent of setting a menu of optional two-part tariffs in the nonlinear pricing literature (Willig 1978, Wilson 1993).[8] Low-demand readers purchase articles individually, while high-demand readers pay the flat fee P_J and enjoy unlimited access to all articles (Figure 2).

Optional two-part tariffs can be either *ex ante* or *ex post* in nature (Mitchell and Vogelsang 1991, page 95). In an *ex ante* arrangement, readers elect to join either the subscriber group or the "article-on-demand" group prior to consumption. Knowing one's *expected* consumption behavior is critical in making the "right" decision. An "article-on-demand" reader who expects to read only a few articles

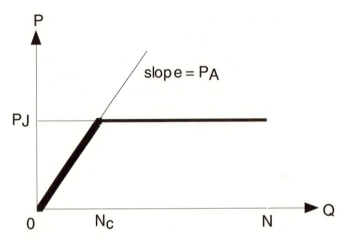

Figure 2 Total outlay vs. number of articles consumed. An *ex post* two-part tariff (in bold) offers a predictable price cap on consumer expenditure.

but ends up reading more than N_c ($= P_J/P_A$) articles would have to pay more than if he/she had become a subscriber in the first place. Many consumers (especially those with fixed budgeting and fund allocation considerations) are reluctant to sign up for these pay-per-use arrangements precisely because of this uncertainty factor. An *ex post* approach eliminates this problem by allowing the consumer to choose the cheaper of the two pricing schemes at the end of the billing period, thereby placing a predictable upper bound on the final bill. However, the need for a final settlement creates an administrative and metering overhead over true pay-per-use models.

4. Modeling Heterogeneity in Consumer Preferences

The *N*-good bundling model departs from the traditional nonlinear pricing model in that consumers are not choosing to purchase *n* units of nondistinguishable articles, as if purchasing *x* kilowatt-hours of electricity or *y* minutes of cellular-phone air time. Instead, each of the *N* articles is unique and distinct from the others. Consumers may value one article dramatically differently from the next. Unfortunately, a complete description of consumer heterogeneity using an *N*-dimensional vector $\{w_1, w_2, ..., w_N\}$ again leads to intractability. We seek a concise way to capture the essence of consumers' willingness-to-pay across the different articles.

Zahray and Sirbu (1990) attempt to capture the heterogeneity in consumer preferences for academic journals, albeit in one variable—the reservation price for the journal. Bakos and Brynjolfsson (2000) take a similar approach, in which they characterize consumers by a single type variable w and assume consumer valuations of goods to be independent and identically distributed. If a single variable is employed, both models can only capture consumer valuations for the bundle in its aggregate. This is adequate in the pure-bundling context, in which journals are sold only in the form of subscriptions. In the mixed-bundling context, however, it is important to account for the correlation of values across the components as well.

Consider, for example, a publisher selling a two-article journal in a market with only two consumers, our friends Alice and Bob. Alice is willing to pay $10 for the first article and $0 for the second, while Bob values the articles at $7 and $5 respectively. A publisher engaging exclusively in pure bundling (i.e., subscription only) is interested only in the aggregate willingness-to-pay of the two consumers. He/she will price the subscription at $10 for a total revenue of $20. A mixed-bundling strategist, on the other hand, will desire additional information on the correlation of values for the component articles. In this example, the publisher will price individual articles at $10 and raise the subscription price to $12, thereby realizing a revenue of $22 and completely extracting the consumer surplus in the process. In effect, the publisher has managed to separate the market into two segments: The segment with high correlation of value across articles (Bob) is sold the subscription; the segment with low correlation (Alice) is offered individual articles.

The present chapter employs two variables, w_o and k, to describe the N-dimensional consumer preference. We allow each journal reader to rank the N articles in the journal in decreasing order of preference, such that his/her favorite article is ranked first, the least favorite is ranked last, and weak monotonicity is observed. The reader may place zero value on any number of the N articles. By assuming a linear demand function for all positive-valued articles, we can plot an individual reader's valuation of all the articles in the journal in Figure 3.

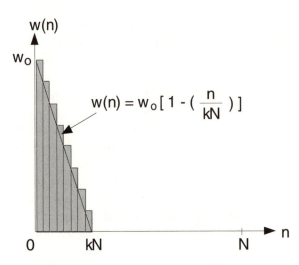

Figure 3 Article valuation by an individual reader indexed by $\{w_o, k\}$.

Each of the articles is positionally ranked between 0 and N along the horizontal axis. The individual's most highly valued article has $n = 0$, so the y-intercept, w_o, represents the WTP for his/her most favored article. The valuation for the subsequently ranked articles is assumed to fall off at a constant rate until it reaches zero at $n = kN$. With the assumption of free disposal, no articles have negative value—readers are free to discard unwanted articles at zero cost. The variable k dictates the slope of the demand curve, and it also indicates the fraction of articles in the journal that have nonzero value to the individual. For example, a reader with $k = 0.01$ is willing to pay a nonzero amount for only one article in a journal with 100 articles, while another reader who positively values half the articles in the journal will have a k of 0.5. If an individual's k is greater than unity, that means he/she places positive value on all N articles in the journal and the demand curve will never cross the horizontal axis. Figure 4 shows a diverse range of consumer preferences that can be described using this two-dimensional $\{w_o, k\}$ index.

Empirical studies performed by King and Griffiths (1995) indicate that the correlation of article valuations is not very high for academic journals (Table 1). Out of the 80 to 100 articles (per subscription period) in an average journal, over 40% of readers surveyed read no more than 5 articles. Only 0.9% of readers read

Network Delivery of Information Goods

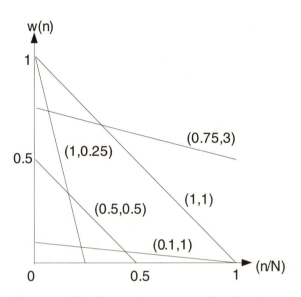

Figure 4 This figure demonstrates the diversity of consumers that can be indexed by $\{w_o, k\}$.

Table 1 Distribution of Number of Articles Read in a Journal (King and Griffiths 1995)

Number of Articles Read in a Journal	Proportion of Readers (%)	Cumulative Proportion of Readers (%)
1 to 5	43.60	43.60
6 to 10	34.40	78.00
11 to 15	8.21	86.21
16 to 20	5.50	91.71
21 to 25	3.37	95.08
26 to 30	1.97	97.05
31 to 40	1.23	98.28
41 to 50	0.82	99.10
More than 50	0.90	100.00

more than 50, or about half of all the articles in the subscription period. This suggests that a majority of readers have small values of k, and very few readers have k-values close to or exceeding unity. This result is incorporated into our analysis below as a fitted probability distribution for k, $f_k(k)$.

Formally, an individual's valuation for the nth article can be expressed as

$$(1) \quad w(n) = \min\left\{0, w_0 \cdot \left[1 - \frac{1}{k}\left(\frac{n}{N}\right)\right]\right\}, \quad 0 \le n \le N-1,$$

with $w_0 \ge 0$ and $k \ge 1/N$. Using this formulation, we can proceed to determine the individual's reservation price of the journal, his/her consumption decision in face of the prices P_A and P_J, and the optimal number of articles consumed in each of the three bundling scenarios.

4.1 Consumer Choice in Pure Bundling

In pure bundling, potential readers can only choose to subscribe to the journal or buy nothing at all. Purchasing individual articles is not an available option. Therefore, an individual's decision is based solely on the price of the subscription, P_J, and his/her reservation price of the journal bundle in the aggregate. This reservation price, W_J, is simply the summation (or integration, if we approximate n as a continuous variable) of his/her reservation prices for all the individual articles:

$$(2) \quad W_J = \int_0^N w(n) \cdot dn.$$

The net benefit U_J derived from subscribing is the difference of the reservation price W_J and the actual subscription price P_J:

$$(3) \quad U_J = W_J - P_J.$$

A potential reader will choose to subscribe only if the subscription results in a positive net benefit $U_J > 0$. The $U_J = 0$ curve, plotted in $\{w_0, k\}$ space in Figure 5, separates the readership population into

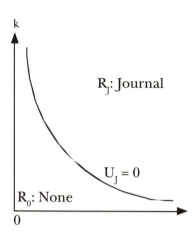

Figure 5 Consumer choice in pure bundling scenario.

two regions. Those who fall in the region R_J will choose to subscribe, while those in region R_0 will opt out.[9]

4.2 Consumer Choice in Pure Unbundling

In the pure-unbundling scenario, all articles are available individually at a unit price of P_A. Consumers are free to purchase as many or as few articles as they desire, up to and including all N articles in the journal. A rational-choice utility-maximizing consumer will consume only those articles with $w(n) \quad P_A$, realizing a net benefit of $w(n) - P_A$ for each of those articles. The marginal article consumed by the consumer, n^*, has a benefit $w(n^*) = P_A$. Therefore, for $w_o \quad P_A$, the optimal number of articles read by an individual indexed by $\{w_o, k\}$ can be expressed as

$$(4) \quad n^* = \max\left\{ N, \ \frac{k \cdot N \cdot (w_o - P_A)}{w_o} \right\},$$

with the maximum capped at N, the total number of articles available in the journal. On the other hand, for an individual with $w_o < P_A$, even the most favored article is deemed unworthy of the price tag P_A. In this case, n^* would be equal to zero and no articles would be purchased. Figure 6 presents the optimal article consumption level in $\{w_o, k\}$ space.

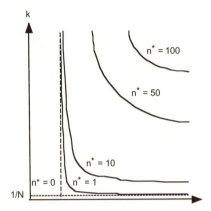

Figure 6 Optimal article consumption level in pure unbundling scenario.

In addition to the optimal consumption level, the net benefit derived from consuming n^* articles, U_A, can also be expressed as

(5) $\quad U_A = W_A - n^* \cdot P_A,$

where the gross benefit, W_A, is

(6) $\quad W_A = \int_0^{n^*} w(n) \cdot dn.$

4.3 Consumer Choice in Mixed Bundling

In mixed bundling, consumers seek to maximize their utility by choosing one of three options: subscribe to journal, purchase individual articles, or neither. Depending on each individual's U_J and U_A measures, as defined above, he/she can fall into one of five regions in Table 2.

This is illustrated in the consumer choice diagram, Figure 7. For example, individuals who value their most favored article at less than the article price (i.e., $w_o < P_A$) have a negative U_A and will not purchase any articles in unbundled form. If their valuation of all the articles in the aggregate is less than the subscription price P_J, they will not subscribe to the journal either. These individuals fall

Table 2   Consumer Choice in Mixed-Bundling Scenario

Region	U_J	U_A	$U_J > U_A$?	Purchase
R_0	< 0	< 0	—	Nothing
R_{A1}	< 0	> 0	No	Article(s)
R_{J1}	> 0	< 0	Yes	Journal
R_{A2}	> 0	> 0	No	Article(s)
R_{J2}	> 0	> 0	Yes	Journal

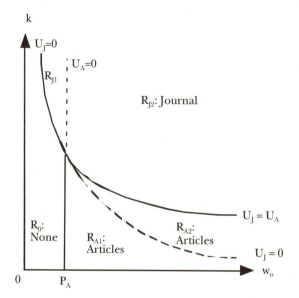

Figure 7   Consumer choice in mixed bundling scenario.

in the R_0 region. On the other hand, if their aggregate valuation is greater than P_J, they will fall in the R_{J1} region and will choose to subscribe to the journal. Individuals with high w_o and low k tend to value only a few articles highly, and will be best off purchasing individual articles. These consumers are found in region R_{A1}. Finally, consumers in R_{A2} and R_{J2} receive positive benefits from either journal subscription or article purchase, and make their respective purchasing decisions based on the relative magnitudes of their U_J and U_A.

5. Production Costs and Economies of Scale

Thus far, we have focused on the demand side of the problem. Now we turn to the supply side, specifically to the underlying technology and production functions of academic journals. As previously noted, the information industry in general and the journal publishing industry in particular are characterized by high fixed costs (FC) and low marginal costs (MC). A producer will stay in the market only if gross margin (gross revenue minus variable cost) is enough to cover FC. As long as total revenue is greater than total cost, the optimal pricing decision is then independent of FC. (Alternatively, we can think of the fixed cost as either zero or sunk.) This assumption allows the treatment of FC as an exogenous variable in the present model.

We incorporate the presence (or absence) of economies of scale (EoS) in the production function by establishing the following relationship between the marginal costs MC_J and MC_A:

$$(7) \qquad MC_J = N^\gamma \cdot MC_A.$$

N is the number of articles in the journal and γ is the EoS index. When $\gamma < 1$, economies of scale are present and a subscription bundle of N articles is cheaper to produce and sell than N individual articles. Therefore, the publisher can realize cost savings via bundling. When $\gamma = 1$, there are no economies of scale in journal production or distribution. No cost savings can be realized by bundling. Finally, if there are diseconomies of scale in the production function, it can be described with $\gamma > 1$. Prior work in bundling almost invariably assumes no cost savings from bundling, that is, $\gamma = 1$. Chae's assumption of extreme economies of scope in the CATV delivery technology translates to a special case of $\gamma = 0$. By treating the extent of economies of scale as an endogenous variable, this model allows a parametric analysis of its influence on the producer's optimal bundling strategy.

Based on the distribution of consumers in the $\{w_o, k\}$ space and the underlying cost structure of journal production, the publisher proceeds to optimize P_A and P_J to maximize gross margin Π:

$$(8) \quad \Pi = \iint_{R_J} \left[P_J - MC_J \right] f(w_o, k) \cdot \partial w_o \cdot \partial k$$

$$+ \iint_{R_A} n * \left[P_A - MC_A \right] f(w_o, k) \cdot \partial w_o \cdot \partial k,$$

where the term $f(w_o, k)$ is the joint probability density function of the readership described in $\{w_o, k\}$ space. It is worthwhile to note that in the case in which the optimal strategy turns out to be pure bundling (pure unbundling), the second (first) integral component will be zero.

6. Analysis and Empirical Results

The N-good bundling model is used to quantify how the choice of the optimal bundling strategy and optimal pricing are affected by MC and γ on the supply side, and by $f(w_o, k)$ on the demand side. Recalling that w_o is an individual's valuation of his/her most favored article in the journal, and k is the fraction of articles in the journal that have nonzero value to the individual, we assume independent distributions for w_o and k. We normalize w_o to be uniformly distributed between 0 and 1. Using the King/Griffiths data in Table 1, k is fitted to an exponential distribution with $\lambda = 13.8758$ or $\mu = 1/\lambda = 0.072$ ($R^2 = 0.97117$). This means that the average reader reads only 7.2% of all the articles in a typical journal. Figure 8 shows, for a journal with $N = 100$ articles, the producer surplus (as measured by gross margin) attainable via each bundling alternative as a function of MC and γ. The marginal cost of a single article, MC, is restricted to be no greater than the highest individual valuation, $\max[w_o]$ (which we normalize to unity without loss of generality). There would be no market participation if it cost more to produce an article than anyone is willing to pay. Given our interest in scenarios in which MC is small but nonzero, these and subsequent figures are plotted on a semilog scale.[10]

In Figure 8(a), there are no economies of scale and the EoS factor $\gamma = 1$. The marginal cost of the journal is N times that of a single article, so no cost saving is realizable from bundling. The pure bundling strategy is clearly dominated by the other two strategies. The mixed-bundling and pure-unbundling alternatives are essen-

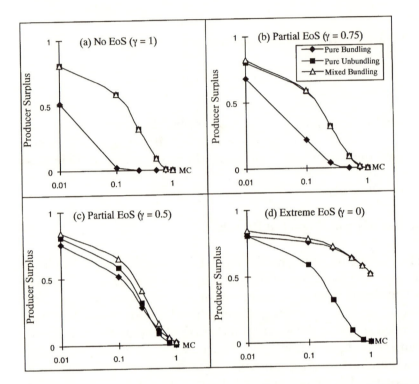

Figure 8 Profit-maximizing bundling strategy: it is clear that mixed bundling is the dominant strategy across all marginal cost and economies of scale conditions.

tially identical. This suggests that even if the publisher opts for a mixed-bundling strategy, virtually the entire revenue will come from article sales. As the production function begins to exhibit some economies of scale, cost-related bundling incentives begin to appear. Yet in Figure 8(b), where $\gamma = 0.75$, the situation remains unchanged. Mixed bundling continues to be the optimal strategy, with pure unbundling slightly inferior at low *MC* levels. As γ continues to fall in the face of stronger economies of scale, mixed bundling becomes the strictly dominant strategy. In Figure 8(c), where $\gamma = 0.5$, pure bundling and pure unbundling trade dominance depending on the magnitude of *MC*, but both are dominated by mixed bundling. Finally, in the case of extreme economies of scale, where $\gamma = 0$ in Figure 8(d), it costs as much (or as little) to produce and sell an entire journal as it does to produce and sell a single article. Mixed bundling strictly outperforms pure unbundling at all MC levels, while pure bundling approaches mixed bundling in capturing producer surplus as MC approaches max $[w_o]$ or unity. In this case, most of the publisher's revenue will be derived from journal subscriptions.

The first conclusion is that mixed bundling is superior to pure bundling and pure unbundling across all values of MC and γ. This extends earlier results for two-good models to the present N-good model. This result makes intuitive sense, since both pure bundling and pure unbundling are boundary cases of mixed bundling, and therefore can do no better than the mixed-bundling strategy. The price discrimination mechanism is at work here, as the mixed-bundling strategy creates an incentive-compatible condition, inducing the high and low demanders to reveal their preferences by self-selecting into the appropriate consumption groups.

In addition, we observe that pure bundling does not necessarily dominate pure unbundling in the N-good scenario. Specifically, the model identifies plausible conditions under which unbundling is actually superior to bundling (in pure forms). When marginal cost is nonzero, pure bundling is undesirable not only in the absence of economies of scale ($\gamma = 1$) but also if the degree of EoS is too weak (as illustrated by $g = 0.75$) for the cost-saving bundling incentive to become a dominating factor. Even in the presence of strong economies of scale ($\gamma = 0.5, 0$), the relative merits of pure bundling and unbundling are still dependent on the magnitude of the marginal cost relative to consumer valuations of the articles. Inefficiency in resource allocation (and loss of surplus) will result if individuals are forced to purchase the bundle and consume some articles that they value below marginal cost. Adams and Yellen label this condition, in which consumption occurs at sub-MC levels, a violation of the "exclusion" assumption. This is of real concern to journal publishers, because the distribution of k (as fitted to empirical data from King and Griffiths) is such that most readers actually place zero value on most of the articles that they read in an average journal. Except for the case of $MC = 0$, or the case of $\gamma = 0$, in which the marginal costs for all but the first article are effectively zero, exclusion is always violated for those readers with $k < 1$. In our numerical analysis, where k is exponentially distributed with a mean $\mu = 0.072$, the probability of k 1, that is, a reader's having positive valuations for all articles in the journal, is on the order of

10^{-6}, or 1 out of 1,000,000 readers. (To place this number in context, *Science,* one of the most widely read academic journals, has a circulation of 165,000; *IEEE Spectrum* and *American Economic Review,* two mainstream periodicals in the electrical engineering and economics disciplines, have circulations of 30,000 and 27,000, respectively.)[11] Therefore, the choice of optimal bundling strategy lies in the balance between cost-savings from bundling and loss of surplus owing to exclusion violation. The proposition by Adams and Yellen (p. 488) that pure unbundling "is a more desirable strategy the greater the cost of violating exclusion" holds true here.

6.1 Optimal Revenue Mix

The mixed-bundling publisher is interested in the optimal pricing of its articles and subscriptions. Figures 9 and 10 show the optimal pricing ratio (P_J/P_A) and the corresponding revenue mix for various marginal cost and EoS conditions, respectively. While the semilog scales preclude the plotting of data at $MC = 0$, we note that when marginal cost is zero, the subscription (to a bundle of 100 articles) should be priced at approximately 10 times that of an individual article, and this optimal pricing ratio would result in a revenue stream that is well balanced between the sale of articles (56%) and of subscriptions (44%). When the marginal cost is non-negligible, however, the optimal ratio becomes sensitive to the economies-of-scale condition. If there are extreme economies of scale $(\gamma = 0)$, the cost-saving incentive induces the publisher to rely more heavily on the sale of bundled subscriptions as MC increases. With strong economies of scale $(\gamma = 0.5)$, the optimal pricing ratio stays constant but the revenue mix shifts decisively toward subscription sales with increasing cost. On the other hand, when the economies of scale are absent or weak $(\gamma = 1, 0.75)$, the publisher is best served by increasing the price ratio, thereby realizing most or all of its revenue through individual article sales.

6.2 Internet-Based Document Delivery Technology

We can characterize the extent to which economies of scale are present in the current set of network-based document delivery technologies. Specifically, we ask what a reasonable value of γ is,

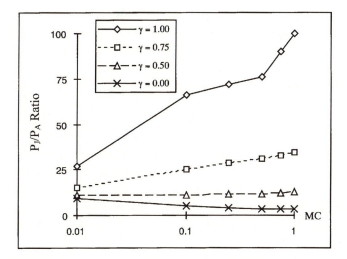

Figure 9 Optimal price ratio for mixed bundling strategy across various EoS conditions.

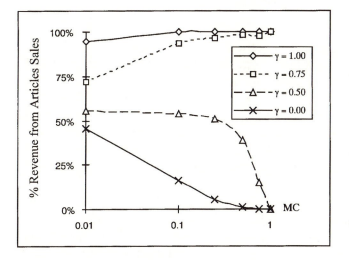

Figure 10 Optimal revenue mix for mixed bundling strategy.

and how it might change with technology. We identify two major components of the marginal cost of delivering a journal or an article. These are the cost of transmitting raw data bits and the transaction costs. Production and data storage are fixed costs to the publisher and should be excluded from consideration in this context.

We consider the scenario in which the publisher outsources both data transmission and fee-collection functions to specialized services. Web hosting services are offered by a multitude of Internet presence providers. Entire digitized archives of journal articles can be hosted on a Web server and made accessible for downloading by scholars. Several micropayment systems are also available to facilitate electronic payment for articles or other information goods sold via the Internet.[12]

We choose to characterize the marginal costs MC_J and MC_A using three cost coefficients:

$$(9) \quad \begin{cases} MC_J = & \kappa_f + \kappa_v \cdot P_J + \mu_s \cdot N \cdot \kappa_d \\ MC_A = & \kappa_f + \kappa_v \cdot P_A + \kappa_d \end{cases}$$

where κ_f, κ_v, κ_d are cost coefficients and μ_s is the expected fraction of articles downloaded by a subscriber. We discuss each variable in turn. Transactional costs are modeled on the two-part fee structure of credit-card transactions. κ_f is a fixed fee levied for each transaction, while κ_v is the variable component charged in proportion to the value of the transaction (P_J and P_A, respectively).[13] This implies, significantly, that the marginal costs are no longer constants, as we have assumed thus far, but have become functions of P_J and P_A, respectively.

The variable κ_d is the cost of transmitting or downloading one journal article. Web hosting services currently charge between $0.05 and $0.50 per MB (megabyte) of data accessed on the server by a client.[14] A journal page, scanned at 600 dpi and compressed in Group 4 Fax/TIFF format, takes up about 100 kB (kilobytes). Assuming a typical journal article has 10 pages, downloading a journal article requires the transmission of 1 MB of data. This translates to a κ_d of between $0.05 and $0.50. With continued improvements in data-transmission and compression technologies, it is reasonable to expect further declines in κ_d.

Most providers sell downloads at a fixed cost per bit, so the publisher enjoys no economies of scale in data transmission per se. However, selling a journal subscription online does not necessarily require the transmission of all N articles to the subscriber. The subscribers are free to download all N articles, but most will choose to download only a fraction of all the articles. This "just-in-time" (as opposed to "just-in-case") delivery paradigm results in an expected transmission cost of $\mu_s \cdot N \cdot \kappa_d$ instead of $N \cdot \kappa_d$ for each journal subscription. We can quantify μ_s as the conditional expectation of the fraction of articles read by the subscribing subpopulation (the region R_J in Figure 7),

$$(10) \quad \mu_s = \frac{\iint\limits_{R_J} k \cdot f(w_o, k) \cdot \partial w_o \cdot \partial k}{\iint\limits_{R_J} f(w_o, k) \cdot \partial w_o \cdot \partial k}.$$

We have shown that the area of integration R_J is a function of the prices set by the publisher. Therefore, μ_s is dependent on the prices as well. Substituting equations (9) and (10) into equation (8) with the appropriate values for the κ coefficients and reoptimizing, we can gain insight into how μ_s and γ are affected by a decline in transmission cost κ_d, which in turn determines the optimal pricing and revenue mix decisions. Figure 11 shows that the optimal subscription price P_J (right-hand axis) varies significantly in the current range of κ_d. The expected fraction of articles read from a subscription copy μ_s (left-hand axis) follows a similar trend, which is not surprising given its dependency on P_J. The higher the price of a subscription, the more articles one will have to read to justify becoming a subscriber. It is interesting to note that even when transmission cost becomes negligible ($\kappa_d = 0$), μ_s is still significantly greater than μ of 0.072 for the overall journal readership.

Figure 12 further illustrates how the economies of scale (γ) and optimal revenue mix are likely to be affected by a declining κ_d. For κ_d greater than \$0.20/MB, there are essentially no economies of scale and most of the revenue is derived from article sales. At κ_d = \$0.05/MB, the current low-end estimate, γ falls to 0.6 and we begin to see a well-balanced revenue mix between article and journal sales. But even when $\kappa_d = 0$, we see that γ will not fall below 0.3, and

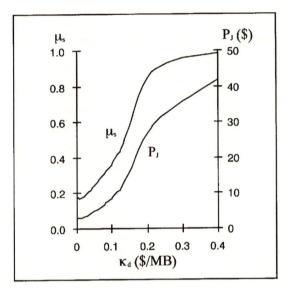

Figure 11 Effect of transmission cost on journal subscription pricing.

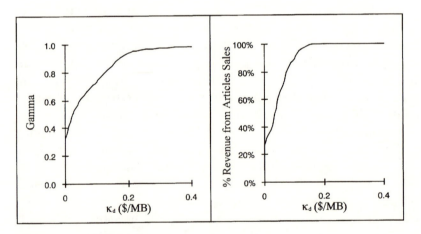

Figure 12 Effect of declining κ_d (transmission cost) on economies of scale and revenue mix.

30% of the revenue is still derived from selling individual articles. Under no circumstances should we expect the entire publishing revenue to come from subscription sales alone.

While we have held κ_f and κ_v constant in our analysis, it is reasonable to expect a decline in these coefficients as well. The Millicent protocol, for example, proposes a lightweight micropayment mechanism with cryptographic operations that cost one-tenth to one-hundredth of a cent (Manasse 1995). Yet one should not expect κ_f and κ_v to fall at a rate similar to that of κ_d. After all, transaction costs are not dictated solely by progress in hardware technology or by the state of the art in cryptography. Other sources of payment system costs, such as customer service, fraud protection, chargebacks, and back-office accounting, may decline only slowly over time, if at all.

7. Conclusions

Several recent independent works suggest that bundling is desirable for information goods (Bakos and Brynjolfsson 2000, Fishburn et al. 2000). This chapter demonstrates, however, that a different conclusion may be drawn when the important distinction between mixed and pure bundling is made. While mixed bundling is always the dominant strategy, our results also show that pure bundling may, under certain conditions, be inferior to pure unbundling. We therefore caution against any wholesale adoption of pure bundling without a thorough analysis of the supply and demand for the information product in question. Specifically, for information goods that at present exist in bundled form (e.g., academic journals), unbundling (i.e., switching from pure bundling to mixed bundling) can actually increase producer surplus. This result suggests that an academic journal publisher should expand its online products by offering to include unbundled articles in addition to traditional subscriptions. By offering a menu of choices that includes both the original bundle and the components, the publisher can extract consumer surplus more completely via consumer self-selection. By extension, the publisher can do even better by simultaneously bundling and unbundling the journal, adding "super-bundles" of multiple journal subscriptions or site licenses to the product mix. Mackie-Mason and Riveros (2000) offer another bundle option in addition to unbundled articles and the traditional subscription, namely the generalized subscription. In this arrangement, the user purchases unlimited access to N units of articles, and is free to select any N articles from the entire archive of M articles (with $M \gg N$).

Our model assumes that a journal is made up of N individual articles. In reality, there are other separable components of a journal subscription, such as the tables of contents, indices, abstracts, and announcements. Readers can assign different valuations for each of these components just as they do for the individual articles. Therefore, these components can be candidates for unbundling as well. RevealAlert, a recent product offered by CARL, delivers via email the tables of contents of up to 50 user-selected journal titles.

A casual survey will reveal that all the major players in the academic-journal publishing industry are actively pursuing the possibility of network access to their journal products. Many have made impressive strides in a very short time. Some publishers provide online access to article abstracts, tables of contents, and indexes to their journal titles; others offer fully searchable text, complete with images and markup tags, of the journal articles. Most publishers have installed (or plan to install) some form of access control and billing mechanism so that charges can be appropriated for the use of these materials. However, lessons learned from various research/demonstration projects indicate that significant economic, behavioral, and institutional barriers need to be crossed before on-demand network delivery of academic journals can become ubiquitous.[15] Intelligent pricing designs must take into consideration the information needs and usage behavior patterns of the journal-reading population, as well as the economies-of-scale characteristics of the underlying technologies.

Notes

1. 17 U.S.C. § 107 (1988 & Supp. V 1993).

2. 17 U.S.C. § 108(g)(2) (1988). Specifically, the CONTU Guidelines (reprinted in 1976, U.S.C.C.A.N. 5810, 5813-14) set forth a copying limit of five copies per year of articles from the most recent five years of any journal article.

3. See Liebowitz (1985) and Besen and Kirby (1989) for detailed treatment of journal photocopying and indirect appropriability; Joyce and Merz (1985) studies the extent of price discrimination by journals across various academic disciplines.

4. Dyl (1983) muses on the applicability and antitrust implications of the Robinson-Patman Act for price discrimination by academic journals.

5. Interested readers can consult Lewis (1989), Byrd (1990), Metz and Gherman (1991), Spigai (1991), and Stoller, Christopherson, and Miranda (1996) for works on the economics of scholarly publishing and serials pricing from the library and information sciences communities' perspective.

6. Carbajo, de Meza, and Seidmann (1990) and Whinston (1990) provide further treatment of this topic.

7. Armstrong (1997) shows that an approximate solution for the optimal tariff problem is a cost-based two-part tariff, that is, a fixed up-front membership fee plus a per-article charge set equal to the marginal cost. However, this approximation reasonably converges only for N in the several-thousands range, and the absence of a price cap may make it unacceptable to consumers who are used to the traditional subscription model.

8. Technically, an $(n + 1)$-part tariff can be made to be Pareto-superior to an n-part tariff. Using the same argument in the bundling context, any mixed-bundling strategy with more than two prices (up to $2N$) will necessarily perform better than a mixed bundling strategy with two prices, and thus better than pure bundling and pure unbundling strategies as well. The extent to which a publisher chooses to offer multiple prices is dependent on its multivariate optimization capabilities and, more important, consumer acceptance of a complex pricing structure.

9. An appendix detailing the formal derivations of consumer choice regions and calculations of producer surpluses is available from the authors on request.

10. In the degenerate case in which marginal cost is zero, the value of g (economies-of-scale factor) becomes irrelevant, and we would naturally expect mixed bundling, pure bundling, and pure unbundling to perform equally well in terms of maximizing producer surplus.

11. Circulation data from *Ulrich's International Periodicals Directory*, 34th ed. R. R. Bowker Publishing Co., 1996.

12. See MacKie-Mason and White (1996) and Sirbu (1997) for surveys of digital payment mechanisms.

13. A typical credit-card operation has κ_f and κ_v set at \$0.30 and 1.66\%, respectively, and is not suited for small-value transactions because of this high κ_f. NetBill (http://www.netbill.com), an experimental electronic micropayment system developed at Carnegie Mellon University, has $\kappa_f = \$0.02$ and $\kappa_v = 5\%$, enabling it to support transactions down to 5–10 cents. This latter set of cost coefficients is used for this analysis. See Sirbu and Tygar (1995) for a description of the NetBill electronic micropayment system.

14. Price schedules for incremental data downloads obtained from a Web-site survey of Web hosting service providers, January 1997.

15. Okerson and O'Donnell (1995) presents an interesting forum discussion, which took place entirely on the Internet, on the future of scholarly journals, drawing experience from various electronic journal endeavors such as *Psycoloquy*, the *Chicago Journal of Theoretical Computer Science*, and the electronic preprint archive for high-energy physics at Los Alamos National Laboratories.

References

Adams, W. J., and Yellen, J. L. 1976. Commodity bundling and the burden of monopoly. *Quarterly Journal of Economics* 90: 475–498.

Armstrong, M. 1997. Price discrimination by a many-product firm. Mimeograph.

Bakos, Y., and Brynjolfsson, E. 2000. Aggregation and disaggregation of information goods In this volume.

Besen, S. M., and Kirby, S. N. 1989. Private copying, appropriability, and optimal copying royalties. *Journal of Law and Economics* 32, no. 2, pt. 1: 255–280.

Burnstein, M. L. 1960. The economics of tie-in sales. *Review of Economics and Statistics* 42: 68–73.

Byrd, G. D. 1990. An economic "commons" tragedy for research libraries: Scholarly journal publishing and pricing trends. *College & Research Libraries* 51: 184–195.

Carbajo, J., de Meza, D., and Seidmann, D. J. 1990. A strategic motivation for commodity bundling. *Journal of Industrial Economics* 38: 283–298.

Chae, S. 1992. Bundling subscription TV channels: A case of natural bundling. *International Journal of Industrial Organization* 10: 213–230.

Dyl, E. A. 1983. A note on price discrimination by academic journals. *Library Quarterly* 53, no. 2: 161–168.

Fishburn, P. C., Odlyzko, A. M., and Siders, R. C. 2000. Fixed-fee versus unit pricing for information goods: Competition, equilibria, and price wars. In this volume.

Hanson, W., and Martin, R. K. 1990. Optimal bundle pricing. *Management Science* 36, no. 2: 155–174.

Joyce, P., and Merz, T. E. 1985. Price discrimination in academic journals. *Library Quarterly* 55, no. 3: 273–283.

King, D. W., and Griffiths, J. M. 1995. Economic issues concerning electronic publishing and distribution of scholarly articles. *Library Trends* 43, no. 4: 713–740.

King, D. W., McDonald, D. D., and Roderer, N. K. 1981. *Scientific journals in the United States: Their production, use, and economics.* Stroudsburg, PA: Hutchinson Ross Publishing.

Laffont, J.-J., Maskin, E., and Rochet, J.-C. 1987. Optimal nonlinear pricing with two-dimensional characteristics. In T. Groves, R. Radner, and S. Reiter, eds., *Information, Incentives and Economic Mechanisms* (Minneapolis: University of Minnesota Press).

Lewis, D. W. 1989. Economics of the scholarly journal. *College & Research Libraries* 50: 674–688.

Liebowitz, S. J. 1985. Copying and indirect appropriability: Photocopying of journals. *Journal of Political Economy* 93, no. 5: 945–957.

MacKie-Mason, J. K., and Riveros, J. 2000. Economics and electronic access to scholarly information. In this volume.

MacKie-Mason, J. K., and White, K. 1996. Evaluating and selecting digital payment mechanisms. In *Proceedings of the 1996 Telecommunications Policy Research Conference.*

Manasse, M. S. 1995. The Millicent protocols for electronic commerce. In *Proceedings of the First USENIX Workshop on Electronic Commerce.*

McAfee, R. P., McMillan, J., and Whinston, M. D. 1989. Multiproduct monopoly, commodity bundling, and correlation of values. *Quarterly Journal of Economics* 104: 371–383.

Metz, P., and Gherman, P. M. 1991. Serial pricing and the role of the electronic journal. *College & Research Libraries* 52: 315–327.

Mitchell, B. M., and Vogelsang, I. 1991. *Telecommunications pricing: Theory and practice.* Cambridge, England: Cambridge University Press.

Okerson, A. S., and O'Donnell, J. J., eds. 1995. *Scholarly Journals at the Crossroads: A Subversive Proposal for Electronic Publishing.* Washington, DC: Association of Research Libraries.

Ordover, J. A., and Willig, R. D. 1978. On the optimal provision of journals qua sometimes shared goods. *American Economic Review* 68: 324–338.

Schmalensee, R. 1984. Gaussian demand and commodity bundling. *Journal of Business* 57, no. 1, pt. 2: S211–S230.

Sirbu, M. A., and Tygar, J. D. 1995. NetBill: An Internet commerce system optimized for network delivered services. In *Proceedings of IEEE CompCon Conference.*

Sirbu, M.A. 1997. Credits and debits on the Internet. *IEEE Spectrum,* February 1997: 23–29.

Spigai, F. 1991. Information pricing. *Annual Review of Information Science and Technology* 26: 39–73.

Stigler, G. J. 1963. United States v. Loew's Inc.: A note on block booking. *Supreme Court Review,* 152–157.

Stoller, M. A., Christopherson, R., and Miranda, M. 1996. The economics of professional journal pricing. *College & Research Libraries* 57: 9–21.

Varian, H. R. 1995. Pricing information goods. In *Proceedings of Scholarship in the New Information Environment Symposium*, Harvard Law School.

Whinston, M. D. 1990. Tying, foreclosure, and exclusion. *American Economic Review* 80: 837–859.

Willig, R. D. 1978. Pareto-superior nonlinear outlay schedules. *Bell Journal of Economics* 9: 56–69.

Wilson, R. 1993. *Nonlinear Pricing*. Oxford: Oxford University Press.

Zahray, W. P., and Sirbu, M. 1990. The provision of scholarly journals by libraries via electronic technologies: An economic analysis. *Information Economics and Policy* 4: 127–154.

Fixed-Fee versus Unit Pricing for Information Goods: Competition, Equilibria, and Price Wars

Peter C. Fishburn, Andrew M. Odlyzko, and Ryan C. Siders

1. Introduction

It is widely expected that electronic commerce, especially in "soft" or "information" goods (such as news stories, software, network games, database access, and entertainment), will move largely to *à la carte* pricing. Consumers will select the items they want and will pay for each through one of the many micropayment schemes that are being developed. However, economic arguments and observations of market behavior show that this is unlikely to be the dominant mode of pricing for established producers. See Odlyzko (1996), Varian (a, b). Information goods are characterized by negligible marginal costs, and therefore arguments in favor of bundling are stronger for them than for physical goods. The combination of matrimonial ads and reports of boxing matches that appears in print newspapers might appear to be caused by the impracticality of producing physically separate editions for each one. However, bundling arguments show that producers can obtain more revenue by combining disparate items, since that allows them to exploit uneven preferences that consumers have for different goods. While it is not true that bundling is always better than offering items separately, in most situations bundling is advantageous to the producers, since it depends only on moderate variations in preferences. See Bakos and Brynjolfsson (2000) and Schmalensee (1982); see also Odlyzko (1996) for various examples. Hence, in the future, we are likely to subscribe to electronic newspapers that carry wide ranges of stories (even though the selection of those stories might be personalized), and not to buy individual stories.

The arguments in favor of bundling are strong, and suggest that *à la carte* or unit pricing will not be the dominant mode of commerce in information goods. However, unit pricing is still likely to be widespread. For many goods, that appears to be the most appropriate approach. Moreover, even if bundling does dominate, as we predict, there are likely to be niches for fixed-fee sales. Newspapers probably will be selling individual stories. All we suggest is that they will contribute a small part of total revenues, just as they do today. One of the few general results about the economics of bundling is the observation of Adams and Yellen (1976) that mixed bundling (in which items are offered for sale separately, as well as in combination, but with the prices of the individual items higher than they would be otherwise) is always better (with proper prices) than pure bundling, in which items are available only in combination. Hence we might see the electronic version of *The New York Times* available through annual subscription for $0.50 per day, a single day's edition for $1.00, and individual stories for $0.25, say. Furthermore, bundling is most appropriate for producers with an established brand. An amateur selling Christmas-card designs is most likely to sell them *à la carte*. The many frustrated authors who feel they are not getting into print because of a conspiracy, or because of the stupidity of publishers, are likely to attempt to sell their works themselves. Even though most of them are likely to be disappointed by the outcome, these attempts will create demand for micropayment systems. (Furthermore, there will be enough successes to keep up the interest. After all, shareware revenues do provide a comfortable living for many programmers, even though shareware is a small factor in the entire software industry.)

Chuang and Sirbu (2000) argue that publishers will benefit from a combination of unbundled and bundled sales of scholarly journal articles. Since the majority of scholarly journals are purchased by academic libraries and not by individuals, and this market is both unstable and full of perverse economic incentives not easily captured by standard economic models (see Odlyzko 1997 for a discussion of this subject), we feel that the Chuang and Sirbu analysis is most appropriate for publications aimed at individuals. Further, even in those cases, the consumer preferences discussed in section 2, which are hard to take into account in the conventional economic utility maximization model of Chuang and Sirbu, suggest that the balance will be tilted more toward subscription pricing than toward individual-article sales.

Most of the discussion of the advantages of bundling in Bakos and Brynjolfsson (2000) and Oldyzko (1996), for example, is about one-time sales of several different items, and the arguments are that bundling is likely to be advantageous to the producers in most cases. In this chapter, we consider *à la carte* versus *prix fixe* approaches to sales of many units of the same or a similar good, for example software or entertainment programs. While most of the sales to consumers are on the fixed-price (for software) or subscription (for cable TV, for example) basis, per-use pricing is frequently discussed. The entertainment industry continues to test such schemes. One of the big attractions of Java, downloadable applets, and the network computer for the software industry seems to be the possibility of charging consumers according to their usage of a particular product. There is a widespread feeling that selling shrink-wrapped software allows heavy users to avoid paying a "fair share" of the development cost. Moreover, even some consumers speak up in favor of per-use pricing. There are many people who do not use Microsoft Word often, but, when they do need to use it, have an urgent need to do so, typically to read documents prepared with Word that are sent to them. These people find it worthwhile to buy (or have their employers buy) the latest version of Word for just such use, and would benefit from per-use pricing. (See, for example, the discussion in Picarille 1996.)

While per-use pricing has obvious attractions, its economic arguments that are based on utility theory are not as clear as for bundling, where those arguments strongly support the idea of selling combinations of items. Producers would (in the absence of competitive alternatives) gather more revenue from heavy users, but less from light users. For some distributions of demands, per-use pricing might be more advantageous than fixed-fee plans. However, in section 3, we present some computations that show that if consumers attach well-defined values to information goods, and know how much of each good they are likely to consume, a monopolist can, for many reasonable distributions of values, obtain more revenue from a fixed-fee pricing plan.

While the simple utility maximization argument might favor per-use pricing in a substantial fraction of cases, what we observe in the market are repeated failures of *à la carte* pricing. Many pay-per-view TV schemes have flopped. Furthermore, there has been tremendous pressure from consumers for subscription plans for information services. The flat-rate Internet access plan may not be viable, since there are substantial marginal costs in providing such services, but the strong consumer preference that has forced even America Online to switch to fixed-fee pricing has to be taken into account. In section 2 we discuss some of the extensive evidence for this preference that is available in the literature, and the reasons for it. This preference is not easy to take into account in standard economic models (other than by saying, as Baumol reportedly did, that consumers derive a positive utility from *prix fixe* pricing), but it appears to be a major factor that will favor fixed-fee schemes, at least for individual consumers. (For businesses, the evidence from market behavior is that they are more willing to accept per-use plans than are consumers.) Content producers can take advantage of this preference by charging higher prices than they would if consumers behaved more as utility maximizers. In section 2 we also discuss other arguments, which are again not easy to cast in quantitative economic terms, as to why even producers might favor flat-rate plans.

While producers of information goods typically have monopolies on their products (after all, there is only one *New York Times*, and in general copyright laws provide protection for the producers), these monopolies are seldom perfect. Readers of *The New York Times* can switch to the *Washington Post*, or rely on online access to Associated Press dispatches, say. Competition is always present, even in muted form, and constrains pricing decisions, including the extent of bundling. Unfortunately, it is hard to model competition in information goods. If two producers offer the same good with zero marginal costs for distribution of an additional unit, then each producer can undercut the other, if only by a small margin, and gain revenue and thus profit. Since the other producer has the same incentive, in the absence of collusion, the only possibility is a ruinous price war that drives prices to zero. To have a realistic model, we would need to include product differentiation, customer inertia, network externalities, and product evolution, all at the same time. Since we cannot do that, we study some much simpler models in section 4, in which one producer offers its product on a per-use basis, and the other a competing and nearly equivalent product on a fixed-fee plan. We do not put any bias toward subscription pricing into our model, and assume that consumers know their usage and choose the cheaper of the two options. We find that in most cases, in the absence of collusion, there is destructive price competition. In those cases in which we find a competitive equilibrium, it typically favors the producers charging on a fixed-fee basis. Furthermore, the competitive equilibria we do find yield much less revenue for the content producers than a monopolist could extract.

What conclusions can we draw from our observations? The models in section 4 show that the simple utility maximization argument does not lead to a clear win for per-use pricing, and (as discussed in section 2) consumers are willing to pay a lot to avoid it. It seems likely, therefore, that subscription or fixed-fee approaches are likely to continue to be more successful in selling software or entertainment goods than per-use schemes. We do not exclude the possibility of various sliding-scale plans (with a charge for each use that declines with the quantity used), but strongly suspect that pure *à la carte* pricing schemes will not be successful in the marketplace.

2. Consumer and Producer Preferences in Pricing Plans

There is considerable evidence of consumer preference for subscription over per-use pricing. Much of it is anecdotal, but there are quantitative measures of just how much extra people are willing to pay for fixed-rate plans. Many of the examples come from telephone service experiments. For example, during the 1970s, the Bell System started offering customers a choice between the traditional flat-rate option, which might cost $7.50 per month and allow unlimited local calling, and a measured-rate option, which might cost $5.00 per month, allow for 50 calls at no extra charge, and then cost $0.05 per call. Anyone making fewer than 100 local calls per month would be better off with the measured-rate option. However, in the numerous trials that were carried out, the flat-rate option was usually selected by over 50% of the customers who were making fewer local calls than the 50 covered by the measured-rate basic charge, even though they clearly would have benefited from per-use pricing. These results are documented in Cosgrove and Linhart (1979), Garfinkel and Linhart (1979), and Garfinkel and Linhart (1980). Similar preference for subscription pricing was observed in the choices made by customers signing up for various AT&T long-distance calling plans in the 1980s, when many people paid for plans that provided more calling than they actually used (Mitchell and Vogelsang 1991). More recently, this same observation has been made about a flat-rate calling plan offered by SBC in the Rio Grande area (Palmeri 1996). In the online service area, it has also been common for customers to pay for larger blocks of time than they use.

There are three main reasons that probably lead consumers to prefer flat-rate pricing, and they were recognized a long time ago (Cosgrave and Linhart 1979, Garfinkel and Linhart 1979, Garfinkel and Linhart 1980): (i) Insurance: It provides protection against sudden large bills. (What happens if my son comes back from college and starts talking to his girlfriend around the clock?) (ii) Overestimation of usage: Customers typically overestimate how much they use a service; the ratio of their estimate to actual usage follows a log-normal distribution. (iii) Hassle factor: In a per-use situation, consumers keep worrying as to whether each call is worth the money it costs, and it has been observed that their usage goes down (Garfinkel and Linhart 1980). A flat-rate plan allows them not to worry as to whether that call to their in-laws is really worth $0.05 per minute.

All three factors are part of a general preference on the part of consumers for simple and predictable pricing.

In addition to the consumer preference for flat-rate pricing, there are reasons for producers, especially in areas such as software, where network externalities are important, also to like these plans. Since per-use pricing does suppress usage (Garfinkel and Linhart 1980), it goes counter to the producer's desire that a software package be used as much as possible in order to lock customers into that product. Producers would like consumers to become so used to the particular features and commands of their software that they will find it hard to change to another system. Producers also want their systems to be easy to try out, and to be widely used, to capture additional customers. Subscription pricing and site licensing promote these goals.

In general, subscription plans also make it easier to develop close relations with customers. If access is on a strict per-use basis, there is no reason to obtain information about the users. On the other hand, subscription pricing lends itself to finding out what the consumers need, and to customization of offerings.

3. Optimal Pricing for a Monopolist

In this section, we argue that a flat fee is better than a metered rate for a monopolist selling information goods on the Internet. We give an example to indicate that in the market of information goods, coexisting companies must differentiate themselves more than in a market with distribution costs.

We restrict our price and demand curves to simplify the monopolist's problem of optimizing profit. The restriction on demand curves implies the restriction on price curves—a company serving consumers represented by our demand curves will optimally set a price curve of restricted type. The restrictions on price and demand curves together imply that each consumer finds it optimal to watch only the price of one quantity, rather than the whole price curve. As some examples show, the monopolist may earn more from a flat fee or from a metered rate, depending on the distribution of consumers; we feel that the population distributions for which a flat fee is most profitable are more natural than the other populations. This contrasts with the situation in many real-world markets, in which a high distribution cost makes the metered rate more profitable. Our restrictions about price curves extend nicely to competitive models: A consumer of our restricted type, when faced with multiple companies offering price curves of our restricted type, still shops simply, making its decisions based on the price at only one quantity rather than the whole curve. So some competitive situations are amenable to our simple analysis as well.

We find that the Internet market requires companies to differentiate their products more than do markets with distribution costs. Similar companies can coexist normally if they face a distribution cost, and their price curves are constrained so that they must split the market: It may be that one company offers better deals on bulk service, while the other is optimal for consumers buying small quantities. Without the distribution cost, the companies must enter a ruinous price war.

It simplifies our computations if each consumer chooses the quantity of service to buy (or not to buy) before examining the available prices. The monopolist serving such rigid consumers can set the price of each quantity of service independently. If no consumer who is shopping for small quantities would consider buying bulk, the monopolist can disregard the price of bulk service when setting the price of a small quantity. We want to simplify the monopolist's problem this way. Under what restrictions on price and demand curves is this consumer behavior reasonable? If the consumers have a constant demand for services up to quantity q (and no demand for more), the optimal price is increasing and has decreasing unit price. The conditions of increasing price and decreasing unit price imply that the price curve is continuous. That the price increase and unit price decrease, and the demand be constant and positive, and then zero, is sufficient to ensure that each consumer maximizes utility by buying either nothing or everything for which it has a positive demand.

Our simple structure for consumers' demands allows a two-dimensional parametrization. Each consumer has demand d for up to quantity q of service; the maximum this consumer will pay is $w = qd$. It is convenient to view the consumers in the q,w plane because price curves and willingness-to-pay curves (the integral of the demand curve) are functions from q to w. If the consumers' density in the plane is $\rho(q,w)$, then (independently for each q) the monopolist sets the price $p(q)$ to maximize $p(q)$ times the population willing to pay more than $p(q)$ for quantity q. If at some q the consumers are uniformly distributed over some interval of w-values, the optimal price is half of the maximal w among consumers or the minimal w among consumers, whichever is larger. This reasoning, applied at every q, determines the monopolist's best price when faced with a population that is uniform in the area between two functions from q to w. To ensure that the resulting price function has diminishing unit price, we could assume that the functions bounding the population of consumers have $f' < f/x$. Or let the population as a function of w be independent of q, but scaled by $f(q) : \rho(q,w) = \psi(w / f(q))$. Let p_0 be that p maximizing $p \int_{w>p} \psi(w)$. Then our monopolist's optimal price is $p = p_0 f$.

In the q,w plane, we can see the price function $p(q) = w$ and the distribution of consumers simultaneously: Those with w values below the price function buy no service; those with w values above it buy their preferred amounts. If ρ is uniform on a rectangle containing the origin, the flat fee is optimal and earns 33% more than the metered rate. But there are two other parameter spaces: q,d and d,w, where $d = w/q$ is the consumer's demand. A uniform population on the same rectangle in d,w-space favors the metered rate by 47%. Finally, a rectangle in $q,d = q,w/q$-space is equivalent to a population in q,w-space that is independent of q but for a scaling factor that is a constant multiple of q. By the last sentence of the preceding paragraph, a metered rate is optimal for this population. So for a uniform population on a rectangle containing the origin in either of our alternate parametrizations, the metered rate is better. Why? The population distribution has three parameters: q, w, and d. A uniform rectangle (containing the origin) in two parameters hides a very wide distribution in the third parameter. Apparently, wide distribution in d, with the other two parameters constrained, favors a flat fee. But if the distribution is widest in one of the other two parameters, the metered rate is better. Which, in reality, is most likely to vary widely? For information goods, d may well have the greatest variation, and a uniform distribution would approximate $\rho(q,w)$ better than it approximates $\rho(q,d)$ or $\rho(d,w)$. For noninformation goods, one of the other parameter spaces may be more reasonable. For non-Internet markets, the cost of distribution may also make the metered rate more attractive. Indeed, the cost of distribution may be simply passed on to the consumers, so that the price of various quantities is the profit plus the linear, or metered, distribution cost.

Distribution cost allows companies to coexist that sell similar or even identical services. If they are free to set arbitrary price curves, each can subtly undercut the other, and a price war is inevitable. So we restrict the price curves to be piecewise linear, with some fixed number of pieces. In the presence of a distribution cost, this allows many companies to coexist, each reaping the same profit, so that none of them is tempted to trade another's price curve for its own. But if there is no distribution cost, the companies must fight a price war. No company alone has found it optimal to set a price schedule that would entice a user to buy any quantity other than its entire desired quantity of service or nothing. Each price curve is increasing, with decreasing unit price. So the minimum over any collection of price curves is also increasing, with decreasing unit price. Equivalent to the condition that unit price decreases is the condition that any ray from any point below the origin on the w-axis intersects the price function only once; clearly this property is preserved under taking the minimum of functions with this property. So each user buys its total desired quantity or nothing at all. Given a collection of price functions, each of which is the minimum of them all at some point, we can introduce a distribution cost that is only slightly less than the minimum of the price functions, so that whichever company lowers its prices to pick up some new consumers begins to serve consumers who are a liability to serve. If we alter the population of consumers, we can create very many of these consumers no one wants to serve. Then we can place profit-yielding consumers barely above the minimal price function, and vary their density with respect to q so that the profit to the various companies is equal. So for any collection of price functions, each of which is somewhere the minimum of them all, there exists a population density and a distribution cost making that collection of price functions a competitive equilibrium. Without any distribution cost, however, each company finds it optimal to undercut one of its neighbors by lengthening or lowering one of the pieces of its piecewise linear price curve. So there is no competitive equilibrium.

4. Fixed-Fee versus Pay-per-Use Competition

We use two models with somewhat different emphases to examine analytically competitive pricing between two companies, denoted by A and B. Company A charges a fixed subscription fee per unit, for example $20 per month, whereas B charges on a per-use basis, for example $1 for each use or hit. We denote A's fee by a, and B's per-use cost by b. It is assumed that a and b are fixed within each time period, whose length equals the time unit for A's fixed fee, but the companies can change their fees from period to period. Such changes are announced prior to the beginning of each new period. At that time, every customer decides whether to use A or B or neither in the next period. Thus, over a succession of periods, an individual customer might choose A, then A, then B, then neither, then B, ...

The models presume characteristics for the population of potential consumers that remain unchanged over time. When a and b are announced for the next time period, every customer chooses A or B or neither for that period on the basis of a straightforward minimum cost calculation according to the particular aspects of the model. Given these choices, we denote by $A(a,b)$ the average revenue per consumer paid to A, and by $B(a,b)$ the average revenue per consumer paid to B. Thus, if there are N potential customers for the service, A earns $NA(a,b)$ and B earns $NB(a,b)$ during the period in which a and b are in effect.

We now describe the two models. In both, a and b are treated as continuous variables for analytical convenience. We assume also that other parameters, such as customer usage rate and willingness to pay, are continuous, and that probability functions or probability density functions defined for these parameters are continuous and differentiable.

5. Model 1

Let x denote the expected number of hits per period for a potential customer if the customer actually uses the service provided by A and B. We assume that x has a probability density function μ over the population of potential customers, with $\int_0^\infty \mu(x)dx = 1$. The probability that a customer chosen at random has $x \in [x_1, x_2]$ is $\int_{x_1}^{x_2} \mu(x)dx$, assuming of course that $x_1 \leq x_2$.

An additional probability overlay for single-customer variability will be avoided by assuming that a customer's expected usage x is its actual usage if it subscribes to the service. We refer to x as the *usage rate* of a potential customer. This usage rate remains constant over time for each customer. If a customer with usage rate x subscribes, it pays a during the period if it uses company A, and pays bx if it uses company B. Thus, assuming that customers are cost minimizers, a customer with usage rate x

pays a to A if $a \le bx$, or

pays bx to B if $bx < a$,

given that it uses the service.

Model 1 incorporates a notion of willingness to pay by assuming that there is a probability function P on $t \ge 0$ such that $P(t)$ is the probability that a customer will actually use the service when it will pay t if it does so. Thus, a customer with usage rate x will subscribe to the service with probability

$$P(\min\{a,bx\}),$$

and will not subscribe, and hence will pay nothing to either A or B, with probability $1 - P(\min\{a,bx\})$. We have $0 \le P(t) \le 1$ for all t, and anticipate that P decreases in t, i.e., that the probability of subscribing decreases as the cost of doing so increases. It should be noted that P is defined independently of x. This may be unrealistic in settings where we expect heavy-usage customers to be willing to pay more. We use this feature in our other model.

It follows from our definitions and assumptions for Model 1 that the average revenues per consumer to A and B for a period in which (a,b) applies are

(1) $A(a,b) = aP(a)\int_{x=a/b}^{\infty} \mu(x)dx,$

(2) $B(a,b) = \int_{x=0}^{a/b} bxP(bx)\mu(x)dx.$

Under the assumption that the companies know μ and P, we are interested in their choices of the cost variable under their control—a for A, b for B—when they desire to maximize their own revenues. We return to this after we describe the second model.

6. Model 2

Model 1 is an all-or-nothing model that says a potential customer with usage rate x either does not use the service at all or subscribes and uses it x times during the period. This may be appropriate for situations in which a third party (parent, company) pays for the usage of the consumer (teenager, employee) but does not control that usage, but it neglects situations in which consumers limit usage to less than their usage rates because of a budget constraint or a limit on their willingness to pay more than certain amounts for the service.

Our second model factors in the latter aspect by assuming that each customer has a willingness-to-pay amount or budget constraint w, which is the most it will pay for the service during each period. With x denoting usage rate as in the first model, Model 2 assumes that (w,x) has a joint probability density function $f(w,x)$ over the consuming population, with

$$\int_0^\infty \int_0^\infty f(w,x)dwdx = 1.$$

The probability that a customer chosen at random has $(w,x) \in [w_1,w_2] \times [x_1,x_2]$ is

$$\int_{w=w_1}^{w_2} \int_{x=x_1}^{x_2} f(w,x)dxdw.$$

We assume for Model 2 that every potential customer actually subscribes, or, alternatively, that f applies only to subscribing consumers. Assuming that customers are cost minimizers, a customer with parameter pair (w,x) in a period in which (a,b) applies will

choose A and pay a to A if $a \leq \min\{bx,w\}$, or

choose B and pay to B if $\min\{bx,w\} < a$.

In other words, if either the willingness-to-pay amount w is less than a or the full-usage per-hit-basis cost bx is less than a, then and only then will the customer subscribe to company B. In this case, if $w < bx$, then the customer limits its hits to y such that $by = w$. On the other hand, a customer that has $a \leq \min\{bx,w\}$ and subscribes to A uses its hit rate x but pays only a.

It follows for Model 2 that the average revenues per consumer to A and B for a period in which (a,b) applies are

(3) $A(a,b) = a\int_{w=a}^\infty \int_{x=a/b}^\infty f(w,x)dxdw,$

(4) $\quad B(a,b) = \int_{w=0}^{a} \int_{x=w/b}^{\infty} wf(w,x)dxdw + \int_{x=0}^{a/b} \int_{w=xb}^{\infty} bxf(w,x)dwdx.$

We assume here that both companies know f and wish to maximize their own revenues by choices of the cost variable under their control.

7. Dynamic Behavior, Equilibria, and Price Wars

As indicated above, companies A and B can change their costs to customers periodically. We will assume this occurs for each period, but no generality would be lost if changes were allowed only sporadically, for example every tenth period. Because each company could gain a competitive advantage if it knew the other company's new fee before it set its own, we will assume that new fees are determined and announced simultaneously. In the absence of collusion, this implies that each company must estimate or guess what the other will charge when it sets its new fee. This casts the price-changing behavior as a repetitive noncooperative game in which the pricing strategies used by the companies could have various forms.

One of these, which we refer to as *naive strategies*, is for each company to set its new price to maximize its revenue under the assumption that the other company will not change its price in the coming period. Naive strategies are obviously myopic and can result in revenues very different from those anticipated when the other company does in fact change its fee. More sophisticated strategies arise when the companies anticipate each other's changes. If this is carried to an extreme, the companies can engage in a succession of changes and counterchanges "on paper" before finally arriving at their to-be-announced new fees.

In this chapter, we will not assume explicit forms or methods for new price determination, but will use an analysis of changes and counterchanges to suggest how the companies' fees might evolve over time, or might be affected by sophisticated computation during a single period. Our procedure begins with a fee pair (a_0, b_0) and determines a series of optimal new prices on an alternating basis for the companies under the assumption that the other company retains its "old price" for at least "one more period." Thus, if A goes first, it computes a_1 to maximize $A(a,b_0)$, then B computes b_1 to maximize $B(a_1,b)$, then A computes a_2 to maximize $A(a,b_1)$, B computes b_2 to maximize $B(a_2,b)$, A computes a_3 to maximize $A(a,b_2)$, and so forth. The result is a series

$$a_0, \ b_0, \ a_1, \ b_1, \ a_2, \ b_2, \ ...$$

of potential changes and counterchanges. We denote the series by S, or by $S(a_0,b_0)$ to note explicitly the initial position.

Among other things, we are interested in the behavior of $S(a_0,b_0)$ as n for a_n and b_n gets large. We write $S(a_0,b_0) \rightarrow (a',b')$ if $S(a_0,b_0)$ *converges* to (a',b'), i.e., if for every $\varepsilon > 0$ there is an $n(\varepsilon)$ such that $|a_n - a'| + |b_n - b'| < \varepsilon$ for all $n > n(\varepsilon)$. And when $S(a_0,b_0) \rightarrow (a',b')$ for a unique (a',b') that is the same for every initial position $(a_0,b_0) \geq (0,0)$, we write $S \rightarrow (a',b')$ and say that S *converges uniquely* to (a',b'). Our experience with a variety of specific assumptions about μ and P in Model 1 or f in Model 2 indicates that unique convergence usually occurs, although other behaviors are possible. We defer consideration of the latter until later and focus for the moment on unique convergence.

Two forms of unique convergence are possible, namely

$S \rightarrow (a^*,b^*)$ with $a^*>0$ and $b^*>0$

and

$S \rightarrow (0,0)$.

In the first case, we refer to (a^*,b^*) as a *strong equilibrium point* (S.E.P. for short). It typically occurs when

$A(a^*,b^*) > A(a,b^*)$ for all $a \quad a^*$,

$B(a^*,b^*) > B(a^*,b)$ for all $b \quad b^*$,

and (a^*,b^*) is the only such point with this property. If the initial position is (a^*,b^*), which might be determined by the companies at the start, neither company has an incentive to change its price and we have $S(a^*,b^*) = a^*,b^*,a^*,b^*,....$ If $(a_0,b_0) \quad (a^*,b^*)$, a succession of revenue-maximizing calculations will drive (a_i,b_i) toward (a^*,b^*).

Natural assumptions about μ and P, or about f, imply that we never have $S \rightarrow (a^*,0)$ where $a^* > 0$ or $S \rightarrow (0,b^*)$ where $b^* > 0$. For example, $B(a^*,0) = 0$ by definition, since $b = 0$ means that B offers its service without charge, whereas $B(a^*,b) > 0$ for small positive b. For a similar reason, the second form of unique convergence, $S \rightarrow (0,0)$ never identifies $(0,0)$ as an S.E.P. We refer to $S \rightarrow (0,0)$ as a *price war* because its typical behavior for $S(a_0,b_0)$ with a_0 and b_0 positive has $a_0 > a_1 > a_2 > \ldots (a_n \rightarrow 0)$ and $b_0 > b_1 > b_2 > \ldots (b_n \rightarrow 0)$. In this case, each company lowers its price to increase its market share and, hopefully, its revenues, but the long-run outcome is that $A(a_i,b_i)$ and $B(a_i,b_i)$ are driven toward zero. To avoid such a ruinous result, the companies might revert to pricing schemes that bypass our form of competitive maximization and that could involve covert or overt collusion, perhaps with a revenue-sharing agreement. We will not discuss the legality of such schemes and will focus on noncollusive competitive pricing. However, effects of collusion or "cooperation" will be noted in examples.

We now describe selected results for the two models. Following usual practice, we refer to (a^*,b^*) as an *equilibrium point* if, for all nonnegative (a,b),

(5) $\quad A(a^*,b^*) \quad A(a,b^*) \quad$ and $\quad B(a^*,b^*) \quad B(a^*,b)$.

Assuming differentiability, the first-order conditions for (5) are

$$\frac{\partial A(a,b)}{\partial a}\bigg|_{(a^*,b^*)} = 0 \text{ and } \frac{\partial B(a,b)}{\partial b}\bigg|_{(a^*,b^*)} = 0.$$

The usual second-order conditions for maxima require concavity, i.e.,

$$\frac{\partial^2 A(a,b)}{\partial a^2} < 0 \text{ and } \frac{\partial^2 B(a,b)}{\partial b^2} < 0 \text{ at } (a,b) = (a^*,b^*),$$

but to ensure that (5) holds globally and not just in the vicinity of (a^*,b^*), it may be necessary to look beyond local concavity.

8. Results for Model 1

When $A(a,b)$ and $B(a,b)$ in (1) and (2) are differentiated with respect to a and b, respectively, we obtain the following first-order conditions for an equilibrium point:

$$(6A) \quad \frac{a}{b}P(a)\mu\left(\frac{a}{b}\right) = \left[P(a) + aP'(a)\right]\int_{x=a/b}^{\infty}\mu(x)dx,$$

$$(6B) \quad \left(\frac{a}{b}\right)^2 P(a)\mu\left(\frac{a}{b}\right) = \int_{x=0}^{a/b}\left[P(bx) + bxP'(bx)\right]x\mu(x)dx,$$

where $P'(x) = dP(x)/dx$. If (a^*, b^*) is an equilibrium point, (6A) and (6B) must hold when $(a,b) = (a^*, b^*)$.

It turns out that there is no (a,b) solution to (6A) and (6B) for many specifications of P and μ, and in most of these cases we have observed that $S \rightarrow (0,0)$, i.e., a price war. But there are other situations with equilibrium points, and in some of these cases they are strong equilibrium points. We begin with an example of S.E.P.s.

EXAMPLE 1. Our first example assumes that P is a negative exponential function with $P(x) = e^{-cx}$, $c > 0$, so that $P(0) = 1$. Changes in c allow us to control the effects of the probability $P(x)$ that a customer with usage rate x will actually subscribe to the service. For example, if $x = 10$, we have $P(10) = 0.905$ when $c = 0.01$ and $P(10) = 0.607$ when $c = 0.05$.

We combine P with the negative power function for μ with parameters k and α defined by

$$\mu(x) = \frac{(k-1)\alpha^{k-1}}{(\alpha+x)^k},$$

with $\alpha > 0$ and $k \geq 2$. The special case of $k = 2$ has limited interest because then the expected value of x, defined by

$$E(x) = \int_0^{\infty} x\mu(x)dx,$$

is infinite. For $k > 2$, $E(x) = \alpha/(k-2)$. For example, if $\alpha = 20$ and $k = 2.5$, the average number of hits per customer during one period equals 40.

The first-order conditions (6A) and (6B) for an equilibrium point simplify when we combine the scale parameters c and α with the decision variables and define p and q by

$p = ca, \quad q = \alpha cb.$

Then (6A) and (6B) reduce to

(7A) $\quad q = \dfrac{p(p + k - 2)}{1 - p},$

(7B) $\quad \displaystyle\int_{z=0}^{p} \dfrac{z\big[(k-1)z - q\big]}{(q+z)^{k+1}} e^{-z} dz = 0,$

respectively. It turns out that (7A) and (7B) have a joint positive solution (p^*, q^*) that depends on k when $2 \le k < 3$, and this solution defines an S.E.P. for each such k with $S \to (p^*/c, q^*/(\alpha c))$. However, when $k \ge 3$, there is no such solution and the situation is a price war with $S \to (0,0)$.

The effect of k, for $2 \le k < 3$, on the a^* value at the strong equilibrium point is as follows: As k increases from 2 toward 3, a^* decreases from about $0.3/c$ to 0, indicating a steady decrease in price at equilibrium as we approach the price war status at $k = 3$. At the same time, the revenue ratio at equilibrium favors A slightly but approaches parity as k approaches 3. We note also that both companies' equilibrium revenues approach 0 as $k \to 3$. Specific calculations show that A's revenue at $k = 2.5$ is 42% of its revenue at $k = 2$; at $k = 2.75$, A's revenue is 22% of its revenue at $k = 2$.

EXAMPLE 2. Our second example involves variations on the price war theme and unusual pricing schemes. We assume throughout that μ is a negative exponential with parameter $\gamma > 0$:

$\mu(x) = \gamma e^{-\gamma x}.$

The expected usage rate in this case is $E(x) = 1/\gamma$.

Before we consider particulars, we note a general result for this μ, namely that if $xP(x)$ is increasing and concave up to a maximum point and then decreases, we have $S \to (0,0)$. Many reasonable P functions have the stated properties for $xP(x)$, which suggests that the price war situation may well be the rule rather than the exception for instances of Model 1.

Now suppose that, as in Example 1, $P(x) = e^{-cx}$. Then $xP(x)$ satisfies the preceding conditions that ensure that $S \to (0,0)$. We consider four pricing schemes that avoid a ruinous price war:

1. A chooses a fixed subscription fee and announces that it will not deviate from this fee. We assume that B maximizes its own revenue, given A's announcement. Suppose a is A's fee and $b = g_2(a)$ is B's best response. Then A chooses a to maximize $A(a, g_2(a))$. Computations show that a is approximately $(0.7)/c$ and $g_2(a)$ for $a = (0.7)/c$ is about $\gamma/(2.86c)$. For example, if $c = 0.05$ and $\gamma = 1/10$, then $a = 14$ and $b = 0.7$, or A charges \$14 per month and B charges 70 cents per hit. As anticipated, B gets the lion's share of the business: The revenue ratio at the solution point is $A(a, g_2(a))/B(a, g_2(a)) = 0.325$.

2. B chooses a fixed per-use fee and sticks to it. Then A maximizes its own revenue with best response $a = g_1(b)$ when B chooses b. We assume that B chooses b to maximize $B(g_1(b), b)$. In this case, b is approximately γ/c and $g_1(b)$ is about $(0.5)/c$, so when $c = 0.05$ and $\gamma = 1/10$, A charges \$10 per month and B charges \$2 per hit. The revenue ratio at the solution is $A(g_1(b), b)/B(g_1(b), b) = 2.784$.

The *sum* of the companies' revenues per potential customer is $(0.19)/c$ for case 1 and $(0.25)/c$ for case 2. Greater totals are possible when A and B collude, to the detriment of consumers. We consider two collusion schemes:

3. The two companies agree to set (a, b) so that their revenues are equal, and do this to maximize what each gets. The (a, b) solution is $(1.38/c, \gamma/(.6c))$ with $A(a, b) + B(a, b) = (0.3034)/c$.

4. The companies collude to maximize $A(a, b) + B(a, b)$, which would be the monopolist solution if A and B were the same company. They then agree to split $A + B$ equally. The maximum occurs here when b is effectively ∞ and $a = 1/c = \arg\max xP(x)$. The total revenue, all of which comes from A's fixed fee, is $e^{-1}/c = (0.368)/c$, a 21% increase over the total of case 3, and a 94% increase over the total of case 1. When $c = 0.05$, A charges \$20 per month in case 4.

We conclude our remarks for Model 1 by considering the unrealistic but analytically interesting situation in which $P(x)$ is constant and positive. In this situation, (6A) and (6B) reduce to

$$\mu(t) = \int_{x=t}^{\infty} \mu(x)dx \text{ and } t^2\mu(t) = \int_{x=0}^{t} x\mu(x)dx,$$

where $t = a/b$. When μ is a negative exponential, as in Example 2, $S \rightarrow (0,0)$, and when μ is a negative power function (Example 1) with parameters $\alpha > 0$ and $k = 2$, a succession of price changes and counterchanges drive (a_i, b_i) the other way, toward (∞, ∞). There are cases in which (6A) and (6B) have a unique solution $t^* > 0$, for example when μ is a specific convex combination of a negative exponential and a negative power function with $k = 2$. In such cases, (a,b) is an equilibrium point if and only if $a/b = t^*$, with $A(bt^*, b) = B(bt^*, b)$, so we have a continuum of equilibrium points. If (a_0, b_0) is not an equilibrium point, a revenue-maximizing change by one company but not the other makes (a_1, b_1) an equilibrium point at which neither company can benefit by a further unilateral change. If both companies change naively and simultaneously in every period, we obtain an alternating pattern in which every other period has $(a,b) = (a_0, b_0)$ and the in-between periods have $(a,b) = (b_0 t^*, a_0/t^*)$. Finally, because t^* is fixed and

$$A(a,b) = a\int_{t^*}^{\infty} \mu(x)dx$$

when $a/b = t^*$, both companies have an incentive to collude and make a and b arbitrarily large.

9. Results for Model 2

Differentiation of $A(a,b)$ and $B(a,b)$ in (3) and (4) with respect to a and b, respectively, gives the following first-order conditions for an equilibrium point for Model 2:

$$(8A) \quad \int_{w=a}^{\infty}\int_{x=a/b}^{\infty} f(w,x)dxdw = a\int_{x=a/b}^{\infty} f(a,x)dx + \frac{a}{b}\int_{w=a}^{\infty} f\left(\frac{a}{b}\right)dw,$$

$$(8B) \quad \int_{x=0}^{a/b}\int_{w=bx}^{\infty} xf(w,x)dwdx = \frac{a^2}{b^2}\int_{w=a}^{\infty} f\left(w, \frac{a}{b}\right)dw.$$

We have examined many instances of Model 2 for specific forms of f, both when w and x are bounded above and when they are unbounded, and have found in most cases that (8A) and (8B) have no feasible (a,b) solution. The predominant result is $S \rightarrow (0,0)$, a price war of successive price reductions toward zero.

A main reason for this finding is brought out by considering the separable case in which

$$f(w,x) = g(w)h(x),$$

where g and h are probability density functions for w and x, respectively. Separability has the defect that the expected usage rate, given w, is independent of w, whereas we anticipate an increase in that rate as w increases. In other words, it seems likely that consumers who are willing to pay more for the service will, on average, have greater usage rates. We will, however, assume separability in what follows because it simplifies matters and facilitates illustrations of key points.

Given separability, let H and h' denote the cumulative distribution function and the first derivative of h, respectively. It can then be shown that (8A) and (8B) have no feasible (a,b) solution, and hence admit no equilibrium point, if

$$(9) \quad \left[h(x)\right]^2 + h'(x)\left[1 - H(x)\right] \geq 0$$

for all x in the domain of the usage rate variable. When x is bounded with domain $[0,K]$, it turns out that (9) holds for most h's that seem reasonable, and it takes some imagination to formulate h's that violate (9) over some subdomain of $[0,K]$. Even then there is no assurance that (8A) and (8B) have a solution. In fact, we have failed thus far to construct a specific example with f separable and w and x bounded that has an S.E.P.

Plausible failures of (9) are easier to imagine when x is unbounded. We conclude with one such case that has an S.E.P.

EXAMPLE 3. For scaling convenience, we define a separable f by

$$f(w,x) = \frac{(1.5)^2}{(1+w)^{2.5}(1+x)^{2.5}} \quad \text{for all } x,w \geq 0.$$

Then $E(x) = E(w) = 2$ in the units used for x and w. For example, if each unit of w represents \$10, and each unit of x represents 7 hits, then the average willingness to pay is \$20 and the mean usage rate, prior to reductions caused by budget constraints, is 14 hits per period. The unit interpretations of \$10 for w and 7 hits for x are presumed in what follows.

Our f admits a unique feasible solution for (8A) and (8B) at $(a^*,b^*) = (0.15,0.13)$, and the solution is an S.E.P. In "real" terms, A charges \$1.50 per month and B charges \$1.30 for 7 hits, or about 19 cents per hit, at equilibrium. The average per capita revenues are $A(a^*,b^*) = 0.0385$ and $B(a^*,b^*) = 0.0365$, so A has a slight edge over B.

The preceding revenues translate into 38.5 cents per consumer for A and 36.5 cents per consumer for B. These amounts, which seem low in view of the average willingness to pay of \$20, are a consequence of competition. For example, if B stopped offering the service, leaving A without a competitor, A would change a from 0.15 to 2, or \$20, and realize a tenfold increase in revenue to \$3.85 per consumer on average. In other words, about 19% of the original consumers would pay A the new fee of \$20 per month, and the others would stop using the service altogether.

Acknowledgments

This is a revised version of a paper first published in *First Monday*, 2(7), 1977, http://www.firstmonday.org. An expanded analysis of the mathematical aspects of this paper appears in Fishburn and Odlyzko (1999). We thank Bill Infosino for his comments on an earlier draft of this work.

References

Adams, W. J., and Yellen, J. L. (1976). Commodity bundling and the burden of monopoly. *Quarterly Journal of Economics*, 90: 475–498.

Bakos, Y., and Brynjolfsson, E. (2000). Aggregation and disaggregation of information goods: Implications for bundling, site licensing and micropayment systems. In this volume.

Chuang, J. C.-I., and Sirbu, M. A. (2000). Network delivery of information goods: Optimal pricing of articles and subscriptions. In this volume.

Cosgrove, J. G., and Linhart, P. B. (1979). Customer choices under local measured telephone service. *Public Utilities Fortnightly*, Aug. 30, 27–31.

Dyson, E. (1994). Intellectual value. First published in Dec. 1994 in *Release 1.0*, republished (in an abbreviated form) in *Wired*, July 1995. Available at <http://www.hotwired.com/wired/3.07/features/dyson.html>.

Fishburn, P. C., and Odlyzko, A. M. (1999). Competitive pricing of information goods: Subscription pricing versus pay-per-use. *Economic Theory*, 13: 447–470.

Garfinkel, L., and Linhart, P. B. (1979). The transition to local measured telephone service. *Public Utilities Fortnightly*, Aug. 16, 17–21.

Garfinkel, L., and Linhart, P. B. (1980). The revenue analysis of local measured telephone service. *Public Utilities Fortnightly*, Oct. 9, 15–21.

Mitchell, B. M., and Vogelsang, I. (1991). *Telecommunications Pricing: Theory and Practice*. Cambridge University Press.

Odlyzko, A. M. (1996). The bumpy road of electronic commerce. In H. Maurer (ed.), *WebNet 96—World Conf. Web Soc. Proc.* (AACE), 378–389. Available at <http://www.research.att.com/~amo>.

Odlyzko, A. M. (1997). The economics of electronic journals. In R. Ekman and R. E. Quandt (eds.), *Technology and Scholarly Communication* (University of California Press), 380–393. Preliminary version in *First Monday*, 2 (8), Aug. 1997, and *J. Electronic Publishing*, 4 (1), Sept. 1998. Available at <http://www.research.att.com/~amo>.

Palmeri, C. (1996). Bully Bell. *Forbes*, Apr. 22, 92, 94.

Picarille, L. (1996). Licensing lessons. *Computerworld*, Dec. 9.

Schmalensee, R. (1982). Pricing of product bundles. *J. Business*, 57: S211–S230. Comments on pp. S231–S246.

Varian, H. R. (a). Pricing information goods. Available at <http://www.sims.berkeley.edu/~hal/people/hal/papers.html>.

Varian, H. R. (b). Buying, renting and sharing information goods. Available at <http://www.sims.berkeley.edu/~hal/people/hal/papers.html>.

Wilson, R. (1993). *Nonlinear Pricing*. Oxford University Press.

Versioning Information Goods

Hal R. Varian

1. Introduction

One prominent feature of information goods is that they have large fixed costs of *production* and small variable costs of *reproduction*. Cost-based pricing makes little sense in this context; value-based pricing is much more appropriate. Because different consumers may have radically different values for a particular information good, techniques for differential pricing become very important.

There are many forms of differential pricing; for a survey see Varian (1989). In this chapter, we will focus on a particular aspect of differential pricing known as *quality discrimination* or *versioning*. These terms describe situations in which the producer provides different qualities/versions of a good that sell at different prices.

As we will see below, the point of versioning is to get consumers to sort themselves into different groups according to their willingness to pay (WTP). Consumers with high willingness to pay choose one version, while consumers with lower willingness to pay choose a different version. The producer designs the versions so as to induce the consumers to self-select into appropriate categories.

2. Observable Characteristics

The fundamental problem in any form of differential pricing is to set prices so that purchasers who are able and willing to pay high prices do so. If willingness to pay is correlated with observable characteristics, such as membership in certain social or demographic groups, prices can be keyed to these observable characteristics. Senior-citizen discounts, student discounts, and AAA discounts are examples of this sort of differential pricing.

The basic theory of this *third-degree price discrimination* is well known. Let's examine a very simple case. Suppose that there are two groups, one with high willingness to pay for "quality," the other with low willingness to pay. In this discussion, *quality* simply refers to some characteristic of the good that is desirable to consumers; in the case of information goods, this could be resolution of a digital image, timeliness of financial news, or speed of operation of a software package.

We assume that the producer can perfectly discern the type of the consumer by observing some exogenous characteristic such as zip code, age, or gender.

Figure 1 depicts the demand curves for quality from the two types of consumers. Note that the demand curve in Figure 1A depicts a lower willingness to pay for the good than the demand curve in Figure 1B for each different quality at which the good may be offered.

For simplicity, we will assume that the marginal cost of producing incremental quality is zero. It is easy to modify the analysis for any nonconstant cost of providing quality.

The profit-maximizing policy for this simple problem is immediate. Since the producer, by assumption, can perfectly identify the type of the consumer, it will price the good so as to extract the entire consumer's surplus. But if the producer is able to extract the entire surplus, it will choose the quality so that total surplus is maximized. Using the notation in Figure 1, the firm would set the quality intended for type 1 to be x_1^0 and charge r_1 = area A; the quality intended for type 2 would be x_2^0 and the price would be r_2 = area B.

It is worthwhile noting that this pricing solution is Pareto-efficient in that there is no way to make the consumers better off without making the producer worse off. In this simple case, differential pricing has allowed the producer to capture the entire consumers' surplus.

3. Differential Pricing Infeasible

What happens in our simple example if price discrimination is not feasible? To be explicit, let us suppose that a fraction π of the

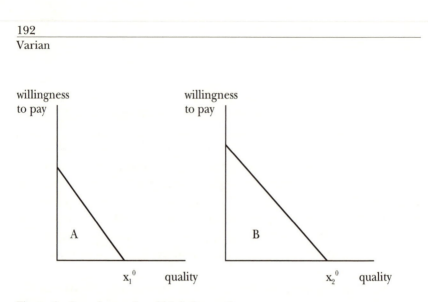

Figure 1 Low-demand and high-demand consumers.

population is the high-WTP type, and a fraction $1 - \pi$ is of the low-WTP type. In this case, the producer can set the price and quality so that only the high-WTP type buys the good or so that both types buy the good.

The profit from the former strategy is πr_2 and the price from the latter strategy is $\pi r_1 + (1 - \pi) r_1 = r_1$. The producer will choose whichever strategy yields greater profit. Note that selling to both types is Pareto-efficient, while restricting the quality to x_1 and selling only to the high-WTP market is Pareto-inefficient—it would be possible to make the low-WTP type better off at zero cost. The seller refuses to do this because selling to that market would reduce the profit it makes from the high-WTP type.

4. Unobservable Characteristics

We continue to investigate the simple example described above in the more interesting case in which the seller knows something about the distribution of willingness to pay in the population, but cannot identify the willingness to pay of a given consumer.[1]

In this case, the seller cannot base its price on an *exogenous* observable characteristic, such as membership in some group, but can base its price on an *endogenous* characteristic, such as the quality of the choice the consumer makes.

The appropriate strategy for the seller in this situation is to choose two qualities and associated prices and offer them to the consumers. Each of the different consumer types will choose one of the two quality/price pairs. The seller wants to choose the qualities and prices of the packages offered so as to maximize profit.

The intention is to get the consumers to self-select into the high- and low-WTP groups by setting price and quality appropriately. That is, the seller wants to choose price/quality packages so that the consumers with high WTP choose the high-price/high-quality package and the consumers with low WTP choose the low-price/ low-quality package.

Figure 2 depicts a possible strategy for this self-selection problem. In this figure, we have superimposed the two demand curves. We start in panel A with the situation examined in the previous section: The seller produces qualities (x_1^0, x_2^0) and sells these at prices $r_1^0 = A$ and $r_2^0 = A + B + C$, respectively. By construction, each consumer gets zero surplus if he chooses the package intended for him.

A careful inspection of Figure 2 shows us that the particular price/quality pairs indicated do not satisfy the self-selection constraints, since the high-WTP consumer can choose the package intended for the low-WTP consumer and achieve a positive surplus. Specifically, if the high-WTP consumer chooses the bundle (r_1^0, x_1^0), he will achieve the surplus represented by area B. The seller's profit would then be $r_1 = A$, just as if price differentiation were infeasible.

In order to prevent this arbitrage, the seller could set a price of $A + C$ for x_2^0. To see that this induces self-selection, note that the high-WTP consumer would be indifferent to purchasing x_1^0 at a price of A, yielding a surplus of B, or purchasing x_2^0 at a price of $A + C$, yielding the same surplus. However, this pricing is definitely more profitable than the original pricing for the seller, since it yields profits of $\pi(A + C) + (1 - \pi)A = A + \pi C > A$.

Using this strategy, the producer is able to capture the incremental surplus to the high-WTP consumer, represented by area C, that is associated with improving the quality from x_1^0 to x_2^0.

However, the story doesn't end here. Although this strategy is feasible, it is not profit-maximizing. It turns out that the seller can

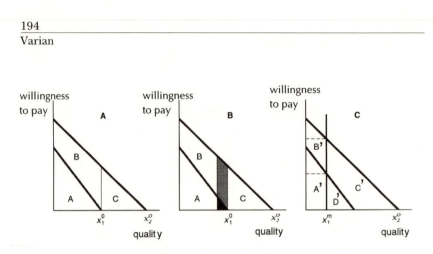

Figure 2 Strategies to induce self-selection.

increase its profit even more by *reducing* the quality available to the low-WTP consumers.

This is illustrated in panel B of Figure 2. By reducing quality offered to the type 1 consumers by a small amount, the seller loses the profit denoted by the small black triangle. However, the quality reduction allows the seller to increase the price charged to the high-WTP consumers by the amount indicated by the trapezoid above the black triangle.

By causing the low-quality bundle to have even lower quality, the seller can charge more for the high-quality bundle. The seller will continue to reduce the quality of the low-quality bundle until the marginal reduction in revenues from the low-WTP consumers just equals the marginal increase in revenues from the high-WTP consumers. This is depicted in Figure 2 for the case of equal numbers of high- and low-WTP consumers ($\pi = 1/2$).

5. Examples of Quality Adjustment

There are many examples of this sort of quality adjustment to support self-selection. Airline pricing is an obvious example. Airlines sell discounted fares that involve various restrictions—advance purchase, Saturday night stayover, and so on. Business travelers choose unrestricted fares, while tourists choose the restricted fares. Even though the cost of carrying a business traveler is essentially the same as that of carrying a tourist, unrestricted fares can sell for three to five times as much as restricted fares.

In this case, reducing the "quality"' of the good by imposing additional restrictions allows the producer to segment the market and induce self-selection so that prices can be based on willingness to pay.

Quality adjustment in transportation in order to induce self-selection is a very old strategy. Consider, for example, this commentary on railroad pricing by Emile Dupuit, a nineteenth-century French economist.

> It is not because of the few thousand francs which would have to be spent to put a roof over the third-class carriage or to upholster the third-class seats that some company or other has open carriages with wooden benches. . . . What the company is trying to do is prevent the passengers who can pay the second-class fare from traveling third class; it hits the poor, not because it wants to hurt them, but to frighten the rich. . . . And it is again for the same reason that the companies, having proved almost cruel to the third-class passengers and mean to the second-class ones, become lavish in dealing with first-class customers. Having refused the poor what is necessary, they give the rich what is superfluous. (Ekelund 1970)

Deneckere and McAfee (1996) contains several other examples of this sort. We describe two: a hardware example and a service example.

• *IBM LaserPrinter series E.* This printer was identical to the standard LaserPrinter, but printed at 5 pages per minute rather than 10. The reason was the presence of a chip that induced wait states.

• *Federal Express.* Federal Express offers to deliver your package the next day, or the next day before 10 a.m. The firm will typically make two deliveries rather than deliver standard packages before 10 a.m..

If we look at (physical) information goods, we can find several more examples:

• *Books.* Popular books are sold first in hardcover; several months later they are reissued in paperback. The cost of paperback binding is only slightly less than that of hardcover binding.

• *Movies.* Movies are issued first for the big screen; several months later, they are reissued on videotape.

Other sellers of information goods and services are just beginning to implement this strategy. Here are some examples:

• PAWWS Financial Network[2] charges $8.95 per month for a portfolio accounting system that measures stock values using quotes that are delayed by 20 minutes. Real-time quotes are available for $50 per month.

• PhotoDisc[3] sells royalty-free stock photographs on the Web. Professional users want high-resolution images that can be printed in commercial journals; nonprofessionals want medium- or low-resolution images for newsletters. PhotoDisc sells different-sized images for different prices; at the time this chapter was written, the firm sold 600K images (72 dots per inch resolution) for $19.95 and 10MB images (300 dots per inch) for $49.95.

• Wolfram Research, Inc.[4] sells Mathematica, a computer program that does symbolic, graphical, and numerical mathematics. At one time, the student version of Mathematica had a disabled floating-point coprocessor so that mathematical and graphical calculations were much slower. The student version sold for a bit over $100; the professional version sold for over $500.

• Windows NT Workstation 4.0 sells for about $260. It can be configured as a Web server, but accepts only 10 simultaneous connections. Windows NT Workstation Server can accept hundreds of simultaneous connections, and sells for $730–$1080, depending on the configuration. According to an analysis by O'Reilly Software,[5] the two operating systems are essentially the same.

6. Welfare Implications of Versioning

Deliberate reduction of quality seems perverse to most casual observers. However, the social-welfare impact of quality discrimination can be judged only relative to its alternatives. In particular, if differential pricing were not allowed, the low end of the market might not be served at all.

Table 1 depicts the total surplus in four different pricing regimes: perfect price discrimination, a flat price at which only the high-WTP consumer purchases, a flat price at which both types of consumer purchase, and the optimal versioning solution.

Table 1 Surplus Comparisons

	Perfect PD	High WTP	Both	Versioning
P_L	A	A + B + C	A	A'
P_H	A + B + C	A + B + C	A	A' + C' + D'
$Surplus_L$	0	0	0	0
$Surplus_H$	0	0	B	B'
Producer surplus	A + π[B + C]	π[A + B + C]	A	A'+π[C' + D']
Total surplus	A + π[B + C]	π[A + B + C]	A + πB	A' +π[B' + C' + D']

Note that the low-WTP consumer always ends up with zero surplus in this model, and so can safely be ignored in the welfare calculations.

We are interested in the welfare effect of versioning. There are three natural benchmarks: perfect price discrimination and the two flat-price regimes. The total surplus calculations are

perfect PD – versioning = $(1 - \pi)D'$ = value of lost quality

versioning – sell to high-WTP only = $(1 - \pi)A'$
= value to low-WTP consumers of incremental consumption

versioning – sell to both = $\pi C - (1 - \pi)D'$
= (incremental consumption of high-WTP consumers) – (reduced quality to low-WTP consumers).

Note that social surplus is always increased by versioning if only the high-WTP consumers would be served under flat pricing. If both classes of consumers would be served under flat pricing, the welfare effect is ambiguous. However, the following observation gives us a clear condition under which welfare will be reduced by versioning.

Fact: *If it is profitable to serve both classes of consumers under flat pricing and*

$\pi B - (1 - \pi)A' > 0,$

welfare will be reduced by versioning.

Proof: If it is profitable to serve both classes of consumers under flat pricing,

$A > \pi[A + B + C]$,

which we can rewrite as

$(1 - \pi)A - \pi B - \pi C > 0$.

Adding the inequality in the hypothesis gives us

$(1 - \pi)[A - A'] - \pi C > 0$.

Substituting $D' = A - A'$ gives us

$\pi C - (1 - \pi)D' < 0$.

The result now follows from the last surplus calculation.

Deneckere and McAfee (1996) analyze the welfare effects of "damaged goods" in a model with exogenous quality. They show that when there are two distinct markets (e.g., tourist travelers and business travelers) and only the high-WTP market would be served in the absence of price discrimination, versioning can easily result in a Pareto improvement: Both classes of customers and the producer will be made better off. When there are many classes of customers with different product valuations, versioning may still result in a Pareto improvement, but the conditions required are much more stringent.

7. Policy

What should antitrust policy be toward differential pricing of this sort? I have examined the welfare effects of differential pricing elsewhere (Varian 1985, 1996), so I will limit myself to a simple summary.

The critical issue turns out to be whether differential pricing increases or decreases total output and/or quality. If the total output in a market decreases under differential pricing, welfare (consumer plus producer surplus) definitely decreases. If total output in a market goes up, differential pricing increases welfare.

Translated into the context of the examples given earlier, the question is whether versioning allows new markets to be served that would not be served in the absence of this pricing strategy. If the answer is "yes," it is likely that versioning increases welfare; if the answer is "no," versioning reduces aggregate welfare.

Unfortunately, existing antitrust law does not seem to show a very clear understanding of these issues. As Huber (1993) puts it:

Almost every marketplace scheme in the information industry today could be construed as illegal under our antiquated antitrust laws. Information just doesn't obey the ordinary laws of economics, so the people who sell it can't obey ordinary antitrust laws. Judges had better get used to that. What we're talking about here is the future of our entire economy.

8. Goldilocks Pricing

We have seen that the number of versions of a product that are offered should be equal to the number of types of consumers in the market. If there are business travelers and tourist travelers in the market, it makes sense to have two broad "versions" of airline tickets.

But what happens if there is no obvious market segmentation? What if the number of "types" is huge? Are there any useful rules of thumb?

A common choice is to have two versions: a "standard" and an "enhanced" version. However, some recent work in marketing suggests that the optimal number of versions in this case is not two but three.[6]

The reason is what psychologists call *extremeness aversion:* If the only two sizes of drinks that you offer are "small" and "large," some consumers will be on the margin between choosing one extreme and the other. Some of these consumers will choose the small version, thereby reducing producer revenues. But suppose the producer adds a jumbo version, and renames the sizes "small," "medium," and "large," making the current "medium" the same size as the previous "large" version. In this case, the "medium" size serves as a focal point for the indecisive: Those who would have chosen "small" end up compromising on "medium," thereby increasing revenues.

Simonson and Tversky (1992) describe a marketing experiment in which two groups of consumers were asked to choose microwave ovens. One group was offered a choice between two ovens, an Emerson priced at $109.99 and a Panasonic priced at $179.99. The second group was offered these ovens plus a high-end Panasonic priced at $199.99. By offering the high-end oven, Panasonic increased its market share from 43% to 73%. More remarkably, the sales of the midpriced Panasonic oven increased from 43% to 60%, apparently because it was now the "compromise" choice. According to Smith and Nagle (1995),

Adding a premium product to the product line may not necessarily result in overwhelming sales of the premium product itself. It does, however, enhance buyers' perceptions of lower-priced products in the product line and influences low-end buyers to trade up to higher-priced models.

If this psychology applies to information goods as well as to physical goods, the producer may be better off providing standard, professional, and "gold" versions than it would be if it just provided standard and professional versions, even if very few consumers choose the "gold" version.

9. Practical Implications

What are the practical implications of this analysis for the producer of information goods?

The first point is the most fundamental: *Make sure that you design the product so that it can be versioned.* That is, the product should be designed in such a way that it is easy to reduce its quality in order to sell it to a particular market segment. In addition to being sound software engineering, modularization can be very useful from the viewpoint of marketing, since it makes it easy to remove features.

The second point is that the right way to to design the product will generally be to *design for the high end of the market first, and then downgrade the product to get the versions for the other segments of the market.* Recall that our analysis implied that the product for the high-demand consumer was chosen so that the marginal willingness to pay for additional quality equals the marginal cost of producing additional quality (which was zero in our example).

If we think of quality as being "additional features," an admittedly dangerous equivalence, this means that the producer should add features until the willingness to pay for an additional feature on the part of the high end of the market just equals the cost of providing that feature. Once the high end has been determined, the producer then removes features to sell to the lower segment of the market, recognizing that each feature it removes allows it to increase the price at which the item is sold to the high-WTP consumers.

The third point applies to information goods that need to be "viewed" using a specific piece of hardware or software. For example, think of a browser used to view online newspaper articles. If the owner of the content controls the browser, it can choose the features of the browser to enhance the quality of consuming the content. For example, if the consumer is viewing page 7 of the article, it is likely that page 8 will be the next piece of content he looks at, so the browser could download page 8 in the background. Controlling the browser allows the seller of content to increase the quality of what it is selling.

But as we have seen, it is also advantageous to reduce the quality of a good in order to segment the market. Hence controlling the browser—or, more generally, the conditions under which the information good is consumed—can be very advantageous to the content owner, since it makes versioning easier. This may well be one of the factors that makes the use of Java-based viewers attractive.

Finally, the discussion of "Goldilocks pricing" suggests that in the absence of any additional information, having three versions rather than two may be attractive due to extremeness aversion on the part of consumers.

Acknowledgments

Research support from NSF grant SBR-9320481 is gratefully acknowledged. Thanks to Dietmar Detering, Fu-Chan Lai, and Char-Ming Yu for comments on an earlier version.

Notes

1. The basic insights in this section were first spelled out by Maskin and Riley (1984). The geometric approach used here seems to have been first used by Varian (1992).

2. http://pawws.com.

3. http://www.photodisc.com.

4. http://www.wri.com.

5. http://software.ora.com/news/ms_internet_andrews.html.

6. See Simonson and Tversky (1992) and Smith and Nagle (1995).

References

Deneckere, Raymond J., and R. Preston McAfee, 1996. Damaged goods. *Journal of Economics and Management Strategy,* 5(2):149–174.

Ekelund, R. B., 1970. Price discrimination and product differentiation in economic theory: An early analysis. *Quarterly Journal of Economics,* 84:268–278.

Huber, Peter, 1993. Two cheers for price discrimination. *Forbes,* September 27, p. 142. Available at http://khht.com/huber/forbes/092793.html.

Maskin, Eric, and John Riley, 1984. Monopoly with incomplete information. *Rand Journal of Economics,* 15:171–196.

Simonson, Itamar, and Amos Tversky, 1992. Choice in context: Tradeoff contrast and extremeness aversion. *Journal of Marketing Research,* 29:281–295.

Smith, Gerald E., and Thomas T. Nagle, 1995. Frames of reference and buyers' perception of price and value. *California Management Review,* 38(1):98–116.

Varian, Hal R., 1985. Price discrimination and social welfare. *American Economic Review,* 75:870–875.

Varian, Hal R., 1989. Price discrimination. In Richard Schmalensee and Robert Willig, eds., *Handbook of Industrial Organization* (Amsterdam: North-Holland).

Varian, Hal R., 1992. *Microeconomic Analysis.* New York: W. W. Norton.

Varian, Hal R., 1996. Differential pricing and efficiency. *First Monday,* 1(2). Available at http://www.firstmonday.dk.

Economics and Electronic Access to Scholarly Information

Jeffrey K. MacKie-Mason and Juan F. Riveros

1. Introduction

Dramatic increases in the capabilities of computers and communication networks, accompanied by equally dramatic decreases in cost, have fomented revolutionary thoughts (if not a revolution itself) in the scholarly publishing community. Much attention is focused on upstart electronic-only journals, and on whether they will successfully displace or competitively discipline the journals managed by traditional professional publishers. Meanwhile, the traditional publishers are developing and testing schemes for electronic access to their body of literature. This chapter concerns a controlled field experiment to investigate the effects of product bundling and pricing structures for electronic access to scholarly literature.

We and our colleagues at the University of Michigan are implementing the field experiment. The host service team is receiving and preparing digital content. The marketing team is recruiting trial participants. We are finalizing the details of the bundling and pricing schemes; the technical structures necessary to provide authorization and authentication, accounting, and other services are being developed. The experimental treatment and data collection had not begun at the time of this writing. The project's current status can be found at http://www.lib.umich.edu/libhome/peak.

Our primary research objective for the field trial is to generate rich empirical evidence on user behavior when faced with various bundling and pricing schemes. This field trial will complement the recent theoretical research of Bakos and Brynjolfsson (2000) and Chuang and Sirbu (2000). However, authors in the bundling literature, including these recent chapters, have restricted their models to rather simplified bundling structures. Although we are severely limiting the design of our trial in order to obtain good data and testable hypotheses, for both practical and intellectual reasons our experimental design calls for bundling structures that have not yet been explored theoretically. We are also working to extend the theoretical work to our more realistic and general structures.

In this chapter, we first provide background on the market economics of the publishing business, and describe some important economic problems facing both research libraries and scholarly journal publishers. We then explain how the opportunity provided by electronic access to use innovative bundling and pricing structures offers some hope of easing the library and publisher problems. New bundling and pricing schemes can uncover new value from both old and new scholarly content. In the next section, we describe our utility-theoretic framework for analyzing the consumer response to the trial conditions, and then briefly survey some related literature on bundling and nonlinear pricing. In the final section, we describe the main features of the experiment, and the rationale behind the design.

2. Economics and Electronic Publishing

2.1 Publishing Economics

Publishing is a value-adding business. This point has been underemphasized by some recent authors. Utopians have suggested that if technology is put in the hands of authors, for-profit publishers can and inevitably will be bypassed.[1] Electronic scholarly journals will arise that are edited, produced, marketed, and distributed by scholars working in the service of scholarship, rather than by professional publishers in the service of profit (e.g., Harnad 1996, Odlyzko 1995).

This striking view conflates two issues: whether or not publishing as a business adds value to authorship, and the industrial organization of the business of publishing. Of course, the way in which value is added, and the structure of costs underlying that value, may determine the efficient and sustainable organization of the industry. Nonetheless, sources of value and industrial organization must be examined separately when technology, costs, and service offerings are drastically changing.

Publishing adds significant value to authoring. The digital revolution is changing sources and amounts of value added, but not eliminating it. The costs of some functions are decreasing rapidly, but other costs are not. Meanwhile, as new information services are developed, there will also be new opportunities for publishers to add value.

Publishers provide many services to authors and readers. For example, they perform copyediting, proofing, typesetting and layout, printing, and binding. The publisher chooses and controls the quality of the medium (paper stock, SGML tagging, etc.) and the production of offprints and supplemental bundles (e.g., CD-ROMs). The publisher also handles fulfillment: billing, accounting, and distribution. Even electronic journals require distribution skill: server administration, backup maintenance, network management, and so on. And even electronic journals have costs that must be covered through some mechanism: Publishers specialize in cost management and recovery.[2]

Perhaps most important, the publisher brings readers to the author: the marketing function. It is quite evident that scholarly journal authors are not writing for direct cash compensation, but to obtain readership (from which indirect compensation may follow). Good scholars are good at research, not at finding readers.[3]

There are at least two implications of the considerable value publishing adds to authorship:

• There is likely a role for an independent publishing industry.

• Competition should ensure efficient provision of publishing services, with only normal (not monopolistic) profits over time.

We expect to see independent publishing because there is enough value added separate from authorship itself that specialization will continue to be efficient: Authors aren't the most fit to provide publishing services. If transaction costs between authors and publishers were high, we might expect integration into single organizations, but there is no obvious reason to think such transaction costs are important. There are some clear economies of scale that publishers can achieve, however (such as in the employment of typesetters, copyeditors, and printers), which are an advantage for large multijournal publishers.

However, we believe that our first claim is not as important (nor as compelling) as our second: Whatever organizational form the industry takes, competition should lead to efficient provision of publishing services. Those providing publishing services should not be able to earn above-normal profits over time.[4] The argument here is quite fundamental and is well understood in the economics of industry: There are low entry barriers and few proprietary advantages to participation in publishing. When entry barriers are low, above-normal profits will attract entry, and entry will continue until the ensuing competition is sufficient to drive returns down to a normal rate.

One type of entry barrier is proprietary control over distinctive intellectual property. It might seem that control over intellectual property is a prevalent characteristic of scholarly publishing: Authors' work, over which the publisher usually has copyright, is unique and valuable. Clearly different research articles are valued differently, or we wouldn't see such wide variation in prices and reputations among journals within similar fields and with similar production quality. However, the key to understanding the steady-state performance of the publishing industry is to recognize that publishers don't *initially* control content; authors do. Publishers who are currently more successful at bringing readers to authors may have an advantage in bargaining for the best new content, but they do not have control. If the publisher charges too much to readers, or degrades production quality, another publisher can easily step up and offer authors a journal that will be more accessible or more appealing to readers.

Of course, reputations rarely depreciate overnight. Thus, a publisher who produces a journal that is considered the best in its field is likely to maintain its subscription base and readership for at least some time. However, academic editorships turn over relatively frequently, and publishers have to compete to attract new editors, who will pay attention to the quality and pricing of a journal. Likewise, libraries and other subscribers do not mindlessly subscribe to every journal. Indeed, there are very few journals, even among the very best, to which *every* potential subscriber subscribes. There are always marginal purchasers who are willing to forgo a subscription if the price is a bit too high or the production quality a bit too low.

The point is simple: Publishers bring little that is unique or proprietary to the table that cannot be well imitated by others. A publisher that is lazy (quality degrades) or fat (profits are abnormally high for a sustained period) will find effective, lean, and hungry competitors luring away its academic editors, its pool of talented authors, and its readership.

The natural competitiveness of the market for publisher services is quite important. First, it is a well-known result in economics that if the market participants behave competitively, the outcome will maximize *consumer plus producer surplus*.[5] Surplus is the difference between value received and price paid. The consumers in the market for publishing services are both readers and authors; the producers are the providers of publishing services. However, competition also ensures that the producers will not receive *excess profits*. That is, producers will generally receive only enough to cover their costs (including a competitive rate of return on invested capital). The rest of the maximized surplus will be enjoyed by readers and authors. A competitive market also has the property that it is Pareto-efficient, which means that no alternative allocation of goods and services can make at least one agent better off without making at least one agent worse off.

In more colloquial terms, the performance of a competitive market in publishing services is quite attractive: Readers get the best combination of quality, price, and quantity possible given the technology and costs of production, and authors get the best readership possible. When new sources of value arise (such as searching over a digital document database), much of the value ultimately accrues to consumers. Of course, at any given moment, a market may not be performing optimally, but in the absence of structural problems (e.g., barriers to entry and externalities), we have much evidence that competitive markets perform very well on average, over time. Many readers will no doubt wonder whether this optimistic view is justified, given apparent problems for readers and authors in the scholarly publishing business. We now discuss some of these problems.

2.2 Electronic Access and Research Libraries

Research libraries have recently faced a number of difficulties. They are often located in institutions of higher education, which have experienced severe budget pressures. In many cases, centrally provided infrastructure services, such as those provided by libraries, have borne more than their share of budget reductions. Concurrent with budget reductions, libraries have faced rapid increases in subscription prices: Some publishers have recently increased prices more than 10% in a year, even after adjusting for inflation. The increasing demand for new services based on digital and network technology have perhaps been making matters worse (although they have also created excitement for information professionals), as they call on already overtaxed human and financial resources.

Given this rather dismal set of problems, we should consider what opportunities might be provided by electronic access to scholarly materials. The first effect that many have hoped for is a reduction in service cost. Unfortunately, although many costs are lower when distribution is electronic, these costs tend to represent only a modest fraction of the total costs of publishing. In any case, even if there are significant cost savings to be made, the question is not very well posed. Electronic access changes both the profile of available services and their quality (which increases in some cases, but decreases in others). Any attempt to compare the costs of paper and electronic publishing must carefully account for these differences in quality and in the services provided: a classic "apples and oranges" problem.

2.3 Electronic Access and Publishers

The fundamental problem facing publishers is clear: high first-copy costs. Odlyzko (1995) reports that it costs $900–$8700 to publish a single math article, with a median of $4000. Of this, 70% is editorial and production first-copy cost, that is, the cost before reproduction and distribution. Thus, most of the the cost to be recovered by a going concern is fixed.

Pricing at marginal cost will not recover first-copy costs. Competition in publishing, however, creates pressure to price at marginal cost. When most publishers are printing on paper, and thus have similar cost structures, an uneasy equilibrium with prices above marginal cost appears to be stable, possibly supported by significant lags in the movement of editors and journal content between publishers in response to competitive pricing changes. However, the advent of electronic publishing brings a medium with potentially lower first-copy costs. In the U.S. telecom industry, local access firms face a similar situation when "bypass" operators that need not pay the fixed costs of universal service can offer large customers lower rates for connection to long distance networks. Likewise, in publishing there is an increasing threat from "bypass publishing."[6] Increased electronic competition pressures print-on-paper publishers to find new ways to recover first-copy costs without loading them all onto per-copy (or per-subscription) pricing.

In part, print-on-paper publishers respond to electronic competition by themselves seeking to develop electronic delivery media. They are also investing to develop various new value-added services based on the investment in first-copy scholarly literature creation, in order to share the recovery of fixed costs across more activities. However, these incremental activities involve development expenditures, and also increase the publisher's risk, since the new products are often untested and of uncertain value.

2.4 Opportunities with Electronic Access: Bundling and Nonlinear Pricing

Although libraries and publishers both face significant problems, some of them the results of developments in electronic access, such access also creates opportunities for dealing with those problems. Electronic access enables both publishers and libraries to engage in new product-bundling and nonlinear-pricing schemes. The first will often involve unbundling of traditional journal components, and then rebundling them in a greater variety of packages, some of them customized for customers or customizable by them. Nonlinear pricing is facilitated by lower transaction costs for fine-grained purchases and by feasible direct usage monitoring by the publisher or library.

New bundling and pricing schemes are enabling technologies: They liberate previously unrealized sources of value from existing content and from new value-added services. For example, bundling can do a better job of extracting revenue from users who value the same content differently. Nonlinear pricing can sort users by their preferences for new services, and extract more of their differing values. Publishers earn returns on their innovations that can offset fixed publishing costs and, by spreading those fixed costs over more streams of revenue, can recover them with less quantity distortion and less vulnerability to competition. In a competitive publishing environment, consumers get to keep most or all of the newly liberated surplus (excess of value over cost).

An example of finding new value in old content would be differential charges to various user types for access to traditional content. Differential charging might be hard to implement for print-on-paper publication, because there is little opportunity to observe actual differences in usage. With electronic access, however, it can be possible to distinguish between, say, retrieval of abstracts or bibliographic records versus retrieval of full text. Since users typically value different uses of content differently, a system of differential charges to recover cost of service can extract more value from a heterogeneous set of uses. There are a variety of different schemes that fall under the general rubrics of *price discrimination* and *nonlinear pricing*. In the economics literature, the general result is that when it is possible to distinguish between different user or usage types, and when resale between parties or uses (arbitrage) is costly or preventable, nonlinear pricing extracts more value than does uniform pricing.

The simplest example of nonlinear pricing is *perfect price discrimination*. Imagine that it is possible for the service provider to perfectly observe exactly how much every different transaction is worth to every user, and to charge accordingly. Obviously, the service provider is then able to extract the maximum possible revenue to recover costs and support new services. In general, such perfect differentiation is not possible. The key to differential pricing is to find observable characteristics (of users, or of their uses of content) that are *correlated* with their willingness to pay, and then to base charges on the value information that is partially revealed. Electronic access provides an opportunity to observe a variety of such characteristics, such as user type (education, business, subscriber or occasional user, determined from authentication records), use type (immediacy of access to current information, volume, full documents or components), and quality (display resolution; text-only or images; plain or formatted text).

The second type of opportunity is to extract value from *new service provision*. The literature is full of new services that may be enabled by electronic access. We will summarize a few here just to illustrate the opportunities:

• *Hyperlinks.* It is possible to prepare documents with embedded hypertext links to referenced material. The electronic version of this article is a simple example: References within the document can be followed quickly—for example, from the table of contents to section text. When more documents are available in electronic archives, it will be possible to embed links to more external references as well, as we have done where possible. For example, some research working papers archived by the Economics Working Papers Archive project include embedded references to other papers stored in the archive, making it possible to simply click on a reference and retrieve a copy.

• *Dynamic Commentary.* Many authors have puzzled about the interaction between electronic publishing and peer review. The main conflict observed is that the peer review process in most disciplines is quite lengthy, and defeats some of the publication timeliness that can be gained by electronic publication and distribution. One novel idea theme that has emerged is that the peer review process may be replaced in part by dynamic, public commentary and response (Harnad 1990, 1996). Readers could post comments and critiques directly to the archive where an article is stored; authors could reply. In response to some comments, revised versions of a paper might be posted. Therefore, the review process might be more open, inclusive, timely, and dynamic (see, e.g., *Psycoloquy*).

- *Social Filtering.* One of the obvious impacts of widespread communication networks is that the geography of community can change. One opportunity provided by virtual communities is the application of networks of like-minded people to the problem of information filtering. Every scholar faces the problem of selecting which articles to read from the vast flow of new material.[7] Social filtering systems collect the ratings of networked users and then, based on some form of cluster analysis, dynamically match one user's preferences to the preferences of others to prepare recommendations. For example, Professor X is matched to 10 other professors who have given similar ratings on articles most of them have read; the system then recommends to Professor X a previously unread article that the match group has liked. Such a system might, for example, supplement asking only one's local colleagues for advice. Firefly™ is a working example of a social filtering system (providing recommendations on audio recordings and films).

3. Bundling and Nonlinear Pricing

3.1 Demand Model

In this project, we will implement an experiment on electronic-access product bundles and nonlinear prices. We wish to learn something about the extra value that can be extracted from existing content. To estimate the responsiveness of consumer demand to new bundling and pricing schemes, we specify a general utility-theoretic model of article demand. This model will form the basis for our econometric estimates once the experimental data are collected. We also review some of the bundling and nonlinear pricing literatures as they relate to the questions raised by the experiment, and describe gaps in the theoretical literature that we hope to fill.

We expect the share of income spent on journal articles to be a small fraction of total income. Further, price and quantity data for demand for other goods will probably not be available. Therefore, we will adopt two-stage budgeting: The consumer first allocates expenditure across broad budget categories (e.g., journal expenditure), then determines budget shares for the commodities within each group.

Economics and Electronic Access to Scholarly Information

Two-stage budgeting requires the first-stage utility function to be weakly separable:

(1) $u(y,x) = U(T_y(y),\ T_x(x,t))$,

where x is the vector of journal articles demanded, y is the vector of demand on other goods, t is a vector of types, and U is an increasing function of T_y and T_x. With two commodity groups, weak separability imposes hardly any restrictions, other than requiring that article demand and "other expenditure" be substitutes (MacKie-Mason and Lawson 1993).

Gorman (1959) derives the conditions under which is possible to solve the first-stage problem without knowledge of all the individual prices. One sufficient condition for top-level budgeting with composite commodities and group price indices is homotheticity of the group subutility functions. This implies that every commodity within a group must have the same income elasticity. Unfortunately, this contradicts all known household-budget studies (Deaton and Muellbauer 1980).

A less restrictive solution to the problem is that the group indirect utility functions take the Generalized Gorman Polar Form (GGPF):

(2) $V_g(M_g,\ P_g) = F_g[M_g/B_g(P_g)] + A_g(P_g)$

for some monotone increasing function $F_g(\ )$, combined with an additively separable top-level utility function:

(3) $U = T_1(Q_1) + T_2(Q_2) + \ldots + T_n(Q_n)$

with $g = 1, \ldots, G$ indexing groups.

Under this formulation, the top-level utility function for journal articles and other goods has the following form:

(4) $U = T_y(y) + T_x(x,t)$.

The GGPF does not impose strong restrictions on the shape of preferences within commodity groups and provides necessary and sufficient conditions for broad group allocation within the framework of weak separability. This is the most general formulation possible for the analysis of the experimental data in this project.

3.2 Product Bundling

As discussed below, we have selected three different bundle types as the products for the experiment. In this section, we review the bundling literature as it applies to each of these products.

Most of the literature on bundling has focused on the case of two goods. Recent research in the area has extended some of the results to more general cases and provided a theoretical framework in which to analyze the bundling of information goods.

The literature on bundling has concentrated on the demand-side incentives that make it a profitable strategy. Examples of these incentives include negative correlations in consumer valuations, complementarity in consumption, and uncertainty in the valuations of the quality of the goods (Hanson and Martin 1990). On the production side, various cost efficiencies may also provide a basis for bundling.

Most of the bundling literature has focused on the two-good case. Stigler (1963) studies commodity bundling strategy for movie distribution. A distributor could increase profits by bundling movies in packages when reservation prices for individual movies are negatively correlated. Adams and Yellen (1976) determine when it is profitable for a firm to bundle and when it is not. Using a graphical tool, they generalize Stigler's example for two goods. They identify three strategies: pure bundling, in which goods are sold only in package form; mixed bundling, in which the goods are sold separately as well as in packages; and pure unbundling, or component selling. They compare these different strategies using examples with a discrete number of customers. When the reservation values for the elements of the bundle are negatively correlated, bundling can serve the purpose of sorting customers into groups with different characteristics. This allows the firm to extract additional consumer surplus.

Schmalensee (1982) studies whether a monopolist can profitably bundle its good with a good provided by a perfectly competitive market. Schmalensee (1984), assuming a bivariate normal distribution for individual demands, shows that bundling can be also profitable when demands are uncorrelated or even positively, but not perfectly, correlated. When goods are added, the variance of the consumer's valuation for the bundle is reduced, allowing the seller to extract more surplus.

McAfee, McMillan, and Whinston (1989) show that mixed bundling is always (weakly) better than pure bundling. A more interesting question posed in their study is whether mixed bundling dominates component selling. They consider two cases: The monopolist can and cannot monitor purchases. When purchases can be monitored, the monopolist can charge more for the bundle than the sum of the component prices. Without monitoring, the bundle price is constrained to be no more than the sum of the component prices. McAfee et al. show that mixed bundling almost always dominates pure unbundling when the seller can monitor. They also derive conditions under which mixed bundling dominates pure unbundling when monitoring is not possible.

Salinger (1995) analyzes the profitability and welfare consequences of bundling. When bundling does not lower cost, it tends to be profitable when reservation prices are negatively correlated and high relative to marginal costs. However, when bundling lowers cost, the incentive to bundle increases when reservation prices are positively correlated and costs are high relative to average reservation values.

The bundling problem becomes increasingly complex as we depart from the two-good formulation. Hanson and Martin (1990) find the optimal bundling strategy by formulating the question as a mixed integer linear program. Their solution method is tested on bundles with up to 21 components. Nevertheless, a typical academic journal contains about 100 articles per subscription bundle. This requires making simplifying assumptions to make the problem analytically tractable.

Bakos and Brynjolfsson (2000) show that pure bundling of zero-marginal-cost goods with independent and identically distributed valuations dominates pure unbundling. This approach reduces the average deadweight loss and increases profits as the number of goods in the bundle increases. They also analyze the consequences of relaxing these assumptions.

Chuang and Sirbu (2000) address the problem by assuming that all articles have identical marginal costs and are priced identically. This reduces the calculation from 2^n optimal prices to just 2 (a per-article price and a subscription price). Their analysis shows that mixed bundling is the dominant strategy: "By offering a menu choice which includes both the original and the components, the producer can extract consumer surplus more completely via consumer self-selection." They also derive conditions under which pure unbundling outperforms pure bundling even when bundling reduces costs. They conclude that more bundling is not always better for the producer.

Chuang and Sirbu model consumer heterogeneity in two dimensions. Each consumer ranks the N articles in the journal in decreasing order of preference. A linear demand function is assumed for all positive-valued articles. The consumer's valuation of the nth article is

(5) $\quad W(n) = \min\{0, W_0 [1 - (1/K)(n/N)]\}.$

Here W_0 represents the willingness to pay for the user's favorite article and K indicates the fraction of articles in the journal that have a nonzero value to the individual. This linear demand equation is consistent with our general formulation. The demand for journal articles does not depend on income, and it is derivable from a quasilinear utility function that is a particular case of the GGPF.

The literature to date on bundling is not sufficiently rich to encompass the products in our field trial. We will discuss the gaps below after we detail the bundles we are implementing.

3.3 Nonlinear Pricing

As discussed below, we will introduce some nonlinear pricing schemes in the experiment. Because of the complexity of the field trial, and because of issues of participant acceptability, we will limit experimentation with nonlinear pricing parameters to individual, single-article purchasing.

Wilson (1993) constructs the optimal multipart tariff by using a menu of optional two-part tariffs, and also characterizes the optimal fixed fee. In the general nonlinear pricing problem formulation, a monopolist seller charges $P(q)$ for an n-vector bundle q of its products. A customer of m-vector type t has a predicted benefit:

Economics and Electronic Access to Scholarly Information

$W(t) = \max\{U(q,t) - P(q)\}$. (The maximum is over q in Q, where Q is the set of possible bundles.) The distribution of type parameters has a density function $f(t)$, with upper support T.

By the Revelation Principle, the monopolist can choose the vectors $q(t)$, $W(t)$. Wilson considered the Ramsey problem of a welfare-maximizing monopolist subject to the constraint of cost recovery. We are interested, instead, in a profit-maximizing monopolist. Thus, for us, the seller's problem is to

(6) $\quad \max_{q(t),W(t)} \int_0^T \big(U(q(t),t) - W(t) - C(q(t))\big)f(t)dt$

subject to

- $W'(t) = U_t(q(t),t)$ (incentive compatibility),
- $W(t) \quad U(0,t) = 0$ (customer's participation constraint),
- $q(t) \quad 0$ (feasibility constraint).

Tirole (1988) analyzes the welfare effects of nonlinear pricing. In the two-type case, he shows that with optimal pricing, the quantity purchased by the high-demand consumers is socially optimal (the marginal utility of consumption of the good is equal to the marginal cost). If the monopolist serves both types of consumers, the quantity purchased by the low-demand consumers is suboptimal. Faced by a continuum of types, a monopolist induces consumers to purchase a suboptimal quantity. The marginal willingness to pay for the good exceeds the marginal cost, except for the highest-demand consumer. These two cases assume quasilinear utility functions.

Katz (1989) shows that nonlinear pricing may yield too little or too much output in comparison with the social optimum. If the single-crossing condition holds, the monopolist generally produces too little output.

4. PEAK: A Field Trial

The University of Michigan has negotiated, with Elsevier, a pricing field trial, "Pricing Electronic Access to Knowledge" (PEAK). This negotiated trial permits Michigan to provide a host service for three years (1997–1999) of all approximately 1200 Elsevier Science scholarly titles. Once the trial is under way, articles will become available as quickly as they do for any Elsevier Electronic Subscriptions customer, which is to say within a few weeks of the mail distribution of the print-on-paper version. Michigan will provide Internet-based delivery to participants in the trial, which will include users both on campus and off.

The PEAK project will be implemented by the same team responsible for Michigan's collaborative digital library enterprise, including its Humanities Text Initiative, the TULIP project, JSTOR, and other efforts. The underlying technologies have been utilized in the TULIP and NSF/ARPA/NASA UM Digital Library projects, among others. The University of Michigan has implemented a full, commercial digital production service, and currently hosts more than a terabyte of indexed document data on high-speed disk systems.[8]

For PEAK, Michigan will create a variety of access models and will administer a pricing system. The agreement is designed explicitly to support experimental field research, and thus there will be experimental variation in the bundles and prices offered to clients. In this section, we will describe in some detail the structure of the experiment. There are three major design components:

1. Economic design: specification of the product bundles and the price structure.

2. Experimental design: implementation of the economic design to obtain statistically informative data.

3. Technical implementation.

4.1 Economic Design: Bundling

Electronic access directly provides the opportunity to unbundle and rebundle scholarly literature. A print-on-paper journal is a bundle of issues, each of which is a bundle of articles and other items, each of which is a bundle of bibliographic information, an abstract, references, text, figures, and so forth. It is often straightforward (though not necessarily costless) to rebundle any of these elements in different ways when the source material is archived in electronic form. For example, one might obtain all abstracts matching a given keyword search, or all citations appearing in a particular article, or just the bibliographic headers from the articles appearing in a given year.

From the beginning, the PEAK project was designed to explore bundling alternatives as well as pricing structures. The specification of product bundles turns out to be a quite difficult task, because the space of possible bundles is extraordinarily large, even if we treat each component of a document as identical across documents (e.g., do not define articles by two different authors to be different commodities for the purpose of bundling). To see this problem, consider bundles defined over just three possible dimensions for electronically accessed scholarly documents:

- *Article component* (abstract, references, text, etc.)
- *Time limit on usage* (unlimited, per use, per year, etc.)
- *Usage rights* (read only, read and print, etc.).

From a rather simple population of the matrix of possibilities, we can postulate 160 possible different bundles (see Figure 1) *before even specifying different bundle quantities.* For example, we might offer a one-year right to read-only N abstracts. If bundles are priced differently for, say, $N = \{1, 10, 100, \text{unlimited}\}$, the space increases to 640 possible bundles.

Although an explicit goal of the field trial was to explore new opportunities afforded by electronic access, feasibility constraints led to a rather limited selection of bundle types to implement. One important constraint is experimental variation: With a somewhat limited number of different observational units, we cannot obtain sufficient variation to explore very many bundle types. A second constraint is customer acceptance: Although this is being operated as a research project by the University of Michigan, the experimental subjects are operational research libraries and individual users who must find the offerings palatable enough for participation to be worthwhile. After numerous meetings with library collection experts and potential participants, the project team decided on three bundles to offer:

- *Per article.* A user can purchase unlimited access to a specific article for a fixed price. This option is designed to closely mimic a

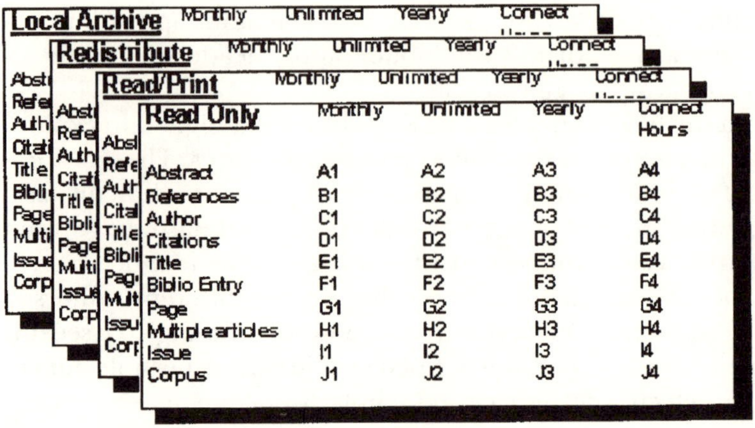

Figure 1 Hypothetical bundling possibilities.

traditional interlibrary loan (ILL) product. With ILL, the individual receives a printed copy of the article that can be retained indefinitely. This is different from the "per–use" pricing model often applied to electronic data sources. The article is retained on the PEAK server, but the user can access a paid-for article as often as desired. This is a buyer-chooses scheme, in that the buyer selects the articles before paying for them.

- *Traditional subscription.* A user or a library can purchase unlimited access to a set of articles designated as a *journal volume* by the publisher. These volumes will correspond to the Elsevier print-on-paper journal titles. Access continues at least until the end of the project. This is a seller-chooses bundle, in that the seller (Elsevier and its editorial associates) decides which articles are delivered to the user after the user has subscribed.

- *Generalized subscription.* A library can prepurchase unlimited access to a set of 120 articles selected by the user. (The number of articles was chosen to correspond approximately to the average number of articles included in a traditional subscription.) Individual users can purchase personal blocks of N articles (where N is less than 120). This is a buyer-chooses bundle. It is the same as a traditional subscription in every regard, except that the buyer selects which articles are accessed, from across all Elsevier titles, after the buyer has subscribed. This bundling approach allows users to capture value from the entire corpus of articles without having to subscribe to all the journal titles. This opportunity is justified by the approximately zero incremental cost of delivering additional articles once the server database is constructed.

The duration for each of the product bundles is the life of the project plus one year.[9] The usage rights for a document will generally be the same as those for an Elsevier article distributed as print-on-paper (e.g., U.S. users can print a copy for personal archival purposes, but may not redistribute it further except as provided under the fair use doctrine).

The first and second products are intended to match as closely as possible the best-known traditional product bundles.[10] This conservatism should promote customer acceptance of the trial, and should also allow better comparisons between electronic and print-on-paper experience. The third option is more novel. The generalized subscription is designed to test the opportunity provided by unbundling and rebundling without straying too far from the other product bundles. Limiting product variations to only one dimension will improve statistical inference about the effects of the different bundling schemes.

Although the planned product bundles do not deviate far from traditional bundles, they do permit some interesting user choices. In particular, generalized subscriptions allow users to prepay and thus obtain the administrative advantage of budget predictability, yet also allow users the flexibility to choose only articles they want. Indeed, users can bundle articles across journals, and even across traditional disciplines. This shares the risk of paying for unwanted articles with the publisher. Consequently, the value per article accessed should generally be higher to the user than under a traditional subscription, and the per-article average price can be correspondingly higher for generalized subscriptions. In short, users trade off an upfront commitment against the benefits of greater customization and the ability to select articles postpublication. Publishers gain by having a significant revenue stream that is predictable, and also by direct feedback on which articles, from across several journals, readers most highly value.

For the experiment, we will vary the mixed bundling opportunities available to users. Some institutions will be offered only traditional subscriptions plus per-article purchase; others will be offered only generalized subscriptions plus per-article purchase. Yet a third group will be offered the opportunity to construct a portfolio from all three: traditional subscriptions, generalized subscriptions, and per-article purchase.

Our products are more complex than those studied thus far in the bundling literature. The differences are largely due to our attempt to maintain plausible comparability to existing print-on-paper offerings while still designing a controlled experiment. For example, our "mixed bundling" is more general than the form studied in the literature. Customers do not need to choose just subscriptions or, alternatively, just individual articles. Our customers might purchase some subscriptions and supplement them with per-article purchases. This feature highlights the other necessary complexity: the fact that subscriptions are actually "sub-bundles." In the Chuang and Sirbu (2000) and Bakos and Brynjolfsson (2000) chapters, only one bundle at a time is considered, which consists of either all or a subset of all articles. In practice, publishers offer several bundles, each as a different journal title. Sizable publishers never limit their bundles to a single, all-article bundle. Thus, the value of per-article and mixed bundling to the provider will necessarily be conditional on the particular set of sub-bundles (journal titles) the publisher offers.[11]

We are focusing on another difference between our formulation and the standard modeling in the bundling literature: uncertainty. With a traditional subscription, the buyer does not know the quality of the bundle before making the purchase decision, but may know the distribution of past quality. With a generalized subscription, the buyer does not know the quality of the individual articles before deciding how many bundles to purchase, but then chooses the articles to be included after their quality has been (at least partially) revealed. With per-article pricing, the buyer knows the quality before committing to any purchases. Therefore, we expect consumer demand for the different bundles to depend on risk preferences and expectations of the heterogeneity of perceived article quality. We are formulating a formal model of consumer demand that incorporates uncertainty on which to base our econometric analysis of the trial. We believe that the ease of offering a variety of different risk-sharing schemes may be an important advantage for electronic access.

4.2 Economic Design: Pricing Structures

The variety of nonlinear pricing structures is essentially unbounded: Any nonlinear, monotonically increasing relationship between total payment and quantity (of something) purchased is admissible. Although a field trial offers some possibility of exploring the space of pricing structures, we again face feasibility and participation constraints. In particular, because we are also varying product bundles, the number of different pricing schemes that we can implement and still obtain sufficient data for statistical inference is very limited.

Within the class of general nonlinear pricing schemes, a large number have been specifically studied and implemented in various industries. These are illustrated in Figure 2, which shows the relationship between revenues and quantity for a linear scheme, second-degree price discrimination (block pricing), a two-part and a three-part tariff, a fixed fee, and a generic nonlinear scheme.

The project team plans to implement two-part tariff pricing (see Figure 3). There is an *entry fee*, an initial payment merely to participate. Incremental access is charged at a flat per-unit price.

4.3 Experimental Design

The PEAK field trial provides an unprecedented opportunity for exploring bundling and nonlinear pricing opportunities afforded by electronic access. The key research objective, however, is generalizability to other user populations and other scholarly materials. Experimental design considerations are therefore paramount, and impose significant constraints on the range of bundling and pricing schemes that can be studied. The fundamental principle of experimental design is that we learn from variation: How do users respond differently when confronted with different alternative bundles or price structures? To obtain a sufficiently rich

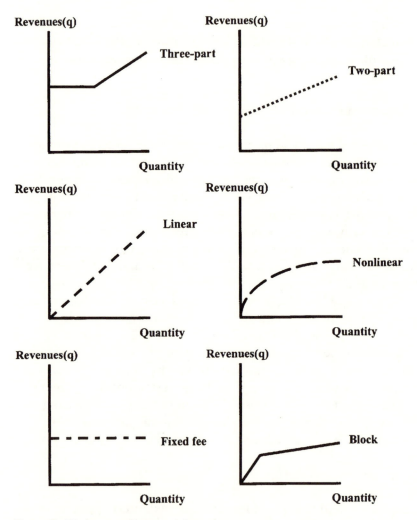

Figure 2 Various nonlinear pricing schemes.

set of observations to draw inferences from the effects of design parameter variation, we must significantly restrict the number of dimensions that vary. These concerns were reflected in the discussion of bundles and price structures above. The experimental design has a number of other interesting features, which we describe below.

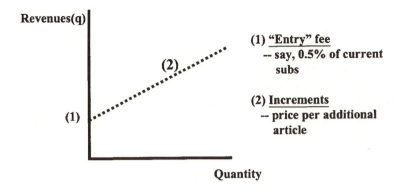

Figure 3 Two-part tariff explained.

1. *Product diversity.* Elsevier is making available approximately 1200 different journal titles for the trial. This corpus includes titles in virtually every academic discipline. The styles, prices, quality, and other features of these journals cover a very wide range. Further, scholarly usage styles appear to differ significantly across disciplines. Therefore, product diversity potentially creates a source of difficult-to-control nonexperimental variation. To limit this problem, the experimental design calls for limiting the trial to a few disciplines in which Elsevier titles have an especially strong presence: engineering, medical science, and economics.[12]

2. *Customer diversity.* Scholarly journals have narrow, specialized audiences. Even within a community as large as the University of Michigan (some 30,000 students, of whom about 10,000 are in graduate school and about 3200 are research faculty), there are likely to be only a few readers for many specialty journals. Only a fraction of these are likely to participate in an electronic-access trial. Therefore, in order to obtain sufficient participation and usage, the project was designed to include clients from a number of organizations outside the University of Michigan. The preliminary participant list includes other research universities and industrial research facilities. Four-year undergraduate colleges may also be participating. Although the sample size of users for each subset of literature is increased by including multiple institutions, broader scope also creates design problems. There will be greater diversity in physical facilities, marketing and communications

to participants, and institutional arrangements. The latter are of special concern Both institutional and individual decisionmakers will participate in the trial. For example, both will be able to subscribe, and both will be able to purchase on a per-article basis. The behavior of a rational and well-informed individual user will be conditioned on the behavior of that user's associated institution.[13] For example, an individual might subscribe to a journal only if the organization's library does not. This complication is probably unavoidable, and will pose challenges for the proper statistical analysis of the results.

3. *Duration and learning.* This trial involves a rather novel access mode for scholarly literature. Although Michigan has substantial institutional experience from TULIP, JSTOR, UMDL, and other projects, most individual users of scholarly literature on campus have little or no experience with electronic access to traditional scholarly journals. Users at the other participating institutions— both individual and institutional—are likely to be even less experienced. The learning process will complicate efforts to uncover generalizable results. The project team will actively educate potential users about the trial, the products, and the pricing. Further, we will be collecting data over a two- or three-year period, and thus will have some chance to isolate learning effects.

There are also a number of technical issues that, although they are not really part of the experimental design, must be overcome to complete the implementation of the PEAK project. These include the implementation of an accounting system, a payment mechanism, and user authentication to the access system. As much as possible, we are relying on off-the-shelf or already implemented local solutions. For example, we have negotiated an agreement with First Virtual, Inc., for bulk provision of user IDs that our client library participants can then redistribute to their individual users. The user need make only one automated phone call to authorize First Virtual to post charges to his/her credit card, and send one email message to link his/her user ID and email address. Users then have a fully refutable and secure method for purchasing bundles and individual articles beyond those paid for by their institutional libraries.

5. Conclusion

It is hard to assert a conclusion when the data have not yet been collected or analyzed. We offer two significant observations based on our experience and theoretical research to date:

• The space for electronic-access product bundling and pricing structures is immense. Many field trials will be required to explore even a limited set of important alternatives.

• The literature on bundling, and to a lesser extent nonlinear pricing, has not yet developed to the point where the models fit actual circumstances very well. We have identified some of the theoretical framework that needs further attention.

Notes

1. Kling and Lamb (1996) offer an insightful discussion of utopian discourse on information technology and electronic publishing.

2. See Fisher (1996) for a good overview of the value-added functions provided by publishers.

3. Hayes (1996) nicely characterizes the publisher's role in bringing readers to authors.

4. "Normal" profits are the ordinary rate of return, adjusted for risk, that an investor could obtain in a competitive financial instrument (such as a government bond). It is a return for the use of capital in the enterprise, necessary since the capital could be invested elsewhere to obtain a normal return.

5. The competitive equilibrium result assumes that there are no externalities. This means that the amount of publishing services received by any one agent does not directly affect how well off any other agent is. A typical externality is water pollution: The more I produce, the worse off the downstream residents are.

6. Some publishers are sufficiently concerned about electronic distribution that they are treating posting of drafts and working papers on the Internet as prior publication, and are refusing to consider for their journals articles that have been thus posted. Most American Psychological Association journal editors have adopted this policy, as have *Neuroscience* and *The New England Journal of Medicine*.

7. Odlyzko (1995) points out that about half of all scholarly literature ever published has been published in just the last 10 years.

8. The University of Michigan was also one of the original host sites and developers of TULIP (The University Licensing Project), sponsored by Elsevier Science.

9. The University of Michigan and Elsevier anticipate that access to paid-for documents and bundles may persist beyond the life of the original project agreement, but that is not guaranteed.

10. Pay per article is traditionally available through at least three vehicles: by paying a per-article royalty to the Copyright Clearance Center; by purchasing an article from a document delivery service (which in turn remits royalties); or, when fair use is invoked, by paying the cost of photocopying.

11. Of course, the selection of the number of sub-bundles, or journal titles, and the guidelines for their specialty content, are endogenous. At a given point in time, mixed bundling might be superior to "traditional subscription only" because reader tastes are sufficiently aligned with journal boundaries. If the publisher responds to this mismatch, the relative value of traditional subscriptions may increase.

12. In 1996, the University of Michigan subscribed to approximately 69 engineering titles at an average cost of about $1000/title, 13 economics titles (~$900/title), and 134 medical titles (~$1200/title).

13. The causality may also run in the opposite direction, of course, but we expect that during the relatively short duration of this trial the purchasing decisions of the institution will likely be relatively predetermined with respect to individual decisions. Over a greater time horizon, the chance that library purchasing would respond to individual choices would likely increase.

References

Adams, W., and Yellen, J. (1976). "Commodity Bundling and the Burden of Monopoly," *Quarterly Journal of Economics*, 90:475–498.

Bakos, Y., and Brynjolfsson, E. (2000). "Bundling Information Goods: Pricing, Profits and Efficiency." In this volume.

Chuang, J., and Sirbu, M. (2000). "The Bundling and Unbundling of Information Goods: Economic Incentives for the Network Delivery of Academic Journal Articles." In this volume

Deaton, A., and Muellbauer, J. (1980). *Economics and Consumer Behavior*. Cambridge, England: Cambridge University Press.

Fisher, J. (1996). "Traditional Publishers and Electronic Journals." In *Scholarly Publishing: The Electronic Frontier*, R. Peek and G. Newby, eds. Cambridge, MA: MIT Press.

Gorman, W. M. (1959). "Separable Utility and Aggregation," *Econometrica*, 27:469–481.

Hanson, W., and Martin, R. (1990). "Optimal Bundle Pricing," *Management Science*, 36:155–174.

Harnad, S. (1990). "Scholarly Skywriting and the Prepublication Continuum of Scientific Inquiry," *Psychological Science*, 1:342–343.

Harnad, S. (1996). "Implementing Peer Review on the Net: Scientific Quality Control in Scholarly Electronic Journals." In *Scholarly Publishing: The Electronic Frontier*, R. Peek and G. Newby, eds. Cambridge, MA: MIT Press.

Hayes, B. (1996). "The Economic Quandary of the Network Publisher." In *Scholarly Publishing: The Electronic Frontier*, R. Peek and G. Newby, eds. Cambridge, MA: MIT Press.

Katz, M. (1983). "Nonuniform Pricing, Output and Welfare under Monopoly," *Review of Economic Studies*, 50:37–56.

Kling, R., and Lamb, R. (1996). "Analyzing Alternate Visions of Electronic Publishing and Digital Libraries." In *Scholarly Publishing: The Electronic Frontier*, R. Peek and G. Newby, eds. Cambridge, MA: MIT Press.

MacKie-Mason, J., and Lawson, D. (1993). "Local Telephone Calling Demand When Customers Face Optional and Nonlinear Price Schedules." *Technical Report*, University of Michigan, 1–33.

MacKie-Mason, J., and Riveros, J. F. (1997). "Economics and Electronic Access to Scholarly Information." Presented at the *Conference on Economics of Digital Information and Intellectual Property*, Harvard University, January 1997.

McAfee, R., McMillan, J., and Whinston, M. (1989). "Multiproduct Monopoly, Commodity Bundling and Correlation of Values," *Quarterly Journal of Economics*, 114:371–384.

Odlyzko, A. (1995). "Tragic Loss or Good Riddance? The Impending Demise of Traditional Scholarly Journals," *International Journal of Human-Computer Studies*, 42:71–122.

Salinger, M. A. (1995). "A Graphical Analysis of Bundling," *Journal of Business*, 68:85–98.

Schmalensee, R. (1982). "Commodity Bundling by a Single Product Monopolist," *Journal of Law and Economics*, 25:67–71.

Schmalensee, R. (1984). "Gaussian Demand and Commodity Bundling," *Journal of Business*, 57:S211–S230.

Stigler, G. (1963). "United States vs. Loew's Inc.: A note on block booking," In *Supreme Court Review*, P. Kurland, ed., Chicago, University of Chicago Press.

Tirole, J. (1988). *The Theory of Industrial Organization.* Cambridge, MA: MIT Press.

Varian, H. (1992). *Microeconomic Analysis.* New York: Norton.

Wilson, R. (1993). *Nonlinear Pricing.* New York: Oxford University Press.

Zahray, W., and Sirbu, M. (1990). "The Provision of Scholarly Journals by Libraries via Electronic Technologies: An Economic Analysis," *Information Economics and Policy*, 4:127–154.

Contributors

Yannis Bakos is Associate Professor of Management at the Leonard N. Stern School of Business at New York University where he conducts research and teaches graduate courses on electronic commerce. In 1989, he co-founded the Workshop on Information Systems and Economics (WISE), which has become the leading forum for research at the intersection of the Information Technology and Economics disciplines.

Erik Brynjolfsson is Associate Professor at the MIT Sloan School of Management and Co-director of eBusiness@MIT. He is also an Associate Member of the MIT Laboratory for Computer Science and researcher at the MIT Center for Coordination Science. His research and teaching focus on how businesses can effectively use information technology (IT) in general and the Internet in particular.

John Chung-I Chuang is Assistant Professor of Information Management and Systems at the University of California at Berkeley. He was a Postdoctoral Fellow in Computer Science at Carnegie Mellon University, where he also received his Ph.D. in Engineering and Public Policy. His research and teaching encompass the technical and economic dimensions of data networking, with particular emphasis on the infrastructural foundations that support scalable and efficient delivery of content to a geographically diverse audience.

J. Bradford DeLong is Professor of Economics at the University of California at Berkeley, a research associate of the National Bureau of Economic Research, a visiting scholar at the Federal Reserve Bank of San Francisco, and the co-editor of the *Journal of Economic Perspectives*. From 1993 to 1995 he was Deputy Assistant Secretary of the Treasury for Economic Policy.

Peter C. Fishburn is a principal technical staff member at AT&T Labs—Research. He received his Ph.D. from Case Institute of Technology in 1962, and joined AT&T in 1978 after serving as a research professor of management science at Penn State. His research interests focus on discrete mathematics and decision theory.

A. Michael Froomkin is Professor of Law at the University of Miami in Coral Gables. He has written a number of articles on e-commerce, e-cash, cryptography, privacy, and internet governance, most of which are online at http://www.law.tm.

Donna L. Hoffman and **Thomas P. Novak** are marketing professors at Vanderbilt University and co-direct eLab, the Electronic Commerce Research Laboratory (http://ecommerce.vanderbilt.edu/). They were recently named the top two Internet Scientists by 600 United States and European scientists and marketing managers in an international survey.

Brian Kahin was founding director of the Harvard Information Infrastructure Project. He recently served as a senior policy analyst at the White House Office of Science and Technology Policy and is currently a fellow at the Internet Policy Institute in Washington, DC.

Jeffrey K. MacKie-Mason is Professor of Information, Economics and Public Policy at the University of Michigan. He is the founding director of the Program for Research on the Information Economy at Michigan, and he holds an IBM University Partnership fellowship for 1998–2000.

Susan M. Mings is a User Education specialist at Microsoft Corporation. Her academic and industry research areas include Internet news, design and use of dynamic HTML in technical documentation, and distance education.

Andrew M. Odlyzko is Head of the Mathematics and Cryptography Research Department at AT&T Labs. He has done extensive research in technical areas such as computational complexity, cryptography, number theory, combinatorics, coding theory, analysis, and probability theory. In recent years he has also been working on electronic publishing, electronic commerce, and economics of data networks. His home page is http://www.research.att.com/~amo.

Juan F. Riveros holds a Ph.D. in Economics from the University of Michigan. He worked as a Research Assistant on a pilot operational service to deliver electronic access to Elsevier Science journals, "Pricing Electronic Access to Knowledge" (PEAK). His current research interests are information economics, in particular the economics of information content and electronic commerce.

Oz Shy teaches economics at the University of Haifa. He previously taught at the State University of New York, Tel Aviv University, University of Michigan, and Stockholm School of Economics. He is the author of *Industrial Organization: Theory and Applications* (1996) and a new book entitled *The Economics of Network Industries*.

Ryan C. Siders is a mathematics graduate student at Princeton University. He wrote his first code in 1985 in a Boca Raton (Florida) public school, and he won the Interservice/Industry Simulation and Training Conference's annual prize for simulations in 1996. His work on this paper was done partially during a summer internship at AT&T Labs—Research in 1996.

Marvin A. Sirbu is Professor in the departments of Engineering and Public Policy, Industrial Administration, and Electrical and Computer Engineering at Carnegie Mellon University. He is also the founder and Chairman of the Information Networking Institute at CMU. His has published widely on information economics, network economics, and telecommunications policy.

Hal R. Varian is the Dean of the School of Information Management and Systems at the University of California at Berkeley, and holds joint appointments in the business school and economics department. He is co-author of *Information Rules* (1998). His homepage is http://www.sims.berkeley.edu/~hal.

Peter B. White is Head of the Department of Media Studies and Director of the Online Media Program at La Trobe University in Melbourne, Australia.

Index